# A structured approach to building programs:

# BASIC
# BASIC
# BASIC

# A structured approach to building programs:

# BASIC BASIC BASIC

# Timothy D. Wells

Yourdon Press
1501 Broadway, New York, N.Y. 10036
15/17 Ridgemount St., London, WD1E 7BH, England

Printed in the United States of America

ISBN: 0-917072-45-6

Library of Congress Cataloging-in-Publication Data

Wells, Timothy.
    A structured approach to building programs.

    1. BASIC (Computer program language)   2. Structured
programming.   I. Title.
QA76.73.B3W44  1985        005.13'3        85-51511
ISBN 0-917072-45-6

This book was set in Times Roman by YOURDON Press, 1501 Broadway, New York, N.Y., using a PDP-11/70 running under the UNIX* operating system.

---

*UNIX is a registered trademark of Bell Laboratories.

*Cover design by George Armstrong*

# DEDICATION

*To Carrie,*

*for her never-ending support, encouragement, arm-twisting, honest love, and deep concern.*

# ACKNOWLEDGMENTS

My thanks to the people of Yourdon Press for their encouragement and support. I am indebted to Ed Yourdon for giving the book a chance. My special thanks to Steve Weiss for reviewing the programs in the text, and, for their editorial guidance and the long hours spent turning my raw manuscript into a readable text, my most grateful thanks to Teresa Ridley, who also designed and typeset the book, Susan Moran, and Janice Wormington.

# CONTENTS

# PREFACE

This book synthesizes two often conflicting objectives, both of them vital, practical skills needed by today's software developer: 1) building an effective design for an application program, and 2) constructing a program using a specific programming language.

For years, it has been widely accepted that the design of computer programs is largely independent of the particular programming language. Whether a programmer is using BASIC, COBOL, or PASCAL is secondary to the definition of the function(s) to be performed by the program(s). Thus, the first objective of any effective course in computer programming is to teach a method of defining requirements and building a good program design.

The second objective is to teach the proper use of the programming language. A course in application development must include ways of implementing and testing modules of code; it must also offer programming style guidelines that help the programmer build readable code. Most texts focus on only one of these objectives; seldom are both topics presented in an integrated manner. The student is thus taught a fragmented approach to the discipline of software development.

This textbook combines the instruction of good software design with effective use of the BASIC programming language. COBOL and PASCAL are each treated as the implementation language in forthcoming books under the same title. Each text is *identical* in form and presentation but unique in specific programming language concerns.

*Timothy Wells*
*Cataldo, Idaho*
*August, 1985*

# Introduction

During the years I have been teaching software development techniques to experienced programmers, I have noticed an interesting phenomenon: Programmers begin coding before they are ready — that is, before they completely understand the problem they are trying to solve. Most programmers are so concerned with the process of coding that they fail to define their objective, much less carry out any other advance planning of the program. An important purpose of this text is to teach readers how to plan a program before they start to write the BASIC commands.

Computer languages are solution-implementation tools, not problem-solving tools. Writing code does not guarantee that the program will do what it is supposed to do. Imagine a chef trying to write down a recipe before he has defined the dish to be prepared, or an artist trying to paint a portrait of Jon Que without having seen Jon Que. Only after identifying the flavors and textures of the new dish can the chef create the culinary delight. Similarly, the artist must determine the image of Jon Que before applying paint to canvas. The recipe and paint are the means of bringing a design to life, but the design is always first.

The same logic applies to building a software program. Before writing the code, the programmer must formulate a program design, which means being able to analyze a problem, design a solution, build code based on the design, and test the resulting programs.

The design method taught in this book enables the programmer to define both the function of the program and the data that flow through it. By clearly stating the proposed results, the programmer is better able to write an accurate program.

Breaking the program down into simpler modules is another important purpose of the program design. When each module is coded individually, a complex program becomes much easier to manage. This part of the model is called the *program outline*.

Another characteristic of software engineering for which students are not always prepared is that needs are often not discovered until after the software has been built. The programmer must be able to add new functions to the existing software, eventually creating a large system of many interrelated programs. Therefore, the programmer must be trained to analyze changes, modify designs, change the code, and test the modified programs. This book has a special section devoted to modifying already existing programs. Beyond that, however, the book's aim is to give readers practical experience in building a system of many programs. Using a single case study throughout, the book starts with a simple program, and each chapter adds a new function related to the initial program. New programs are built, but earlier programs must be modified as well. The result is a set of interlocking programs that store and analyze data and produce reports.

In order to teach problem definition, this book presents a broader spectrum of software engineering than is typical in programming language books. It gives some idea of the analysis and design phases which can, in simplified form, be used by the beginner. It also teaches the reader how to keep a data dictionary, estimate the size of a program, and create test cases. These are useful skills which help instill professional habits early.

Readers will learn a system of principles, concepts, and techniques as they progress through the text. This book is written for the novice programmer who has taken an introductory BASIC programming course and has written several programs. Even those with more experience, however, will discover performance-improving techniques.

### The organization of the book

The text takes a "learn by example" approach. A single case study is used throughout the book to illustrate the process of building a program. Readers will build a second case study in a series of exercises.

The book consists of twelve chapters, each containing two sections, A and B. The first chapter presents the basic process of building software. It introduces the basic tools of software engineering and gives the reader a feel for things to come.

Each remaining chapter presents a new program which performs a software function, such as carrying out basic arithmetic calculations, accessing a random file, producing a report, and doing maintenance on a program. In each chapter, section A demonstrates how to model the function and design a program outline; this corresponds to defining the problem to be solved. This initial section follows the same procedure in each chapter. First, a problem is described. Based on the description, a diagram is built labeling the function to be performed by the computer and showing inputs and outputs. Second, the data used and produced by the function are precisely defined. Third, the text uses the model and the data definitions to estimate the size of the program. Fourth, the data definitions are used to build test data for verifying the program. Fifth, an outline of the program is built showing all modules. Section B shows how the program outline is used to build the BASIC program.

At the end of each chapter is an exercise that allows readers to model a function and build code using the techniques illustrated in the sections. Suggested answers to exercises are located in Appendix C. Before proceeding to the next chapter, readers should do the exercises and review the suggested answers to be sure they completely understand the ideas presented in each chapter.

After working through the text and exercises, the reader will be able to analyze the goals of a program, estimate the size of the job, build test cases to verify the program's accuracy, design a solution, and map the solution into a programming language.

### Student portfolio

I ask readers to keep a record of the work done for these exercises; this record is called a *portfolio*. Readers can use the portfolio to review their progress and to demonstrate it to others. More importantly, they can use pieces of past programs stored in the portfolio to help complete current projects. Reusing suitable modules from old programs makes building new programs quicker and easier.

Finally, the portfolio includes a record of the time taken to build each program. Readers can use this record to estimate how long it will take to complete a new project. An outline for the portfolio is provided in Appendix A.

### Assumptions about the reader

In this text, I make some assumptions about readers. I assume that they have access to a computer. The type of computer doesn't matter; I assume readers have worked with the computer before and that they are comfortable with it.

After readers have defined a particular problem, they will write programs. This means they must type the program and make changes and corrections to what they have typed. They will also have to compile or interpret the program and execute it. I assume none of this will cause readers any trouble.

The biggest assumption I make is that readers have some familiarity with the BASIC language. They don't have to know much about files or arrays, but they should understand loops, IF...THEN...ELSE statements, assignment of variables, and arithmetic calculations. In fact, as long as readers can understand a block of BASIC code, they need little experience actually writing programs. The text will fully introduce BASIC commands used for building and manipulating files and arrays.

The examples in this text use Microsoft™ BASIC. BASIC, one of the most popular languages, has a number of variations, but it is not important that readers have the same version of BASIC used in this text. What is important is that they have a reference manual for the BASIC they use. Readers should develop the habit of using reference manuals to resolve differences between BASIC dialects and to refresh their memory about the many BASIC commands.

# Modeling a Computer Program

## 1A: Building the Model

A good computer program carries out the intent of the user. It makes entering data and receiving correct, usable results easy. The data should flow smoothly from the user, through the program, into storage files, out of storage files, and back to the user.

This book will illustrate a process for designing good programs. Your knowledge of a programming language gives you the tool needed to write a program, but writing the commands is only a small part of creating a good program. You must build a model of the program before writing even your first line of code.

This model has several parts. It contains a simple diagram naming the function performed by the program and showing the data the program receives and produces. Detailed definitions of these data are given in another part of the model. The definitions of data leaving the program clearly show the program's objective. Since you know what the program should produce, you can more easily determine what activities are needed to generate each piece of data.

The program outline shows the different activities that comprise it. By breaking the program into small pieces and allowing you to work on one segment at a time, this part of the model makes program writing much easier.

### Data flow diagrams

The first part of the model is called a *data flow diagram* because it shows the data going into and leaving the program.

The following example introduces the data flow diagram and other tools used to model programs. In this example, you will write for a high school guidance counselor a program that computes a student's grade point average (GPA).

The guidance counselor keeps each student's courses and grades in a separate folder, which is identified by the student's ID number and stored in a file cabinet. When a student asks the counselor to look up her grade point average, he must first find out what data he needs to compute it. That piece of data is the student's ID, since that number indicates the correct folder with the grades inside.

Now you know that the student ID number goes into the program and the GPA results from it. With this information you begin building the model. In other chapters, you will begin by modeling the program itself; however, in this case you begin by modeling the counselor's current, noncomputerized method of finding the GPA. Because the steps followed by the counselor closely match those in the future program, you will be able to base the program code on this model. Professional programmers often begin designing a program by looking at the current operation, but usually they must alter their model before coding.

First, build the data flow diagram. You begin by drawing a circle to represent the program's function, which you can also think of as the program's goal or the one large task it accomplishes. The name of the function is written inside the circle — in this case, Determine Student GPA. To represent the student's ID, you draw an arrow going to the function and label it. An arrow called student ID pointing to the circle tells you that the student's ID will be a necessary input to the program. Figure 1.1 shows this much of the data flow diagram.

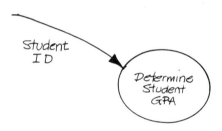

**Figure 1.1. Beginning data flow diagram for Determine Student GPA.**

Using the student's ID number, the counselor can go to the file cabinet and retrieve the student's folder. The data flow diagram depicts the file as two parallel lines with the file name written between them. The student's record inside the folder is a collection of data that is used to perform the function, so it too is shown as an arrow going to the circle. Both the student's file and her record from the file are added to the data flow diagram, shown in Figure 1.2.

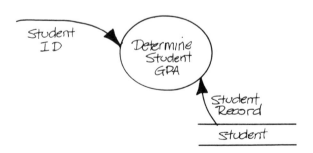

**Figure 1.2. More complete data flow diagram for Determine Student GPA.**

Once the counselor has computed the GPA, he gives this number to the student and places the folder back in the file cabinet. Thus, the GPA and student's record are pieces of data leaving the function. The GPA goes out to the student and the record goes onto the file. Both data flows are recorded in the completed data flow diagram in Figure 1.3.

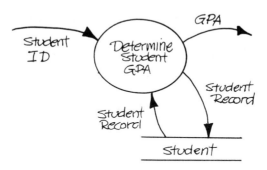

**Figure 1.3. Data flow diagram for Determine Student GPA.**

If a computer performed the function instead of a human being, the program would not need to store the record back in the file. As a program reads a record, it gets a copy; therefore, the record never actually leaves the file. The only time a record is put back is when some of its data have been changed. In this example, however, the function places the record back into the file.

## Data definitions

After identifying the function's incoming and outgoing data, you should define each data flow, which means recording in a notebook the values each piece of data can have. For instance, the data flow called Student ID is an integer, but not just any integer. An ID number of -15 doesn't make sense. For this example, the student ID can be any number between 1 and 100.

The data flow called GPA must also be defined. In most schools, a grade of F is worth zero points and a grade of A four points. The average is found by adding the points and dividing by the number of grades. Because of the division, the average often contains numbers to the right of the decimal point. So, the data item called GPA is defined as a real number between 0.0 and 4.0.

To define the data flow Student Record, you study the information in the student's folder. If the record contains the student's ID number, name, class year, and grades for six courses, you should note that Student Record consists of these data items and then define each item separately.

These definitions will help when you write and test the program. When writing the program, you inspect the definitions to find out which kinds of data the program should reject. For example, you will want the program to accept only student IDs that are between 1 and 100. If the user enters the number 210, the program should report an error. When you test the program, the data definitions indicate what the correct results should be. According to the definition of GPA, the resulting grade point average should always be between 0.0 and 4.0. If the program produces any other number, a malfunction exists. The testing process is explored throughout this book.

## The program outline

Once you have modeled the function in a data flow diagram and defined the data, you are ready to outline the structure of the program. The program outline shows the activities that make up the program and indicates which activity coordinates the others.

A program performs its function by stepping through a series of activities. The five major types are listed below:

- getting data from the outside world

- retrieving data from internal files

- manipulating or transforming data from both the outside world and internal files

- reporting data to the outside world

- storing data on internal files

Think of these activities as small subtasks needed to complete the overall function. You build the program outline by deciding which of these five activities are necessary to complete the function.

For each data flow coming from the outside world, there is an activity to get that data into the program. In this example, the program needs an activity to get the data flow called Student ID. You call this activity Get Student ID. In the program outline, the activity is shown below the main function, as in Figure 1.4.

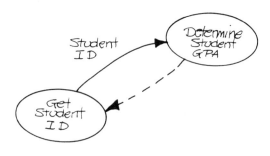

**Figure 1.4. Beginning program outline for Determine Student GPA.**

The top circle containing the name of the function no longer represents the entire function or program, but a kind of boss activity. This new activity coordinates the activities below it. The dotted line tells you that the person or section of code performing the top activity tells the lower activity when to begin. This may be confusing in the example: Since the counselor does both activities, he tells himself to get the student ID. The relationship between the top circle and the lower ones is clearer when you design an actual program, because each activity is carried out by a different piece of code. The data flow called Student ID, with the arrow pointing toward the top activity, tells you that the activity Get Student ID provides the function with the student ID.

For each data flow coming from a file, add another activity to the program outline. Student Record is stored on the student file; therefore, you should declare an activity that is responsible for retrieving it from the file. Figure 1.5 shows that a data flow with two labels and an arrowhead on both ends goes between Get Student Record and the boss activity. This data flow is actually two combined data flows. The label Get Student ID next to the arrowhead going into Get Student Record indicates that this activity uses the student ID number to find the right record. The other data flow, Student Record, is the result of this activity.

You should also declare an activity for each of the two outgoing data flows in Figure 1.3. One reports the result to the student and the other stores the student record on the file. These two activities also appear in Figure 1.5.

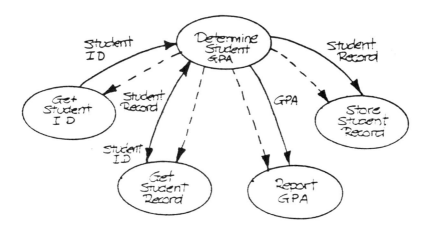

**Figure 1.5. More complete program outline for Determine Student GPA.**

Declare a final activity for any data manipulation needed to turn the incoming data into the desired results. In this example, the counselor computes the average of grades in the student record. After declaring an activity for this computation, you show the data that flow to and from it. The double-headed arrow in Figure 1.6 indicates that the activity uses the grades from the student record and produces the GPA.

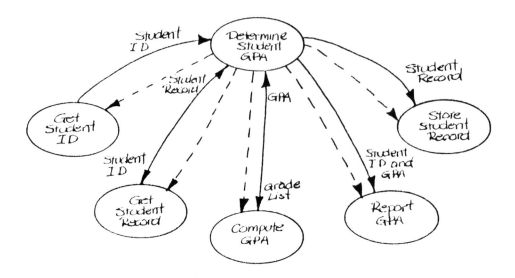

**Figure 1.6. Program outline for Determine Student GPA.**

In this summary, the program outline for this example shows five activities:

- Get Student ID (getting data from the outside world)

- Get Student Record (retrieving data from internal files)

- Compute GPA (transforming the data from the student's record into the student's GPA)

- Report GPA (reporting the student's GPA to the outside world)

- Store Student Record (storing data in an internal file)

The structure in Figure 1.6 outlines the program. Each circle denotes an activity. The lower-level activities carry out their own task, and the top circle coordinates those activities. For each activity, you will write a small piece of code.

This completes the modeling process. The data flow diagram and data definitions make up the model for the function; this model helps you identify the data that flow into and out of the program. The program outline is the model of the program and helps organize the code into small, understandable modules.

# 1B: Building the BASIC Program

In this section, you will use the program outline to construct the BASIC code for a function. Rather than working on one large piece of code, you are able to work on a series of small, simpler activities because of the program outline. These small, almost self-contained blocks of code are also called *modules*.

You build the program by writing a group of statements to carry out each activity on the lower level of the program outline. The code for the top activity causes the lower blocks of code to be carried out in sequence. If all activities perform correctly, the program will complete its function.

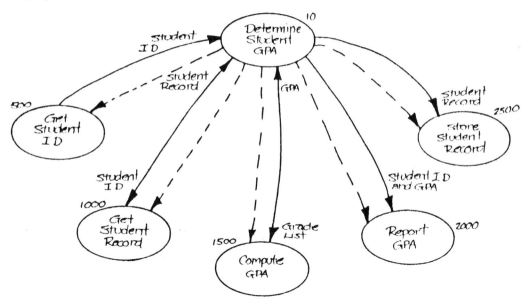

Figure 1.7. Program outline for Determine Student GPA.

Since BASIC requires a line number for each line of code, a starting line number for each activity has been added to the program outline. The program steps through the lines of BASIC code in sequence, starting with the lowest number.

Begin coding with the top activity. When you need to initiate a lower-level activity, use the GOSUB command followed by the starting line number of that activity. This tells the computer to go to the activity's starting line and proceed until the activity is completed. In BASIC, the command RETURN marks the end of an activity. When the computer hits that command, it jumps back to the top module.

The code for the top activity is shown below. You do not need to understand every command at this point. Read through it and the following code examples to get a feel for how BASIC code is constructed. The other chapters explore the process and commands in greater detail.

```
10 REM ----- DETERMINE STUDENT GPA -------------------
20 REM
25 DIM GR$(5)
30 REM
105 OPEN "R",1,"STUDENT"
110 FIELD #1, 2 AS F1$, 20 AS F2$, 10 AS F3$, 2 AS F4$, 6 AS F5$, 1 AS FX$
115 GOSUB 500
120 GOSUB 1000
125 GOSUB 1500
130 GOSUB 2000
135 GOSUB 2500
140 CLOSE #1
145 END
150 REM - END DETERMINE STUDENT GPA -------------------
151 REM
```

The OPEN and FIELD statements tell the computer to get the STUDENT file ready for processing. Using the GOSUB command, the program sequentially initiates the lower-level activities. Finally, the top module closes the file and ends.

The top module checks that the steps are taken in their proper order. For example, it retrieves the student's record before the GPA is calculated, since it would make no sense to try to calculate the GPA before the grades on the record are available.

The REM in lines 10 through 20 stands for REMark. It allows you to make comments about the program or add white space that makes the program easier to read. The DIM statement, line 25, is discussed in Chapter 2 and the OPEN and FIELD statements in Chapter 3.

To see how the rest of the program is put together, look at the BASIC code for the subtasks. The code for Get Student Number is shown below. Again, you're not expected to understand every line. Line 525 tells the computer to display the message "ENTER STUDENT NUMBER:" and to call the user's response S%, a name given to whatever the user types on the keyboard.

Line 530 checks whether the number is greater than or equal to 1 and less than or equal to 100. If not, the computer displays the message "# MUST BE 1 TO 100." Lines 520 and 535 tell the program to repeat the enclosed statements until the user has entered a valid number.

```
500 REM ----- GET STUDENT NUMBER -------------------
505 REM      PROMISES S% CONTAINING STUDENT NUMBER BETWEEN 1 AND 100
510 REM
515 I%=1
520 WHILE I%
525   INPUT "ENTER STUDENT NUMBER: "; S%
530   IF (S% >= 1) AND (S% <= 100) THEN I% = 0 ELSE PRINT "# MUST BE 1 TO 100"
535 WEND
540 RETURN
541 REM - END GET STUDENT NUMBER -------------------
542 REM
```

At the command RETURN, the computer goes back to the top module and executes the next statement at line 120. This sends the computer to line number 1000, the start of the Get Student Record activity. Line 1025 retrieves the student's record. The remainder of the module places the student's grades into an array called GR$.

An *array* is a series of data items of the same type — in this case, a series of grades. Every item in the array has the same BASIC name. To distinguish between them, a number called a *subscript* identifies each element in the array. In this example, the first grade is called GR$(0), the second grade GR$(1), and the sixth grade GR$(5). The statements 1030 and 1040 tell the computer to repeat line 1035 six times. That line takes the next grade on the record and puts it into the next spot in the array.

```
1000 REM ----- GET STUDENT RECORD --------------------
1005 REM      ASSUMES S% CONTAINS VALUE BETWEEN 1 AND 100
1010 REM           STUDENT FILE IS OPEN
1015 REM      PROMISES ARRAY GR$() CONTAINS 6 GRADES FROM STUDENT RECORD
1020 REM
1025 GET 1, S%
1030 FOR I% = 0 TO 5
1035   GR$(I%) = MID$(F5$,(I%+1),1)
1040 NEXT I%
1045 RETURN
1046 REM - END GET STUDENT RECORD --------------------
1047 REM
```

Next, the top module calls the Compute GPA activity, which starts at line number 1500. Here, the program computes the average of the six grades by adding the value of each grade to a data item called A! and then dividing A! by 6.

```
1500 REM ----- COMPUTE GPA --------------------
1505 REM      ASSUMES ARRAY GR$() HAS 6 GRADES
1510 REM      PROMISES A! CONTAINS THE AVERAGE OF 6 GRADES
1515 REM
1520 A!=0
1525 FOR I%=0 TO 5
1530   IF GR$(I%) = "A" THEN A! = A! + 4.0
1535   IF GR$(I%) = "B" THEN A! = A! + 3.0
1540   IF GR$(I%) = "C" THEN A! = A! + 2.0
1545   IF GR$(I%) = "D" THEN A! = A! + 1.0
1550   IF GR$(I%) = "F" THEN A! = A! + 0.0
1555 NEXT I%
1560 A! = A! / 6
1565 RETURN
1566 REM - END COMPUTE GPA --------------------
1567 REM
```

The module starting at line 2000 displays the results on the screen. This module does all its work in one line, number 2020. You should add some text to this line to make the results more readable to the user.

```
2000 REM ----- REPORT GPA -------------------
2005 REM        ASSUMES S% IS STUDENT NUMBER AND A! IS THE GPA
2010 REM        PROMISES TO DISPLAY S% AND A!
2015 REM
2020 PRINT "STUDENT # " S% " HAS A GRADE POINT AVERAGE OF " A!
2025 RETURN
2026 REM - END REPORT GPA -------------------
2027 REM
```

The last activity stores the record back on the file. It is not necessary in this example, since the program has been working with a copy of the student record and the data on the record have not been changed. The module Store Student Record has been included to illustrate the process.

In the module, the array that contains the grades is formated into a single piece of data called X$. Line 2515 defines a data item called X$ with zero characters. The loop at line 2520 places each grade in turn into X$. After the loop, X$ contains all six grades. Line 2535 then places the grades back on the record, and the next line puts the record back onto the file. The data item S% tells the computer which record to store.

```
2500 REM ----- STORE STUDENT RECORD -------------------
2505 REM        ASSUMES S% RECORD IS IN BUFFER AND GR$() IS TO BE STORED
2510 REM
2515 X$=""
2520 FOR I% = 0 TO 5
2525    X$ = X$ + GR$(I%)
2530 NEXT I%
2535 LSET F5$ = X$
2540 PUT #1, S%
2545 RETURN
2546 REM - END STORE STUDENT RECORD -------------------
2547 REM
```

These six modules do a lot of work for one small function. You can see how building software becomes very complex. This brief run-through shows how dividing a program into activities makes writing it far more manageable.

This chapter has given you a quick tour of the software development process. The remaining chapters will follow the same procedure: They will introduce a function, model the function, define its data, build a program outline, and construct the BASIC program. Beginning with the next chapter, you will also build test cases and estimate the size of your programs.

# 2

# Performing a Calculation

## 2A. Building the Model

In this section, you will work through the entire program-building process in greater detail, using a smaller, simpler example that allows you to concentrate on the tools and techniques. This simple program performs a calculation — it computes the grade point average for an individual student.

This chapter introduces two new steps in the method for building a program: estimating the time needed to complete the program and building test cases. Including these new procedures, the basic approach to building software now consists of the following steps, given in order:

- defining a function to be performed by the program

- defining the data flowing into and out of the function

- estimating the size of the job

- building test data that will verify the program

- building an outline of the program

- building the program by writing the program language syntax, following the outline

You will work through these activities one at a time. At the end of section 2B is an exercise that allows you to work through the same process using a different case study.

**Defining the function**

The school guidance counselor has asked you to build a small program that computes the grade point average for a student's semester grades. Your first step is to define the function performed by the program, working directly from the description given by the counselor. In his statement, you find the name of the function: Compute Grade Point Average. You represent that function by drawing a circle and labeling it with the function name.

Next, you declare the data needed by the function and the data produced by it. To compute the GPA, the function uses the student's semester grades, so these must be entered into the program. You show this by drawing an arrow into the function labeled Grade List. As its name indicates, the program produces a grade point average. This piece of data is represented by an arrow flowing out of the function.

**Figure 2.1. Data flow diagram for Compute GPA.**

## Defining the data

Before writing a program, you must know exactly what is inside every package of data represented by an arrow. You may be tempted to say that the function needs only a list of grades, since everyone knows what grades are. However, your definition and the counselor's definition of a grade list may not be the same. For example, a list of grades could contain four grades or nine. To you, the letter I might be a valid grade meaning incomplete, but to the counselor, *I* may be invalid. To be sure the program works according to the counselor's instructions, you need a precise definition of each data flow.

You arrive at data flow definitions after consulting with the counselor: He wants to enter a list of exactly six letter grades. Each grade is one of the letters A, B, C, D, F, or W. To calculate the GPA, you also need to know how many points each grade is worth. Each A is worth four points, each B is worth three points, and so on until F, which is worth zero points. A grade of W stands for withdrawn and is ignored in the grade point average calculation. This defines the incoming data flow; now look at the outgoing one. Obviously, you won't be able to list all possible values of the grade point average. Instead, give its range: GPA is a real number between 0.0 and 4.0. You need a convenient way of writing the numerous data definitions in larger programs. For future reference, these definitions should be recorded alphabetically in a notebook called the *data dictionary*.

They could be written as follows:

Grade can be A, B, C, D, F, or W.

Grade List is a series of exactly six grades.

Grade Point Average is a real number between 0.0 and 4.0.

Since writing out the definitions may be cumbersome, a special, simpler notation is suggested. Table 2.1 shows the definition of the data items using this notation, followed by an explanation.

---

## DATA DICTIONARY

Grade = [ A | B | C | D | F | W ]

      Grade can be only one member of the set enclosed in square brackets.
      The vertical bar separates the different choices.

Grade List = 6 {Grade} 6

      The curly braces around Grade indicate a series of grades.
      The 6 to the left of the brace means at least six grades, while the 6 to
           the right means no more than six grades.
      In other words, the series must contain exactly six grades.

Grade Point Average = Real number between 0.0 and 4.0

      This comment describes the data type (real or integer)
          and its range.

---

**Table 2.1. Data dictionary for Compute GPA.**

The data dictionary contains information about the composition and value of data. The definition of Grade List is an example of composition; it tells you that Grade List is composed of exactly six individual grades. Grade and Grade Point Average define the possible values of those data items. The definition of Grade shows the correct values of a grade, while Grade Point Average is any number within a range.

In Chapter 3, you will see definitions of nonnumeric data items. For this type of data item, give the number of characters that make up the length of the data item. The portfolio in Appendix A contains a summary of the symbols used in the data dictionary. Refer to this summary as you work through the coming chapters.

The primary purpose of the data dictionary is to give you a more precise understanding of the program's function. These definitions, however, are useful in many other situations. They are used to build test cases and to estimate the size of the program, as they are needed to build the code that edits incoming data flows and manipulates data on files. Even after the program is completed, the definitions are required for future improvements and modifications to the program.

**Estimating the size of the program**

With the function and data defined, you have the necessary information for estimating the time needed to build a computer program. You may feel this is unnecessary, since you will get the job done eventually. Estimates, however, are useful for several reasons. You may want to decide whether you can meet a deadline. For example, you want to build a program that helps with income tax preparation and want some assurance that you will be able to finish the project well before April 15. Estimates will also prevent the frustration of trying to do a ten-day job in three days.

Estimates can sometimes save you from building inefficient programs. Suppose you decide to build a program for storing recipes and planning meals. You project that it will save two hours each week in household chores. If you estimate the program will take 100 hours to build, it will take almost a year of use to accrue any benefit. Of course, an estimate may help to justify building a program. Perhaps the recipe program could save five hours a week. If you estimate that the program will take fifteen hours to build, the program will pay for itself in three weeks.

Professional programmers are required to predict how long a job will take to complete. If they have no way of estimating the size of the job and no data on which to base predictions, they are forced to make up numbers and hope they can live up to them.

Reaching an estimate requires that you first estimate the program's size, which is roughly equivalent to its complexity. You measure complexity by inspecting the data flow diagram and data definitions. The more data flowing into and out of the function and the more complex the data definitions, the more complex the program will be. A function that processes five packages of data will be larger than a function that processes two. Also, the more complex the program, the longer to build it.

To compute a rough measure of size, count the incoming and outgoing data flows on the data flow diagram, assigning points to them called *tokens*. Because each data flow represents one package of data that the function must process, each data flow is counted as one token. The diagram for this example has two data flows, so the initial token count is two.

Next, look at the data dictionary definitions, noting the braces and brackets. The braces tell you that the function works with a series of data items, in this case a series of grades. Processing a list of data requires fairly complex code. You account for this complexity in your estimate by adding one to the token count for each set of braces. Since the data dictionary shows one set of braces, you add one.

Similarly, a program requires fairly complex code to process a data flow defined as a choice of several options. Therefore, each set of brackets should be counted as one token. The current example shows one set of brackets in the data dictionary. So, you add one to the token count.

The final token count for the Compute GPA function is four. Enter this number on a performance log like that shown in Table 2.2.

PERFORMANCE LOG

| Function | Token Count | Estimate | Actual Time | Rate Token/Time |
|----------|-------------|----------|-------------|-----------------|
| 1 | 4 | | | |

**Table 2.2. Performance log for Compute GPA.**

The amount of time taken to complete a project depends on both the size of the project and your programming speed. The figure used for your programming speed, or rate, is based on past experience. Keep track of the time taken to complete your programs and record the total amount of time in the performance log under Actual Time. With the size estimate and previous time, you compute your speed by dividing the sum of all token counts from past projects by the sum of the times taken to complete them. Future estimates can then be made by dividing the token count of the current function by your past rate.

Enter both your calculated rate of programming and the estimate into the performance log, which is part of your portfolio. The log, along with the other parts of the portfolio, will help to track your progress.

**Identifying the test cases**

After coding the program, you test it to verify that it does what it should. Testing means entering data, running the program, and checking the results. A set of input data, along with the result you expect from the program, is called a *test case*. You will need several to test a program thoroughly. Building the test cases is your next task.

You want to test as many values of data as you can while keeping the number of test cases reasonably low. Because you can test only a limited number of values, they must be carefully selected. Here, again, you work from the data definitions. The definition for the data flow Grade List tells you that the program will get six grades. You must build a test case for each separate valid grade, being sure to include the correct result. If you enter six A's, you would expect a grade of 4.0, since the grade A is worth four points. If the program gives something else, you know that it contains an error.

You should be able to enter six B's and get a result of 3.0 and six F's for a result of 0.0. You should also design a test case that combines different grades. A test case of three A's and three F's should give you 2.0.

The grade W is a special case because it isn't counted in the GPA. You need two test cases for W, one that consists of W's only, which produces a correct result of 0.0, and one that combines a W with valid grades. If you include a W along with five A's, the result should be 4.0, since W should be ignored. If you get some other answer, the program is handling the W grade incorrectly.

In addition to checking valid values of incoming data, you must include at least one test case that contains an invalid piece of data, one not defined in the data dictionary. Invalid data should cause the program to give an error message. A grade of X is not part of the definition, so you can design a test case containing only the letter X.

As you identify test data, record them in your portfolio's test case log.

---

### TEST CASE LOG

| Test Case | | | | | | Result |
|---|---|---|---|---|---|---|
| A | A | A | A | A | A | 4.0 |
| B | B | B | B | B | B | 3.0 |
| C | C | C | C | C | C | 2.0 |
| D | D | D | D | D | D | 1.0 |
| F | F | F | F | F | F | 0.0 |
| W | W | W | W | W | W | 0.0 |
| A | A | A | F | F | F | 2.0 |
| A | A | A | W | A | A | 4.0 |
| X | | | | | | Error message |

---

Table 2.3. Sample test case log for Compute GPA.

Building test cases helps to clarify the function performed by the program. While constructing test cases, you often find unfamiliar situations. For example, you may not have realized that W's are not counted in the GPA. The question, however, would probably have occurred to you if you tried to calculate the result of entering a grade of W along with five A's. When you have questions like this, ask the user what he wants. Projecting results before you start to program will prevent many errors.

**Building the program outline**

You are now ready to build the program outline. Recall from Chapter 1 the five basic activities performed by computer programs. Look at the arrows in the data flow diagram and determine which activity is needed to process each arrow. The program gets the data flow Grade List from the user and reports the data flow GPA to the user. Getting the grade list and reporting the GPA are two activities which the program performs. The program is not using a file, so it does not need activities that retrieve and store data on internal files. To compute the average, the program uses the third type of activity, manipulating data. The program outline is complete once this activity has been added. To summarize, this function has three activities: getting the grades from the user, computing the average of these grades, and reporting the result to the user.

Construct the program outline by drawing one circle for each activity under a circle representing the Compute GPA function. Compute GPA is the top activity and directs the others. As the dotted lines indicate, it coordinates the subordinate activities to perform the function. Each circle represents a block of code.

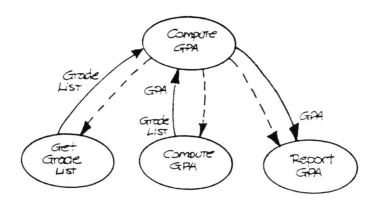

**Figure 2.2. Program outline for Compute GPA.**

Through the modeling process, you have defined the function and its data. You have estimated the size of the project and defined test cases that will verify the accuracy of the final program. The program outline is your guide to code construction. Section 2B completes this example by building the language commands for each activity on the program outline.

# 2B. Building the BASIC Program

After building a model of the program to compute the average of six grades, you have a thorough understanding of the job ahead. You know the function to be performed, the data necessary to perform it, the size of the job, and the organization of the program. Everything is ready for you to write the BASIC commands.

Each activity on the program outline will become one module of code. The lower-level modules will be initiated in order by the top module, which uses a GOSUB command followed by the module's starting line number. So, before you can code the top module, you must assign a starting line number to each activity on the program outline.

One convenient numbering system is to assign a starting number of 10 to the top module and to number the remaining modules in increments of 500. This leaves enough numbers available for the lines of code within each module. Figure 2.3 shows the activities in the Compute GPA function numbered according to this system.

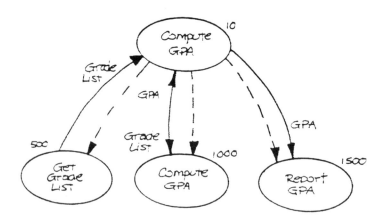

**Figure 2.3. Program outline for Compute GPA.**

The top activity coordinates the lower-level activities by stepping through a series of GOSUB commands. It first invokes the Get Grade List module with a GOSUB 500, then the Compute GPA module with a GOSUB 1000, and finally the Report GPA module with a GOSUB 1500.

```
5 REM ----- COMPUTE STUDENT GPA -------------------
6 REM
10 DIM GR$(5)
100 REM
105 GOSUB 500
110 GOSUB 1000
115 GOSUB 1500
120 END
121 REM - END COMPUTE STUDENT GPA -------------------
122 REM
```

Line number 100 tells the computer about the data flow Grade List. The data dictionary defines Grade List as a series of individual grades. A series of similar data items such as grades is called an *array*. Arrays are indicated in the data dictionary by curly braces. In a BASIC program, the series of data items is called by one name, and each data item is identified by a number called a *subscript*, which is attached to the name of the array. The purpose of the dimension statement is to tell the computer the size and name of the array. The size of an array is the number of data elements in it.

In this example, there are six grades in the array. The DIM statement in line 100 shows a size of five instead of six because BASIC starts with 0 when numbering the elements of an array. Therefore, the first grade is Grade (0), making Grade (5) the sixth element of the array. The diagram below shows how each grade in the grades array corresponds to a number, also referred to as the grade's position in the array.

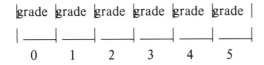

Line 100 names the array GR$. The letters GR make up the data name. It would be clearer to name the array Grade or Grade List, but most BASIC interpreters allow only two-character data names.

The name also includes the type of data in the array. BASIC recognizes four types of data: integers, real numbers up to seven digits, real numbers with eight or more digits, and strings of characters. The symbol after the data name tells the computer what data type is in the array. The dollar sign means that the grade is a string of characters.

Like an array, each item in the data dictionary needs a BASIC name used for written code. After assigning a name to a piece of data, you record that name in the data dictionary, a central place for keeping track of data names used in your programs. Simply write the BASIC data name under the corresponding definition. A sample data dictionary for the Compute GPA program is illustrated in Table 2.4.

---

## DATA DICTIONARY

Grade = [ A | B | C | D | F | W ]
    G$

Grade List = 6{Grade}6
    GR$()

Grade Point Average = Real number between 0.0 and 4.0
    A!

---

**Table 2.4. Data dictionary with BASIC data names.**


According to the table, the grade point average has the data name A!, and the data item that contains an individual letter grade has the data name G$. All data names must end with a symbol indicating the type of data. The exclamation point in A! defines the data item as a real number with seven digits or less.

The first module invoked by the top module is Get Grade List (starting at line number 500). You decide to write this module first, although in fact you can write the modules in any order you choose. The objective of Get Grade List is to prepare the Grade List array for processing, which means it has to get each grade from the user and place it in the array GR$. Always keep the module's function in mind; writing program syntax can confuse you if you lose sight of it.

The code for this activity goes through the process of getting a grade and putting it in the array six times, once for each grade. You use a counting loop to repeat the process. Below is a very rough sketch of the module showing only the code that controls the loop. Line numbers are ignored until the logic of the module is defined.

```
500 REM
505 REM ** GET GRADE LIST **
    FOR C%=0 TO 5
        get a valid grade
        put the grade in the array
    NEXT C%
    RETURN
```

The counting loop starts by setting an integer (C%) equal to a low value (0 in the example). Each time the program completes the instructions inside the loop, it adds one to the integer. Thus, the statements inside the loop are executed once for each value of the integer. The loop ends when the integer is greater than the upper limit (5 in the example).

Add the details after the module has been outlined. First, build the code that gets a single valid grade. This code asks the counselor to type a grade on the keyboard. An INPUT statement displays the word GRADE? and then waits for the user to type in a string of characters (G$).

Any program should check that the data entered by the user are valid. This process is called *editing*. In this case, the program checks that the grade is A, B, C, D, F, or W. If the grade is not one of these, the program displays an error message and asks for another grade.

```
500 REM
505 REM ** GET GRADE LIST **
   FOR C%=0 TO 5
    E%=0
    WHILE E%=0
     INPUT "GRADE";G$
     E%=0
     IF G$="A" THEN E%=1
     IF G$="B" THEN E%=1
     IF G$="C" THEN E%=1
     IF G$="D" THEN E%=1
     IF G$="F" THEN E%=1
     IF G$="W" THEN E%=1
     IF E%=0 THEN PRINT "UNRECOGNIZED GRADE.  REENTER."
    WEND
     Put the grade in the array
   NEXT C%
   RETURN
```

Each time the counselor enters an invalid grade, the program repeats the process of asking for a new grade and checking that it is valid. Therefore, you set up another loop that repeats until the counselor has entered a valid grade. Since you do not know how many times the program will go through the loop, use a general loop construct with the WHILE command. The statements between the WHILE and WEND will execute over again as long as the integer E% is equal to 0. If the user enters a valid grade, the value of E% is changed to 1 and the program exits the loop.

Inside the loop, the program gets the grade and the IF statements check that it is valid. The program compares G$ with the valid values. If one of them equals G$, the program sets E% to 1. If E% equals 0 after the grade has been checked, the input is not good and the program displays an error message. If E% equals 1, the input is good and the program can leave the loop.

The program puts the valid grade into the Grade List array. This is done with the single statement *GR$(C%)=G$*. G$ contains the grade just entered. C% points to the next element in the grades array. Remember, C% increases by 1 each time the counting loop is performed. Therefore, every time the program puts a grade into the array, C% increases by 1 over the last grade entry. Thus, each grade is placed immediately after the last grade entered.

The module that gets the grades is almost complete. You should display some instructions to guide the counselor. You can display messages to the user with the PRINT statement. Below is the complete module, including remarks. The blank REM statement on line 500 separates Get Grade List from the preceding module in the program by adding white space between modules of code.

```
500 REM ----- GET GRADE LIST --------------------
505 REM        PROMISES GR$ CONTAINING 6 GRADES
510 REM
515 PRINT "ENTER 6 GRADES.  PRESS <ENTER> AFTER EACH GRADE."
520 FOR C%=0 TO 5
525   E%=0
530   WHILE E%=0
535    INPUT "GRADE";G$
540    IF G$="A" THEN E%=1
545    IF G$="B" THEN E%=1
550    IF G$="C" THEN E%=1
555    IF G$="D" THEN E%=1
560    IF G$="F" THEN E%=1
565    IF G$="W" THEN E%=1
570    IF E%=0 THEN PRINT "UNRECOGNIZED GRADE.  REENTER."
575    WEND
580    GR$(C%) = G$
585 NEXT C%
590 RETURN
591 REM - END GET GRADE LIST --------------------
592 REM
```

Once all grades have been entered, the program averages them.  According to the program outline and data dictionary, module 1000 uses an array of six grades to produce a GPA.  The module begins by adding the values of the grades.  It sets the data field called A! to 0 and then adds the value of each grade to it.  The counting loop construct used in module 500 can be used here.

```
1000 REM
1005 REM ** COMPUTE GPA **
    A!=0
    FOR C%=0 TO 5
      add the grade's value to A!
    NEXT C%
    divide A! by 6
```

This loop allows the module to look at each of the six grades one at a time.  IF statements determine the value of the grades.  If the grade is A, 4.0 is added to the total.  If the grade is B, 3.0 is added to the total. If the grade is F, 0.0 is added.  A rough sketch of this code is shown below.

```
1000 REM
1005 REM ** COMPUTE GPA **
    A! = 0
    FOR C% = 0 TO 5
      IF GR$(C%) = "A" THEN A! = A! + 4.0
      IF GR$(C%) = "B" THEN A! = A! + 3.0
      IF GR$(C%) = "C" THEN A! = A! + 2.0
      IF GR$(C%) = "D" THEN A! = A! + 1.0
      IF GR$(C%) = "F" THEN A! = A! + 0.0
    NEXT C%
    divide A! by 6
```

This code is not complete because it does not take into account the grade **W**. If one of the grades is W, the module must divide the total by five, not six. In other words, the program counts the number of completed grades and divides the total by that count. Each time the program sees a completed grade (not W), it adds 1 to a count, N%. The complete module is shown below.

```
1000 REM ----- COMPUTE GPA -------------------
1005 REM       ASSUMES GR$() WITH 6 GRADES
1010 REM       PROMISES A! CONTAINS AVERAGE
1015 REM
1020 A!=0
1025 N%=0
1030 FOR C% = 0 TO 5
1035   IF GR$(C%) = "A" THEN A! = A! + 4.0: N% = N% + 1
1040   IF GR$(C%) = "B" THEN A! = A! + 3.0: N% = N% + 1
1045   IF GR$(C%) = "C" THEN A! = A! + 2.0: N% = N% + 1
1050   IF GR$(C%) = "D" THEN A! = A! + 1.0: N% = N% + 1
1055   IF GR$(C%) = "F" THEN A! = A! + 0.0: N% = N% + 1
1060 NEXT C%
1065 IF N% > 0 THEN A! = A! / N%
1070 RETURN
1071 REM - END COMPUTE GPA -------------------
1072 REM
```

Note that line 1065 checks the count (N%) to see if it is greater than 0. If all the grades were W, the count would be equal to 0. Dividing by 0 causes most BASIC interpreters to abort. The check on line 1065 guards against this possibility. If all grades are W, the average (A!) equals 0.

The final module in the program outline is Report GPA. Its task is simply to display the average to the counselor. This is done with the PRINT statement as shown below.

```
1500 REM ----- REPORT GPA -------------------
1505 REM       ASSUMES A! IS THE GPA
1510 REM       PROMISES TO DISPLAY A!
1515 REM
1520 PRINT "THE AVERAGE OF THE GRADE LIST IS: "A!
1525 RETURN
1526 REM - END REPORT GPA -------------------
1527 REM
```

The program is now ready to be typed into your computer and tested. After you have typed the program, run it with the test data in section 2A. Any result other than that expected points to an error in the program. Check that the code was entered properly. If there are no typing errors, check that all modules are doing what the program outline says they should do.

Once the program has been tested, you record in the performance log how long you took to build the program and then calculate your programming speed by dividing the token count by the hours worked. For example, if this program took three hours and you estimated the size to be four tokens, you worked at a rate of 1.33 tokens per hour. You will probably be able to build the next error-free program at a rate of 1.33 tokens per hour; this rate will improve as you gain experience.

You have just completed the entire process of building a program. You saw how a function is modeled with a data flow diagram and data dictionary. You have been introduced to the process of building test cases and estimating the size of a program. You also saw how the program outline is formed and used to build BASIC code.

You are now ready for the following exercise. The problem is similar to the one you just worked through. If you need assistance, refer back to the examples in this chapter. For consistency, this first exercise is labeled "II" to correspond to the chapter number. The remaining exercises will be numbered accordingly.

## EXERCISE II

The case study used for the exercises throughout the book concerns a community theater that puts on four or five productions each year. The president of the theater tells you that one of its members has volunteered to take ticket reservations for upcoming shows. Unfortunately, the old gentleman never learned his multiplication tables and has trouble calculating ticket charges.

The regular ticket price is $5. A special price of $3 per ticket is given to students and senior citizens. The president has asked you to build a program that accepts the number of regular and special tickets requested by the patron and displays the total price for regular tickets, the total price for special tickets, and a grand total.

Your assignment is to build the program by doing the following:

1.  define the program's function by drawing a data flow diagram; name the function and identify the incoming and outgoing data flows

2.  write data dictionary definitions for all data flows

3.  calculate the token count for this function and enter the count in your performance log

4.  build four test cases that will test the program after it is written

5.  build a program outline by identifying all activities needed to perform this function

6.  construct the BASIC code for each activity on the program outline

Suggested answers and a discussion of the exercise are located in Appendix C. Check your work against the suggested answers. If there are any differences, review the material and examples in this chapter.

*3*

# Creating a Random File

## 3A. Building the Model

One of the most important functions performed by computers is the storage and retrieval of data. Data entered into a program can be retained on internal files and then recalled when needed. In this section, you will see how the program-building process is used to create a program that remembers data.

A file built and used by a computer program can be compared to a file cabinet. The file contains folders or records, and each record contains a set of related data. A person can go to the file and retrieve any folder directly. Similarly, computer files consist of records that the user can ask for individually by name. A file from which any record can be taken directly is called a *random* file. You will build this type of file for the guidance counselor.

The counselor was so impressed with the program you built for him that he wants you to build a program that stores data about his students. This small program will store student names, ID numbers, class years, and grades. Each student has been assigned an ID number ranging from 1 to 100 and takes six classes in a semester, with a grade awarded for each class.

**Defining the function**

Before a file can be used by a program to store data, the file has to be created. Just as the counselor would have to buy a file cabinet, folders, and paper before he could store records, you will have to create a blank computer file containing a blank record for each student ID number. The function to create an entire file of blank records is represented in Figure 3.1.

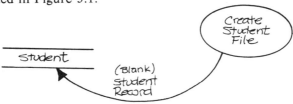

**Figure 3.1. Data flow diagram for Create Student File.**

The next step is to store the information on the blank file. While you create the file only once, the counselor needs to store new data many times — every time a new student enrolls or an old student changes courses or class year. Therefore, this function not only stores the original data on the file, but also updates it.

To define this function, work directly from the description given by the counselor: a small program that will store student name, ID number, class year, and grades. You decide to call the function Store Student Data and start modeling it with the data flow diagram in Figure 3.2. So far, this diagram looks much like the previous examples.

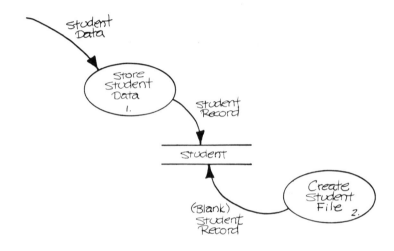

**Figure 3.2. Data flow diagram for Store Student Data.**

Now, try to visualize how the counselor would use the new program to update and store student data. He would enter the student's ID number and the program would display the student's record, containing all data for that student. If no record existed yet for that student, nothing would appear on the screen. In either case, the counselor would then enter the new data, and the program would place the record with the new data back on the student file.

The preliminary data flow diagram shows data flowing only into the function and the file. Now, however, you see that data must flow both ways. To provide a more accurate picture of the function, the data flow diagram needs four data flows, as shown in Figure 3.3, bubble 1. The user must tell the program which record he wants by entering the student ID. The old data from the student file are displayed, and the new or changed data are entered onto the record, which is stored back on the file.

The numbers in the bubbles in Figure 3.3 are merely a convenient way of referring to the functions. In later chapters, the data flow diagrams will be larger, and the numbered bubbles will be easier to recognize.

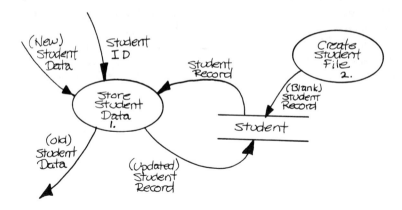

**Figure 3.3. Revised data flow diagram for Store Student Data.**

### Defining the data

The data flows represented by the arrows around the function must now be defined with the counselor's help. The data flow labeled Student ID is a number that identifies a particular student. Because there are a maximum of 100 students, the numbers range from 1 to 100. This information is recorded in the data dictionary, shown in Table 3.1.

---

## DATA DICTIONARY

Class Year = [ FR | SO | JR | SR ]

First Name = Maximum length of 10 characters

Grade = [ A | B | C | D | F | W ]

Grade List = 6{Grade}6

Student ID = Integer between 1 and 100

Last Name = Maximum length of 20 characters

Student Data = Student Name + Class Year + Grade List

Student File = 100{Student Record}100

Student Name = First Name + Last Name

Student Record = Student ID + Student Name + Class Year + Grade List

---

**Table 3.1. Data dictionary.**

You were told earlier that the counselor wants to store the student's name, ID number, class year, and grades. In talking with the counselor, you now find that he wants both the first and last name of the student stored on the file. This information makes up the student's record, also defined in the data dictionary. Now, you define the data items making up the student record. According to the counselor, there will be six grades (A, B, C, D, F, or W). Class Year is a code identifying the student as a freshman (FR), sophomore (SO), junior (JR), or senior (SR).

Notice that you define the maximum size for the first and last names. When writing a record to the file, you need to know the size of each data item. On a record, each piece of data occupies a fixed space, and you must assign a certain amount of space to each data item in advance. Since this limits the number of characters in each data item, you define the record so that it contains the maximum size of all data items.

Both (New) Student Data and (Old) Student Data consist of the student's name, grades, and class. Because both have the same content, list only Student Data in the data dictionary. In the data flow diagram, the parentheses around the adjectives *Old* and *New* tell you that the definition for these data flows are found under Student Data. Similarly, the data flow produced by bubble 2 (Create Student File) has the same definition as the student record in bubble 1. The only difference is that the (Blank) Student Record has blanks in each data item. The dictionary defines the student file as a series of student records. The file is built initially with 100 blank records. As the counselor works with the file, the records are updated with real data, but the file always has 100 records.

**Estimating the size of the program**

Now, you can estimate the program's size by building a token count for each function shown on the data flow diagram. By counting each data flow that goes into or out of bubble 1 as one token, you get a total of five tokens. The remaining tokens are found by inspecting the data dictionary for braces and brackets.

Although Chapter 2 implied that each set of braces or brackets is counted as one token, that isn't usually true. You ignore a set if the material inside is not manipulated by the function. Look at each data flow's definition. If it contains a set of braces or brackets, imagine yourself performing the function and ask yourself if the function needs to know what data are inside it. If it does manipulate the data one or more times, add one to the token count. The following examples should make this clearer.

The data flow (New) Student Data contains a set of braces around Grade. The function handles each grade from the new student data as it is entered by the user, checks that the grade is valid, and places it in its correct place on the record. This adds one to the token count.

(New) Student Data also contains two sets of brackets: one around Grade and one around Class Year. The brackets mean that the function must choose a single data item from a set of items. When the function gets new student data, it verifies the content of Grade and Class Year. You must build two blocks of code to check the validity of both the incoming grade and the class year. Count each set of brackets as one token.

The Student Record and (Updated) Student Record data flows both contain braces. Do you count these braces or not? If you retrieved the student record from a file cabinet, you would go to a file drawer and pull out a single object — the folder. You would not look at the data while getting the folder. At that time, the exact contents of the folder, including the individual grades in braces, would not matter to you. The same is true of the Store Student Data function when it takes the student record out of the file or places the updated student record back onto the file. Because the function treats each record as one single set of data, you do not count these braces in your token count. The function does not affect the data inside the set of braces, so you do not build code to manipulate that series of data items.

The total token count for function 1 is calculated at nine tokens. It is not important that you totally agree with this estimate. What is important is that you begin to get a feel for the process. As long as your own estimates are consistent, you will be able to determine how much time you need to complete a job.

Function 2 (Create Student File) writes out only 100 blank records, and the data flow diagram shows only one data flow connected to it. The function does not refer directly to the grade list, the individual grade, or the class year codes, so do not count the braces or brackets in the data definition. Bubble 2 has a token count of one, and the entire job program has a token count of ten, as recorded in the sample performance log in Table 3.2.

PERFORMANCE LOG

| Function | Token Count | Estimate | Actual Time | Rate Token/Time |
|----------|-------------|----------|-------------|-----------------|
| 1 | 9 | | | |
| 2 | 1 | | | |
| TOTAL | 10 | | | |

Table 3.2. Performance log.

## Identifying the test cases

You need to build test cases containing both valid and invalid data. To be sure the program treats invalid data as errors, create one test case with invalid data for each type of data. Use test data that are just below the lowest allowable value and just above the highest value. Table 3.3 shows that if you enter a student ID equal to 0 and another equal to 101, the result should be an error message. The next two test cases verify that the program will not accept a first or last name with too many characters. You also build test cases to ensure that an invalid class year or grade is reported as an error.

## TEST CASE LOG

| Test Case | | | | | | | | | | Result |
|---|---|---|---|---|---|---|---|---|---|---|
| Student ID | Characters Last and First Name | | Class Year | Grade List | | | | | | |
| 0 | | | | | | | | | | Error message |
| 101 | | | | | | | | | | Error message |
| | 21 | | | | | | | | | Error message |
| | | 11 | | | | | | | | Error message |
| | | | FX | | | | | | | Error message |
| | | | | X | | | | | | Error message |
| 1 | Smith | John | FR | A | A | A | A | A | A | Updates record 1 |
| 100 | Jones | Mary | SO | B | B | B | B | B | B | Updates record 100 |
| 10 | Peters | Jon | JR | C | C | C | C | C | C | Updates record 10 |
| 11 | Pike | Sue | SR | D | D | D | D | D | D | Updates record 11 |
| 2 | Adams | Al | FR | F | F | F | F | F | F | Updates record 2 |
| 3 | Baker | Wes | SR | W | W | W | W | W | W | Updates record 3 |

**Table 3.3. Test case log.**

After covering the invalid cases, you can start on the valid ones. When selecting valid test data for a certain data item, you can test every value if there aren't too many. For example, since the data item called Class Year has four values, you can make sure the program accepts all four. You can also test all six grades, although certainly not all combinations of those grades. To save work, use the same test cases here that you built in Chapter 2. The reason you record the test cases in the portfolio is to avoid the work of recreating them for future testing.

In many cases, it would take you too much time to test every possible value of a data item. Instead, you should carefully select two or three values. Because programming errors often occur when the program is working on the lowest or highest value of a piece of data, you should always include lowest and highest values in your test data. You can identify these values by looking at the data dictionary. For example, since the student ID number must be between 1 and 100, you should test the program with a student ID equal to 1 and another equal to 100. In both cases, the program should display the content of these records.

Group together as many valid cases as possible. For instance, the seventh test case in Table 3.3 checks that the smallest ID is accepted, FR is accepted as a class code, and A is accepted as a grade. Doubling up on valid test cases is a good way of keeping the total number of test cases at a manageable level.

## Building the program outline

The last task before writing code is building the program outline. You need to identify the activities that carry out the functions you have just defined. Using the data flow diagram, pick the combination of activities that get data and report it to the outside world, store it on files and then retrieve it, and manipulate it.

Draw an activity on the program outline for each of the two incoming data flows. One is responsible for getting a valid student ID number, and the other does everything necessary to get a good set of new student data.

Another activity retrieves the student record from the file, using the student ID number to identify the correct record. You also need an activity to store the student record back on the student file.

A fifth activity reports data to the user. That is, you build a piece of code to display the current student data to the counselor.

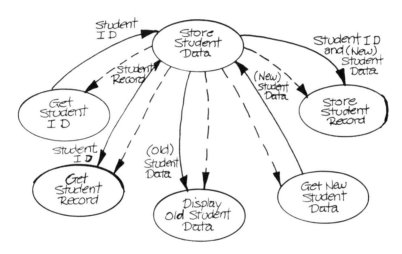

**Figure 3.4. Program outline for Store Student Data.**

Observe that the activities shown on the outline correspond to the data flows around bubble 1 in the data flow diagram in Figure 3.3. The program outline is based on the data flow diagram, since each data flow in the diagram is handled by an activity in the program outline.

Now, turn your attention to Create Student File. Figure 3.3 showed no direct data flow between the two bubbles. When you see two independent functions such as these, you should build two separate programs. Although they are part of the same system, they do not have to be in the same program. Also, since the counselor needs to create a blank student file only once, there is no reason for him to create another each time he runs the program to store student data.

As its data flow diagram clearly shows, Create Student File's program outline needs an activity to store blank records on the file. While that covers the single data flow in Figure 3.1, it does not take care of all activities in the program outline.

Another activity is needed because the blank records have to come from somewhere. Since they don't come from outside the function, the function needs an activity to create a blank record. This activity comes under the category of activities that manipulate data.

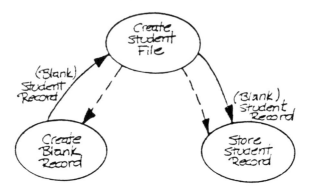

**Figure 3.5. Program outline for Create Student File.**

In this section, you have built a function model that creates and uses a random file. Based on your token counts, the model is 2.5 times larger than the one built in Chapter 2. Although function sizes vary, the process of building software remains the same.

# 3B. Building the BASIC Program

In section 3A, you explored the function of building a random file. The models are now complete, and you are ready to build the BASIC programs that perform the function. As before, you will build small blocks of code to carry out the activities on the program outline.

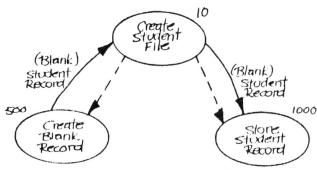

**Figure 3.6. Program outline for Create Student File.**

You start with the program that creates the student file because that program is smaller and because the file must be created before the program that stores student data will work. Figure 3.6 shows the starting line numbers assigned to the activities used in creating the file. Before the program can use a random file, it must first open the file and define the layout of a record. So, besides initiating the lower activities as usual with the GOSUB command, the top module also carries out these two new tasks using the OPEN and FIELD commands.

```
5 REM ----- CREATE STUDENT FILE --------------------
6 REM
10 OPEN "R",#1,"STUDENT"
15 FIELD #1, 2 AS F1$,20 AS F2$,10 AS F3$,2 AS F4$,6 AS F5$,1 AS FX$
20 GOSUB 500
25 GOSUB 1000
30 CLOSE #1
35 END
36 REM - END CREATE STUDENT FILE --------------------
37 REM
```

A BASIC program must give the file a name and number. The number is used in other statements to refer to the file. The OPEN statement at line 10 tells the computer it is dealing with a random file "R" that has file #1 and the name STUDENT.

The FIELD statement on line 15 tells the computer how a record on file #1 is organized. It allots space to each piece of data on the record; such a space is called a *field*. The name of the field follows the symbol AS and the length of the field (number of characters allowed for the data item) precedes the AS.

| | Student ID | Last Name | First Name | Class Year | Grade List | Status |
|---|---|---|---|---|---|---|
| Field Name | F1$ | F2$ | F3$ | F4$ | F5$ | FX$ |
| | \|-- | \|-------------------- | \|---------- | \|-- | \|------ | \|- \| |
| Characters | 2 | 20 | 10 | 2 | 6 | 1 |

**Table 3.4. Student file record layout.**

You decide to name the first field in the record F1$ and make it two characters long, as you will place the student's ID number there later. The second field, labeled F2$, is the future location of the student's last name. It is twenty characters long, since the data dictionary gives twenty characters as the maximum length of the last name. Similarly, the field for the first name (F3$) is allotted ten characters. The two-character class year will go into the fourth field, and the six grades into the fifth field. The sixth field (FX$) contains only one character, whose purpose is discussed below. Note that the length of each field matches the length of the corresponding data item defined in the data dictionary for Student Record:

Student Record = Student ID + Last Name + First Name + Class Year + Grade List
Characters:                    2                20            10             2              1

Each record on the file remains blank until the user enters data onto it. This means that at any point in time there are records that contain new data and others that are still blank. You need to distinguish a blank record from one that has real data. To indicate the status of the record, use the sixth field, FX$. You put an X in this field to indicate that the record is blank. When new data are entered onto the record, the program puts an A into the field to tell you that the record is active.

After carrying out the OPEN and FIELD commands, the program invokes the subroutines that complete the work of creating the file. Once the file is ready and the program is done, it must close the file. The statement on line 30 tells the computer that the program is finished with the student file (file #1).

You should record in the data dictionary the BASIC names assigned to the data, as shown in Table 3.5. Each data item has been assigned two names. In BASIC, edits and arithmetic operations cannot refer directly to the field name, so a second name is needed. For example, when the user enters the student's class year, the program calls this piece of data CL$. The program can then check CL$ to be sure it contains a valid code before placing the code in the record field named F4$. CL$ is the name of the data item entered by the user, F4$ is the name of the field on the student record.

## DATA DICTIONARY

Class Year = [ FR | SO | JR | SR ]
        F4$ or CL$

First Name = Maximum length of 10 characters
        F3$ or NF$

Grade = [ A | B | C | D | F | W ]
        G$

Grade List = 6{Grade}6
        F5$    GR$()

Student ID = Integer between 1 and 100
        F1$ or ID%

Last Name = Maximum length of 20 characters
        F2$ or NL$

Student Data = Student Name + Class Year + Grade List

Student File = 100{Student Record}100
        STUDENT

Student Name = First Name + Last Name

Student Record = Student ID + Student Name + Class Year + Grade List + Status

Status = [ A | X ]
        FX$ or AX$

**Table 3.5. Data dictionary with BASIC data names.**

Notice that the definition of status has been added to the data dictionary. This piece of data is now a permanent part of the student file and must be recorded as part of the student record.

The module at line 500 is responsible for building a blank record. Using the command LSET to move data into a field, it fills the empty fields with blanks. This command takes a string of characters and puts it into the designated field.

```
500 REM ----- CREATE BLANK RECORD --------------------
505 REM        PROMISES A BLANK RECORD IN STUDENT RECORD
510 REM
515 LSET F1$=MKI$(0)
520 LSET F2$="                    "
525 LSET F3$="          "
530 LSET F4$="  "
535 LSET F5$="      "
540 LSET FX$="X"
545 RETURN
546 REM - END CREATE BLANK RECORD --------------------
547 REM
```

In BASIC, integers stored on a record are compressed into two characters. In the FIELD statement, therefore, you make the field for the student ID (an integer) two characters long, even though a student ID could have three digits. The command to compress an integer is MKI$(integer). In the blank record, put the value of 0 in the student ID field.

Lines 520 through 535 put blanks (spaces) into the fields. In the computer, a blank takes up space like any other character. You put twenty spaces in F2$, ten spaces in field F3$, two spaces in F4$, and six spaces in F5$. An X is placed in field FX$ to tell you that this is a blank record.

After a blank record has been built, the program must create 100 copies of it and place them on the student file.

```
1000 REM ----- STORE STUDENT RECORD -------------------
1005 REM      ASSUMES STUDENT FILE IS OPEN
1010 REM      PROMISES TO WRITE 100 RECORDS TO STUDENT FILE
1015 REM
1020 FOR C%=1 TO 100
1025   PUT #1,C%
1030 NEXT C%
1035 RETURN
1036 REM - END STORE STUDENT RECORD -------------------
1037 REM
```

To create 100 copies of the blank record, you set up a counting loop on lines 1020 through 1030. Each execution of the loop simultaneously creates a record and puts it onto the student file. The command to write a record to a file is PUT. It specifies the file number assigned in the OPEN statement and the number of the record that is being written. The first time through the loop, the number of the record C% equals 1, so the program puts record #1 on the file. The second time through, it puts record #2, and so on, until 100 records have been written to the file.

This completes the code for the first program. If you enter and run it, you will create a file called STUDENT with 100 blank records on it. Be sure to save this program before starting the second one. The program that stores student data will be built as a separate program.

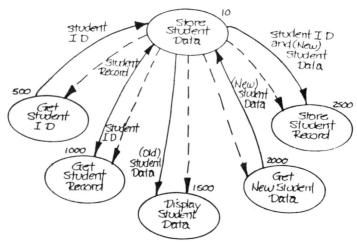

**Figure 3.7. Program outline for Store Student Data.**

In the program outline for Store Student Data in Figure 3.7, the top module, as in the first program, opens the student file and declares the field organization of the student record. Simply copy the statements from the first program. The top module then defines the array for the grades and executes the lower-level modules with the GOSUB statement. The first activity gets a student ID number, and the second gets the associated record. After the third activity displays the data from the record, the fourth gets a new set of student data. The data are then restored onto the file.

```
10 REM ----- STORE STUDENT DATA --------------------
11 REM
15 OPEN "R",#1,"STUDENT"
20 FIELD #1, 2 AS F1$,20 AS F2$,10 AS F3$,2 AS F4$,6 AS F5$,1 AS FX$
25 DIM GR$(5)
100 GOSUB 500
105 GOSUB 1000
110 GOSUB 1500
115 GOSUB 2000
120 GOSUB 2500
125 CLOSE #1
130 END
131 REM - END STORE STUDENT DATA -----------------
132 REM
```

Module 500 is responsible for getting a valid ID number and will not return without one. You set up a general loop in lines 515 through 535. As long as the integer E% is equal to 1, the program will ask for an ID number. When the user enters an ID number between 1 and 100, the program stops the loop by setting E% to 0.

```
500 REM ----- GET STUDENT ID NUMBER --------------------
505 REM        PROMISES STUDENT ID% BETWEEN 1 AND 100
510 REM
515 E%=1
520 WHILE E%=1
525   INPUT "ENTER STUDENT ID";ID%
530   IF (ID%<1) OR (ID%>100) THEN PRINT "BETWEEN 1 AND 100" ELSE E%=0
535 WEND
540 RETURN
541 REM - END GET STUDENT ID NUMBER --------------------
542 REM
```

If you want to check data for validity or use them in a calculation, they must be in a data name other than the field name. As a standard practice, you move the values of the FIELD items to other data names (defined earlier in the data dictionary) so that you can manipulate these pieces of data as you choose. When finished, you move the data back to their fields and PUT them back on the file.

The activity that gets the student record starts at line 1000. First, the program must get the record for the given ID number; this is done on line 1030 with the GET command. Then, the values of all fields are copied into separate data names. The statement on line 1035 tells the computer to take the content of the data field called F2$ and put that same data in the data item called NL$. Data field F2$'s contents are the same; a copy, however, has been placed in NL$.

```
1000 REM ----- GET STUDENT RECORD -------------------
1005 REM        ASSUMES ID% TO BE BETWEEN 1 AND 100
1010 REM            STUDENT FILE IS OPEN
1015 REM        PROMISES NF$, NL$, CL$, GR$() AND AX$ FILLED WITH DATA
1020 REM            FROM STUDENT RECORD ID%
1025 REM
1030 GET #1,ID%
1035 NL$=F2$
1040 NF$=F3$
1045 CL$=F4$
1050 FOR C%=0 TO 5
1055   GR$(C%)=MID$(F5$,C%+1,1)
1060 NEXT C%
1065 AX$=FX$
1070 RETURN
1071 REM - END GET STUDENT RECORD -------------------
1072 REM
```

The activity that gets new student data edits each grade as the user enters it. To make this process easier, you place the grades into an array. This means taking each of the six characters in F5$ and placing them in a corresponding array element. To do this, you use a counting loop and the MID$ command.

The statements from lines 1050 through 1060 make up a counting loop that executes six times. The MID$ command on line 1055 tells the computer to look at the string called F5$ and then pick out the substring that not only starts with the character in the C%+1 position, but is also one character in length. The first time through the loop, C% equals 0. The substring, therefore, starts at the first character of F5$; this is the first grade. In other words, the first time through the loop, line 1055 has the program put the first character of F5$ into GR$(0). The second time through the loop, the second character is placed in GR$(1), and so on until the last time, when the program puts the sixth character of F5$ into GR$(5). Now, all data items from the student's record are in usable data fields.

The next activity (starting at line 1500) displays these data items. You use the PRINT statement to display the data to the user. The line of dashes at the bottom of the module makes the screen more readable by marking the end of the display.

```
1500 REM ----- DISPLAY STUDENT DATA -------------------
1505 REM        ASSUMES STUDENT DATA NF$,NL$,CL$,GR$(),AX$,ID%
1510 REM
1515 PRINT "DATA FOR STUDENT ID ";ID%
1520 PRINT "LAST NAME ",NL$
1525 PRINT "FIRST NAME ",NF$
1530 PRINT "CLASS     ",CL$
1535 PRINT "GRADES   ",
1540 FOR C%=0 TO 5
1545   PRINT GR$(C%);" ";
1550 NEXT C%
1555 PRINT
1560 PRINT "STATUS    ",AX$
1565 PRINT
1570 PRINT "-----------------------------------------"
1575 PRINT
1580 RETURN
1581 REM - END DISPLAY STUDENT DATA -------------------
1582 REM
```

The module called Get New Student Data (line 2000) gets the new student data from the user and makes sure that they are valid. It has the same type of processing as the module that gets the student ID, so you build code similar to that module for each data item the user enters.

From the data dictionary definition of Student Data you know the user will be entering four pieces of data: first name, last name, class year, and grade list. Rather than write one large block of code to handle all four pieces of data, you break the Get New Student Data module into four smaller modules, each responsible for one piece of data. Smaller blocks of code tend to be less complex, and less complex code has fewer errors.

The process of putting a piece of work into its own module is called *factoring*. When factoring a module, you must update the program outline so that it remains an accurate model of the program.

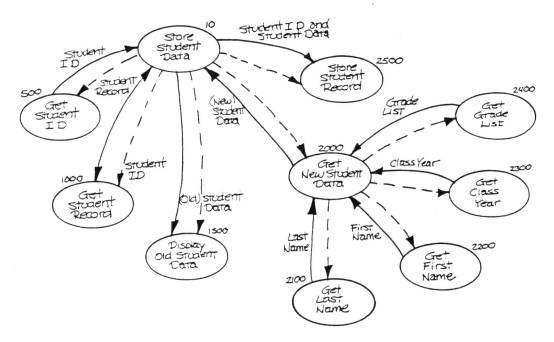

**Figure 3.8. Factored program outline for Store Student Data.**

The code for Get New Student Data is shown below. Notice the basic pattern that is repeated in each module: A general loop is set up that loops until a valid piece of data is entered, just as in the Get Student ID module. The code starting at line 2400 should look even more familiar because it is the same code used in the Chapter 2 example. Since you have written a module that does the same work, why write it again?

```
2000 REM ----- GET NEW STUDENT DATA --------------------
2005 REM      PROMISES VALID VALUES IN STUDENT DATA
2010 REM
2015 GOSUB 2100
```

```
2020 GOSUB 2200
2025 GOSUB 2300
2030 GOSUB 2400
2035 RETURN
2036 REM - END GET NEW STUDENT DATA -------------------
2037 REM


2100 REM ----- GET A VALID LAST NAME (NL$) -------------------
2105 REM
2110 E%=1
2115 WHILE E%=1
2120  INPUT "ENTER STUDENT'S LAST NAME ",NL$
2125  IF LEN(NL$)>20 THEN PRINT "ONLY 20 CHARACTERS" ELSE E%=0
2130 WEND
2135 RETURN
2136 REM - END GET A VALID LAST NAME -------------------
2137 REM


2200 REM ----- GET A VALID FIRST NAME (NF$) -------------------
2205 REM
2210 E%=1
2215 WHILE E%=1
2220  INPUT "ENTER STUDENT'S FIRST NAME ",NF$
2225  IF LEN(NF$)>10 THEN PRINT "ONLY 10 CHARACTERS" ELSE E%=0
2230 WEND
2235 RETURN
2236 REM - END GET A VALID FIRST NAME -------------------
2237 REM


2300 REM ----- GET A VALID CLASS YEAR (CL$) -------------------
2305 REM
2310 E%=1
2315 WHILE E%=1
2320  INPUT "ENTER CLASS YEAR",CL$
2325  IF CL$="FR" THEN E%=0
2330  IF CL$="SO" THEN E%=0
2335  IF CL$="JR" THEN E%=0
2340  IF CL$="SR" THEN E%=0
2345  IF E%=1 THEN PRINT "MUST BE FR, SO, JR, OR SR"
2350 WEND
2355 RETURN
2356 REM - END GET A VALID CLASS CODE -------------------
2357 REM


2400 REM ----- GET GRADE LIST -------------------
2405 REM
2410 PRINT "ENTER 6 GRADES.  PRESS <ENTER> AFTER EACH GRADE."
2415 FOR C%=0 TO 5
2420  E%=0
2425  WHILE E%=0
2430   INPUT "GRADE";G$
2435   IF G$="A" THEN E%=1
2440   IF G$="B" THEN E%=1
2445   IF G$="C" THEN E%=1
2450   IF G$="D" THEN E%=1
2455   IF G$="F" THEN E%=1
2460   IF G$="W" THEN E%=1
2465   IF E%=0 THEN PRINT "UNRECOGNIZED GRADE.  REENTER."
2470  WEND
```

```
2475  GR$(C%)=G$
2480 NEXT C%
2485 RETURN
2486 REM - END GET GRADE LIST -------------------
2487 REM
```

Lines 2125 and 2225 use the command LEN to determine the number of characters in a string. You want to be sure that the first and last names entered by the user fit on the record.

The last activity in the program returns the data prepared in the Get New Student Data module to the student file.

```
2500 REM ----- STORE STUDENT RECORD -------------------
2505 REM        ASSUMES VALID STUDENT DATA, ID% BETWEEN 1 AND 100
2510 REM              STUDENT FILE OPEN
2515 REM        PROMISES TO STORE STUDENT DATA ON RECORD ID%
2520 REM
2525 LSET F1$=MKI$(ID%)
2530 LSET F2$=NL$
2535 LSET F3$=NF$
2540 LSET F4$=CL$
2545 G$="''"
2550 FOR C%=0 TO 5
2555   G$=G$+GR$(C%)
2560 NEXT C%
2565 LSET F5$=G$
2570 LSET FX$="A"
2575 PUT #1,ID%
2580 RETURN
2581 REM - END STORE STUDENT RECORD -------------------
2582 REM
```

The MKI$ command on line 2525 formats the integer ID% into the two-character string F1$. Lines 2545 through 2560 put the Grade array back into a single string. The statement $G\$=$ "" creates a string with zero characters. The counting loop adds each grade in turn to the data item G$, which now contains all six grades and is put into the record field.

Remember that field FX$ indicates the status of the record. Line 2570 puts the code A into the field to mark it as active.

You are now ready to type the programs into your computer and test them. You cannot test the first program directly because it does not produce results you can see, since the file it creates is blank. Only by testing the program that stores student data can you test the program that creates the file.

If the test cases perform as you expect, you are assured of an error-free product. Should one of the test cases produce unexpected results, find the activity that should have caught the error and check the code for a mistake. The program outline is helpful in this task. If the BASIC interpreter reports a syntax error, check your BASIC reference manual to be sure you are using the right syntax for your particular interpreter.

In this section, you have worked through the code needed to build and use a random file. BASIC code was built for each activity of the program outline. You also saw how the program outline can be refined during the coding process by factoring subactivities into their own modules.

The following exercise continues the theater case study you started in Chapter 2. Work through the exercise and then compare your work with the suggested answers in Appendix C.

### EXERCISE III

The community theater was not impressed with your first program, since a cheap calculator can do the same thing. Your new job is to build a set of programs that record the names of ticket purchasers as well as other information now being kept in a ticket sales log.

The ticket seller tells you that most patrons buy more than one ticket to a performance. The largest single order he can remember was seven tickets, and the average purchase is about three.

For each new play, the ticket seller gets a packet of 200 envelopes. Each envelope has a serial number between 1 and 200 printed on it. When a patron asks for a certain number of tickets, the ticket seller finds that number of seats and places the tickets in a small envelope. He then records in the log the envelope number, the patron's name, the number of regular tickets, the number of special tickets, the total amount the patron paid, and a list of seat numbers assigned to the patron.

The theater house has twenty rows (lettered A - T) with twenty chairs in each row (numbered 1 - 20). A three-character seat number is printed on each ticket. The first character specifies the row, and the last two characters specify the chair in the row. So, ticket B5 is for the fifth chair in the second row.

The president of the theater wants a program that replaces the ticket sales log now being kept by the ticket seller.

1.  draw a data flow diagram showing the functions to be performed by the programs; name the functions and data flows

2.  write data dictionary entries for the incoming and outgoing data flows

3.  estimate the size of the project by counting the tokens for each function; enter your results in the performance log

4.  build at least eight test cases to verify the programs after they are written

5.  look at each function and determine which activities must be performed; build a program outline showing a circle for each activity and the organization of the activities

6.  build BASIC code for the activities on the program outlines

# Producing a Report

## 4A. Building the Model

The functions built in Chapter 3 allow the user to look at and update any single record stored on a random file. You can also build functions that produce reports listing and summarizing all records on the file. In this chapter, you will learn how to build such a program.

With the programs in Chapter 3, the guidance counselor can add and change data on any record on the student file. The counselor is happy with the programs but not yet content. After entering dozens of student records, he realizes that he needs a list on paper of all active records on the file. He tells you that the report should list the data from each student record as well as the student's grade point average. A summary at the end of the report should list the average grade for each class.

### Defining the function

As in previous chapters, you build a data flow diagram of the function. This time, however, there are no data flowing in from the outside world. As shown in Figure 4.1, the only piece of data used by the bubble is the Student Record from the Student File.

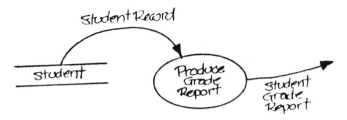

**Figure 4.1. Data flow diagram for Produce Grade Report.**

Since the counselor's description refers to only two sets of data, the Student Record and the Grade Report, the data flow diagram shows only two data flows. The function retrieves the active records from the student file, and includes their data on the outgoing data flow called Student Grade Report.

## Defining the data

Your second task is to define in the data dictionary all data flows and files around the process. You have already defined the Student File and Student Record in Chapter 3. The Student Grade Report contains previously defined data items — Student ID, Student Name, Class Year, Grade List — as part of each line on the report.

---

### DATA DICTIONARY

Class Year = [ FR | SO | JR | SR ]

Class Averages = FR Average + SO Average + JR Average + SR Average

Detail Line = Student ID + Student Name + Class Year + Grade List +
        Grade Point Average

First Name = Maximum length of 10 characters

Grade = [ A | B | C | D | F | W ]

Grade List = 6 {Grade} 6

Grade Point Average = Real number between 0.0 and 4.0

Student ID = Integer between 1 and 100

Last Name = Maximum length of 20 characters

Student File = 100 {Student Record} 100

Student Grade Report = {Detail Line} + Class Averages

Student Name = First Name + Last Name

Student Record = Student ID + Student Name + Class Year + Grade List

---

**Table 4.1. Data dictionary for Produce Grade Report.**

This borrowing from previous work illustrates an important concept: The models you built in the past form the basis for new functions. Just as old test cases can be used to test new programs, so, too, pieces of the data flow diagrams and data dictionary form parts of new programs as the system gets larger. Similarly, you can identify reusable modules of code by inspecting the program's structure depicted in the program outline. This information is found in your portfolio.

### Estimating the size of the program

Since there are two data flows in Figure 4.1, your initial estimate of program size is two token counts. Next, look in the data dictionary for data items that the function will be directly manipulating. You need to determine with which sets of braces and brackets the function is working.

Student Record contains a set of braces around Grade List and two sets of brackets, one around Class Year and one around the choices for grades. You already know from Chapter 3 that when the program retrieves a record, it doesn't look at the series of grades or the class year. Therefore, you do not include them in the token count — at least, not yet. They may still be counted if used later in the program.

In fact, the program does manipulate data inside one of these braces. You discover this by imagining yourself preparing the outgoing data flow, Student Grade Report. When preparing the report, you compute the grade average of each student by adding the series of six grades. You need to know the grades inside the braces, and once you have the GPA you write individual detail lines in the report, so the braces around Detail Line count as well. Including these two sets of braces, the token count is now up to four.

Next, look at the data flow and identify and count any new pieces of data that are not identical to an incoming data flow or that cannot be derived directly from only one of them. The GPA of each student and Class Averages are the only new outgoing data items. GPA is excluded because it is a one-for-one transformation from the grades on the Student Record, since each student record results in a single grade point average.

The Class Averages, however, are counted because each one is a new piece of data accumulated from many student records. Because the four pieces of class averages form such a simple data structure, a sequence of data items as opposed to a series or a selection, you count the set as one token. The total token count for this function is five.

## PERFORMANCE LOG

| Function | Token Count | Estimate | Actual Time | Rate Token/Time |
|----------|-------------|----------|-------------|-----------------|
|          |             |          |             | 2 tokens/hr.    |
| 1        | 5           | 2.5 hr.  |             |                 |

Table 4.2. Performance log entry for Produce Grade Report.

Now, build an estimate of the time needed to build this program. By dividing the token count of five by the previous rate of two tokens per hour, you achieve a rough estimate of about two and one half hours to build the program outline, write the code, and test the program.

When calculating estimates, be sure to use your own figures based on your own experience; different people work at different rates.

### Identifying the test cases

In order to test this program, you use the Store Student Data program to place test records onto the student file. If the Store Student Data program was not tested properly, you will not be able to verify that the Produce Grade Report program is correct. An imperfect Store Student Data program could put incorrect data onto the file, causing the report program to have inaccurate results when tested even though that program may have no bugs.

The first test runs the report program with a blank student file to be sure that the program starts and stops and that it does not report inactive records. Each subsequent test adds a set of two test records to the file and runs the report program again. Each new set of records tests different values of data — a different class year and different grades.

Many programming errors involve the processing of the first and last pieces of data, so a test record should be placed on records 1 and 100. As in this case, any time you see curly braces in the data dictionary you should build test cases containing the first and last values in the series. Table 4.3 shows one possible test case log for Produce Grade Report.

## TEST CASE LOG

| Test Case | Test Data | | | Result | |
|---|---|---|---|---|---|
| | Record | Class Year | Grade List | GPA | Class Average |
| 1. no records on file | | | no detail lines and 0.0 averages | | |
| 2. add records 1 and 100 | 1 100 | FR FR | A A A A A A B B B B B B | 4.0 3.0 | FR avg. = 3.5 all others 0.0 |
| 3. add records 2 and 99 | 2 99 | JR JR | C C C C C C D D D D D D | 2.0 1.0 | FR avg. = 3.5 JR avg. = 1.5 |
| 4. add records 3 and 98 | 3 98 | SR SR | F F F F F F W W W B B B | 0.0 3.0 | SR avg. = 1.5 |
| 5. add records 4 and 97 | 4 97 | SO SO | A A A B B B B B B C C C | 3.5 2.5 | SO avg. = 3.0 |

Table 4.3. Test case log for Produce Grade Report.

After the program is run for each set of test cases, check that the data are printed in an orderly format. The student's name should appear on the report exactly as it was entered. The class code and grades should be printed near the name, and the student's GPA after the grades. The class averages should be neatly printed at the end of the report.

### Building the program outline

To build the program outline, you identify the activities used by Produce Grade Report, looking for activities that match one of the five types in Chapter 1. Two of these activities correspond to the two data flows in Figure 4.1. The first one retrieves data from an internal file (it gets the student record from the student file), and the second reports data to the outside world (it prints the student grade report). The data flow diagram in Figure 4.1. shows that Produce Grade Report does not get data from the outside world or store data on internal files.

The third type of activity manipulates data from internal files or from the outside world. The program does manipulate data when it computes averages for each student and each class, so Compute Averages is the third activity placed on the program outline. Figure 4.2 shows a module for each of the three activities identified so far.

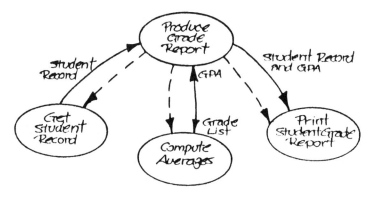

**Figure 4.2. Program outline for Produce Grade Report.**

Several data flows are missing from Figure 4.2. Get Student Record uses the Student ID to retrieve a Student Record, so the program outline must be updated to show the Student ID flowing from the top module into Get Student Record.

There are also missing data flows between Produce Grade Report and Compute Averages. These are not obvious, and to see them you have to think carefully about how this program works. This activity uses the grades from the student record to calculate the student's GPA, but it also computes class averages. To do this, Compute Averages adds the student averages for each class and divides that sum by the number of students in each class. Therefore, Compute Averages must keep track of the combined average for each class and the number of students in each class. Each time Compute Averages is invoked, it must add the student's GPA to the Class Average Total and add one to the Class Count. The data flows Class Average Totals and Class Counts are added to the program outline.

Figure 4.3 now shows all data flows around the main activities that Produce Grade Report performs.

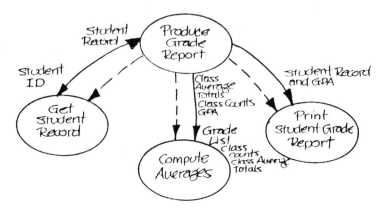

**Figure 4.3. Revised program outline for Produce Grade Report.**

Because Class Average Totals and Class Counts now appear on the program outline and the program must work with these data flows, they must be added to the data dictionary.

Class Counts = FR Count + SO Count + JR Count + SR Count

Class Average Totals = FR Total + SO Total + JR Total + SR Total

The Print Student Grade Report activity can be broken into small modules. The data dictionary shows that the report is made up of Detail Lines and Class Averages. To complete the program outline, you show the activity that prints a detail line and the activity that prints the totals at the end of the report. Separating these two activities makes the structure of the program clearer, since the program must perform Print Detail Line many times and Print Totals only once.

The report should have a heading to help the user identify the data. The first lines of the report print the title and label each piece of data on the detail line, as shown below.

STUDENT GRADE REPORT

Student ID   First and Last Name   Class   Grade List   GPA

1            Tom Jones             SR      A B A A C A  3.5

The module Print Student Grade Report has disappeared from the program outline. Its removal is slightly unusual. More often, when a module is broken into pieces, it is left in the outline with its component modules placed below it. In this case, however, that would have been unworkable. To see this, go through the activities and decide their order.

After the program gets a record, computes the GPA, and updates the totals, does it get another student record and go through the process again? Or, does it write a detail line and then get a record? Actually, it is much more efficient for the program to write a detail line for each record as soon as it finishes computing the student's GPA. Otherwise, the program would have to store dozens of GPAs until the report was ready to be printed.

Because the program will print a detail line each time a student's GPA is computed, you cannot include the activity Print Heading under the activity Print Student Grade Report. The latter activity would be carried out after the GPAs are computed, while the heading must be printed before any GPAs are computed and printed. Thus, Print Heading should be the first activity performed.

Another way to explain this is to say that activities are always placed under the module that knows when to invoke them. Print Student Grade Report does not know whether it is working on the first active record or the last; therefore, it does not know when to print the heading or the averages. The only activity that knows when to print the report heading is the top one. It can initiate Print Heading at the beginning of the program and take care of the report totals at the end.

Print Heading becomes a new activity on the completed program outline in Figure 4.4.

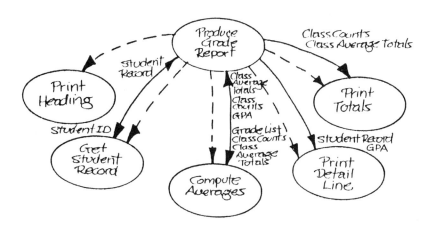

**Figure 4.4. Program outline for Produce Grade Report.**

In this section, you learned how to model a report-producing program. You've seen how data flows defined in previous examples are used to model a new function and how to write a program outline with activities that print a report heading and report summary. In section 4B, you will expand the program outline into a finished program.

# 4B. Building the BASIC Program

In this section, you will see how records are read from a file and how data from these records are made into a report. Figure 4.5 repeats the program outline with a starting line number for each activity.

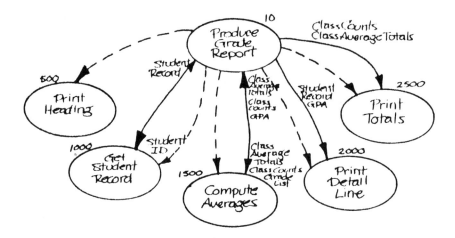

**Figure 4.5. Program outline for Produce Grade Report.**

For those data items in this program that are the same as those in the Store Student Data program, you use the same BASIC data names. The new data items, Class Counts and Detail Line, must now be given names. Note in Table 4.4 that Class Averages and Class Average Totals have the same BASIC data names. This is because the program accumulates the grade values in Class Totals that will be divided by Class Counts to compute Class Averages.

---

## DATA DICTIONARY

Class = [ FR | SO | JR | SR ]
     F4$ or CL$

Class Averages = FR Average + SO Average + JR Average + SR Average
     FR!  SO!  JR!  SR!

Class Average Totals = FR Total + SO Total + JR Total + SR Total
     FR!  SO!  JR!  SR!

Class Counts = FR Count + SO Count + JR Count + SR Count
       FR%   SO%   JR%   SR%

Detail Line = Student ID + Student Name + Class + Grade List
       + Grade Point Average
       A!

First Name = Maximum length of 10 characters
       F3$ or NF$

Grade = [ A | B | C | D | F | W ]
       G$

Grade List = 6 {Grade}
       F5$   GR${ }

Grade Point Average = Real number between 0.0 and 4.0

Student ID = Integer between 1 and 100
       F1$ or ID$

Last Name = Maximum length of 20 characters
       F2$ or NL$

Student File = 100 {Student Record} 100
       STUDENT

Student Grade Report = {Detail Line} + Class Averages

Student Name = First Name + Last Name

Student Record = Student ID + Student Name + Class + Grade List

Status = [ A | X ]
       FX$ or AX$

**Table 4.4. Data dictionary with BASIC data names.**

     As in the Store Student Data program, the top module declares the student file. It can use the OPEN and FIELD statements in the Store Student Data program. If you simply copy these statements from the program in Chapter 3, you won't run the risk of using different definitions for the same file. To average the grades you put them in an array, so use the previous DIM statement to define the array.

```
10 REM ----- PRODUCE GRADE REPORT --------------------
11 REM
15 OPEN "R",#1,"STUDENT"
20 FIELD #1, 2 AS F1$,20 AS F2$,10 AS F3$,2 AS F4$,6 AS F5$,1 AS FX$
25 DIM GR$(5)
30 GOSUB 500
35 FR%=0: SO%=0: JR%=0: SR%=0
40 FR!=0: SO!=0: JR!=0: SR!=0
45 FOR ID%=1 TO 100
50   GOSUB 1000
55   IF AX$="A" THEN GOSUB 1500: GOSUB 2000
```

```
60 NEXT ID%
65 GOSUB 2500
70 CLOSE #1
75 END
76 REM - END PRODUCE GRADE REPORT -------------------
77 REM
```

On line 30, the top module initiates the module that prints the report heading.

You must be careful when writing the instructions that invoke the next three sub-routines. Simply writing three lines of code saying GOSUB 1000, GOSUB 1500, and GOSUB 2000 will not work. As you know from thinking about the program outline, the program will go through these three modules repeatedly, one after the other, until detail lines for all records have been written. For this reason, the GOSUB instructions for the three modules must be inside a loop. Lines 45 through 60 use a counting loop to retrieve each of the 100 records on the file. After it retrieves a record, the program uses an IF statement to check if the record is active or blank. If the record is blank, nothing happens. If the record is active, the Compute Averages module returns the grade point average, and the Print Detail Line module prints the student record and average. When all records have been processed, the loop exits and the report totals are printed (GOSUB 2500). The program closes the file and ends.

According to the program outline, the top module sends the Class Average Totals and Class Counts to the Compute Averages activity to be updated with a student's grades. On the first invocation, the values in Class Average Totals and Class Counts must be 0. Therefore, lines 35 and 40 of the top module initialize these data items by setting them to 0.

The first subordinate module to be invoked is the Print Heading module, which prints the title of the report and, beneath it, the column heads for the student's ID number, last name, first name, class year, grade list, and GPA. The only command the module needs is LPRINT. Its syntax is the same as the PRINT statement's, but it prints the output on the printer instead of on the screen.

```
500 REM ----- PRINT HEADING -------------------
505 REM
510 LPRINT SPACE$(25); "STUDENT GRADE REPORT"
515 LPRINT
520 LPRINT "STUDENT ID   FIRST AND LAST NAME        CLASS";
525 LPRINT "   GRADES     GPA"
530 LPRINT
535 RETURN
536 REM - END PRINT HEADING -------------------
537 REM
```

You want the title centered at the top of the report. First, you figure out how many characters are printed on a line. You assume that the printer can print about 70 characters on an 8½" sheet of paper after leaving room for margins. Because the title is 20 characters long, that leaves 50 spaces remaining on the line, half of which should go in front of the report title. The command LPRINT SPACE$(25) enters the report title by putting 25 spaces in front of it. You must also check that there are enough spaces between column heads to accommodate the longest possible data item.

The activity to get a student record is the same function used in the Store Student Data program. You do not need to rethink that module; you can copy the code for the Get Student Record module in Chapter 3 into the new program. That module is repeated below.

```
1000 REM ----- GET STUDENT RECORD -------------------
1005 REM        ASSUMES ID% TO BE BETWEEN 1 AND 100
1010 REM               STUDENT FILE IS OPEN
1015 REM        PROMISES NF$, NL$, CL$, GR$(), AND AX$ FILLED WITH DATA
1020 REM                FROM STUDENT RECORD ID%
1025 REM
1030 GET #1,ID%
1035 NL$=F2$
1040 NF$=F3$
1045 CL$=F4$
1050 FOR C%=0 TO 5
1055   GR$(C%)=MID$(F5$,C%+1,1)
1060 NEXT C%
1065 AX$=FX$
1070 RETURN
1071 REM - END GET STUDENT RECORD -------------------
1072 REM
```

You can also borrow from past work when building the Compute Averages module. The calculation of the student's grade point average is the same as that used in the example in Chapter 2. As in that chapter, the module uses a counting loop to add the grade values together and then divides that sum by the number of grades. For the Compute Averages module, you must add code to update the Class Average Totals and Class Counts. The code adds this student to the count of students in the class and adds the student's GPA to the sum of GPAs in the class.

```
1500 REM ----- COMPUTE AVERAGES -------------------
1505 REM        ASSUMES GR$() WITH 6 GRADES, CLASS,
1510 REM              CLASS TOTALS, AND CLASS COUNTS
1515 REM        PROMISES A! CONTAINS AVERAGE AND COUNTS/TOTALS ARE UPDATED
1520 REM
1525 A!=0
1530 N%=0
1535 FOR C% = 0 TO 5
1540   IF GR$(C%) = "A" THEN A! = A! + 4.0: N% = N% + 1
1545   IF GR$(C%) = "B" THEN A! = A! + 3.0: N% = N% + 1
1550   IF GR$(C%) = "C" THEN A! = A! + 2.0: N% = N% + 1
1555   IF GR$(C%) = "D" THEN A! = A! + 1.0: N% = N% + 1
1560   IF GR$(C%) = "F" THEN A! = A! + 0.0: N% = N% + 1
1565 NEXT C%
1570 IF N% > 0 THEN A! = A! / N%
1575 REM
1580 REM ** UPDATE CLASS TOTALS AND CLASS COUNTS
1585 IF CL$ = "FR" THEN FR% = FR% + 1: FR! = FR! + A!
1590 IF CL$ = "SO" THEN SO% = SO% + 1: SO! = SO! + A!
1595 IF CL$ = "JR" THEN JR% = JR% + 1: JR! = JR! + A!
1600 IF CL$ = "SR" THEN SR% = SR% + 1: SR! = SR! + A!
1605 RETURN
1606 REM - END COMPUTE AVERAGES -------------------
1607 REM
```

The first part of the module (lines 1525 through 1570) was copied from the Compute GPA program in Chapter 2. Lines 1580 through 1600 determine in what class year the student belongs and then add 1 to the student count for that class. Notice that a comment has been put in the middle of the module. Since the module has two parts, each with a slightly different function, the comment makes the code easier to understand by separating the two parts and stating what the second part does.

The code for the Print Detail module is not very complicated, but getting the program to print the data in the correct position can be difficult. In order to align the headings with the data, it helps to write down the number of spaces required to hold a piece of data and the number of spaces desired between data items.

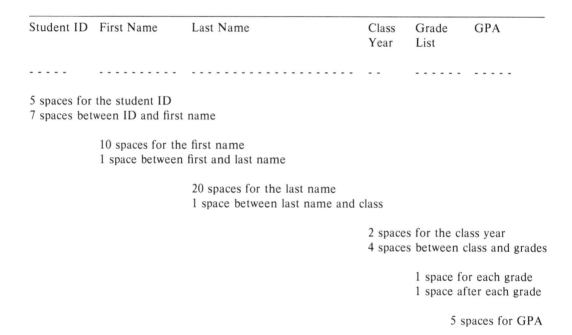

**Table 4.5. Spacing for Detail Line.**

For each data item, you must allot enough spaces to hold the longest value and adjust the number of spaces between data items and headings so that the data align under the correct heading. Once this is done, you may want to go back to the Print Heading module and refine the spacing in lines 520 and 525. It usually takes some experimentation to define a good, readable report layout.

In the code below for the Print Detail module, you use the LPRINT USING command, which allows you to format more readable detail lines by aligning the column of integers on the right-hand side, and the column of decimal numbers by the decimal points. For example, to make the student IDs align on the right, line 2015 has five number symbols following LPRINT USING, three for the digits in the number and two to indent the number two spaces to the left. The command on line 2055 aligns decimal points by telling the program to print the average with two digits to the left of a decimal point and two digits to the right. Because two spaces are allotted to the left of the decimal point and a GPA has only one digit to the left, the left-most "#" has the effect of adding another blank space between the grades and GPA. You will see other formating commands later in the text. You will also find useful information in your BASIC reference manual under the topic LPRINT USING.

```
2000 REM ----- PRINT DETAIL LINE --------------------
2005 REM        ASSUMES STUDENT RECORD AND A!
2010 REM
2015 LPRINT USING "#####"; ID%;
2020 LPRINT "       "; NF$;
2025 LPRINT " "; NL$;
2030 LPRINT " "; CL$;
2035 LPRINT "    ";
2040 FOR C%=0 TO 5
2045   LPRINT GR$(C%); " ";
2050 NEXT C%
2055 LPRINT USING "##.##"; A!
2060 RETURN
2061 REM - END PRINT DETAIL LINE --------------------
2062 REM
```

The code for Print Heading and Print Detail produces a report similar to the following:

---

### STUDENT GRADE REPORT

| Student ID | First and Last Name | Class Year | Grade List | GPA |
|---|---|---|---|---|
| 1 | Timothy Lenahan | FR | A W W W W W | 4.0 |
| 2 | Barbara Harkins | SO | A B C B B B | 3.0 |
| 99 | Gail Insock | JR | B B B C C C | 2.5 |
| 100 | Michael Salzman | SR | A B B A B A | 3.5 |

---

**Table 4.6. Partial sample Student Grade Report.**

The Print Totals module prints the class averages at the end of the report. It must also do the final calculation just before the averages are printed. After all student records have been printed, the program has the number of students in each class under the names FR%, SO%, JR%, and SR%, and the sum of the students' grade averages under the names FR!, SO!, JR!, and SR!. To compute the class average, the program divides the class average total by the class count.

```
2500 REM ----- PRINT REPORT TOTALS -------------------
2505 REM      ASSUMES CLASS TOTALS AND CLASS COUNTS
2510 REM      PROMISES TO COMPUTE AND PRINT CLASS AVERAGES
2515 REM
2520 IF FR% > 0 THEN FR! = FR! / FR% ELSE FR!=0
2525 IF SO% > 0 THEN SO! = SO! / SO% ELSE SO!=0
2530 IF JR% > 0 THEN JR! = JR! / JR% ELSE JR!=0
2535 IF SR% > 0 THEN SR! = SR! / SR% ELSE SR!=0
2540 LPRINT
2545 LPRINT SPACE$(44); "FR   AVERAGE IS   ";
2550 LPRINT USING "##.##"; FR!
2555 LPRINT SPACE$(44); "SO   AVERAGE IS   ";
2560 LPRINT USING "##.##"; SO!
2565 LPRINT SPACE$(44); "JR   AVERAGE IS   ";
2570 LPRINT USING "##.##"; JR!
2575 LPRINT SPACE$(44); "SR   AVERAGE IS   ";
2580 LPRINT USING "##.##"; SR!
2585 RETURN
2586 REM - END PRINT REPORT TOTALS -------------------
2587 REM
```

A class may have no members listed on the file. For example, at the end of the program you may have a freshman count of 0. If the program tries to divide the class average total by 0, BASIC will stop the program. To prevent this, use an IF statement to check the class count for 0 before computing the class average. A 0 class count causes the program to perform the instruction after ELSE, which sets the class average to 0.

To print the class average, you use LPRINT USING "##.##" just as you did in the Print Detail module. Each class average is identified by printing its class year in front of it. The command SPACE$(44) places the class year for the totals in the same columns as the class year in the detail lines, as shown in Table 4.7. This makes the report neater and more readable for the user.

## STUDENT GRADE REPORT

| Student ID | First and Last Name | Class Year | Grade List | GPA |
|---|---|---|---|---|
| 1 | Timothy Lenahan | FR | A  W  W  W  W  W | 4.0 |
| 2 | Barbara Harkins | SO | A  B  C  B  B  B | 3.0 |
| 99 | Gail Insock | JR | B  B  B  C  C  C | 2.5 |
| 100 | Michael Salzman | SR | A  B  B  A  B  A | 3.5 |
|  |  | FR | average is | 4.0 |
|  |  | SO | average is | 3.0 |
|  |  | JR | average is | 2.5 |
|  |  | SR | average is | 3.5 |

**Table 4.7. Complete sample Student Grade Report.**

In this section, you went through the process of building a BASIC program that produces a report. You will find that the hardest part of building a report is aligning the data with the headings. Practice is the best way to master this skill; the following exercise gives you the opportunity to try it yourself.

## EXERCISE IV

The ticket seller for the community theater likes the program you wrote, but he does have one problem. He needs a report that lists all patrons who have purchased tickets and how much they paid. This will help him balance the records against the actual money taken in.

The theater's president asks you for a printed report listing the patrons. The report should list the envelope number, the patron's name, the seats assigned, the number of regular tickets purchased, the number of special tickets, and the total price. The end of the report should have a summary showing the total number of regular and special tickets sold as well as the total amount of money received from ticket sales.

1.  draw a data flow diagram of the function and all incoming and outgoing data

2.  write data dictionary entries for each data flow; use the data dictionary entries from the last exercise wherever possible

3.  estimate the size of this project; enter your estimate in the performance log; try to estimate the amount of time it will take you to finish the project

4.  build at least five test cases to verify the program's accuracy

5.  determine the activities needed to perform the function and show them on a program outline; be sure to show all data flows between activities; do not forget the report heading and report totals

6.  build a BASIC program that carries out the activities shown on the program outline, and run the program using the test cases built in step 4

# 5

# Modifying the Programs

## 5A. Building the Model

Programs seldom remain unchanged for long. The user's needs change and the programs must change along with them. The same models used when the program was first built are used to change and test the modified program. The previous chapters demonstrated methods of building new programs; in this chapter you will learn how to make changes to existing programs.

**An example**

After using his new programs for awhile, the counselor asks you to make three improvements. First, he has no way of deleting a student's record. When the student leaves the school, his record remains on the file and is reported along with all records marked active. The counselor's first improvement is to add a way to delete a record. Second, the counselor has no way of changing individual fields in a student's record. As the Store Student Data program is set up now, he must reenter all data even if he wants to change only one field. The program would be much more convenient if it allowed the user to indicate those pieces of data, including individual grades, to be replaced.

The third change affects the report program. When the counselor had only 20 or so student records on the file, the entire report fit on one page. Now that he has almost 100 active records, the report goes onto a second page. To make the report easier to read, the counselor wants the program to reprint the heading along with the page number at the top of each page.

There are two rules to follow when changing a program: First, you can do only one thing at a time. Even though you have several changes, address them individually. Second, to change a program you follow the same steps used to build the program. The only difference is that you modify an already existing model instead of creating a completely new one.

First, review the data flow diagram and make any necessary changes to the data flows, although occasionally you may need to start a new diagram from scratch. You update the data dictionary to include new or changed pieces of data. A token count of these new or changed pieces of data gives you your estimate. Next, you check that the existing test cases contain data needed to test the changed programs, and add new test cases if necessary. Once you have changed the program outline to reflect the altered structure of the program, the model is complete. Of course, you also change the program code of those modules altered in the program outline.

Unless there is some pressing reason to implement a particular change first, you are free to address the changes in any order you wish, as long as you address each change separately. This section focuses first on the change to the report program.

## CHANGES TO PRODUCE GRADE REPORT

### Defining the function

You plan to add a heading and page number to each report page. Your first step is to inspect the data flow diagram for the Produce Grade Report program in Figure 4.1. Will you need to change any data flow?

After you add the headings and page numbers, the function continues to retrieve student records from the student file and produce a student grade report. The data flow diagram is unchanged, so no new data flows need to be added. However, the request does affect the definition of Student Grade Report.

### Defining the data

Consider what you want the student grade report to look like. It will consist of a series of pages, and each page will contain a series of detail lines and a page number. The definition of Student Grade Report must change to show the page number and the number of detail lines on a page.

The program must know the number of detail lines on a page in order to know when one page ends and the next begins; this tells it where to put the heading. To determine the number, you check the paper on which the report will be printed. For example, if you are using standard 8½" x 11" paper, and your printer prints 6 lines per inch, you have 66 lines per page. From this number, you substract the space in lines needed for the margins and heading. To leave a 1" margin at the top of each page, the first line of the report heading should be 6 lines from the top edge of the page. The heading includes the title, the column heads, the space between them, and the space between the heading and first detail line; it takes 4 lines. You can print the page number on the same line as the report title. You should leave a 1" margin (6 lines) at the bottom of the page. That leaves 50 lines for the detailed student data.

---

### DATA DICTIONARY

Line Count = Integer betwen 1 and 66

Student Grade Report = 1 {Page} + Class Averages

Page = Page Number + {Detail Line}50

Page Number = Integer greater than 0

---

**Table 5.1. Additional data dictionary definitions.**

The previous definition of Student Grade Report (Student Grade Report = Detail Line + Class Averages) is replaced by a new definition that consists of one or more pages and class averages. A page becomes a major element in the definition of the report and is itself defined afterward. It must become part of the definition because the new elements of the report, page numbers and headings, are its components.

**Estimating the size of the change**

In building estimates, you know that a program that manipulates five pieces of data is less complex than one that manipulates ten pieces. Similarly, if a change affects five pieces of data, it is smaller than a change that affects ten pieces. The more data items added or changed, the more work involved to implement the change.

When estimating the size of a change, you base your calculation on changed data flows and definitions. In the example, the data flow Student Grade Report has changed, so the initial token count is one. Add one token for the added brace around Page in the report's definition, making two the final token count for this program.

**Identifying the test cases**

All tests for the original program should be reused after the change is made to check that the program still performs the old functions correctly. You must also test whether the report program puts information on the correct page. A good test case has exactly 50 records on the file. For this, you expect the first page to show all 50 records and the second to contain the class averages. Another condition to test is a file with 51 records. In this case, the first page should have 50 detail lines; the second should have one detail line and the class averages.

You must now decide whether the class averages can ever be split between two pages. If the file contains 47 records, should the program print some class averages on the first page and the remainder on the second? Or, should the report always print all class averages together on the same page?

Most likely, the user wants all class totals on one page. A report that breaks a set of information between two pages is more difficult to read. So, you should plan on all the class averages being printed together.

| TEST CASE LOG | | |
| --- | --- | --- |
| Test Case | Result | |
| | No. of Pages | Class Averages Printed |
| 50 records on file | 2 | on second page |
| 51 records on file | 2 | on second page |
| 47 records on file | 2 | on second page |

**Table 5.2. Test case log.**

### Building the program outline

You must modify the current program outline to reflect the changes. The data flow diagram contains nothing new, so start by thinking about the changes to the data dictionary. How will the new data affect the program outline?

The program must keep track of a new piece of data, the page number. You can have the Print Heading activity print the heading and page number at the top of each page, and this same activity can increase the page number by 1 each time the heading is printed. The program outline shows data that flow between modules. The Print Heading module does not create the page number, so the page number must be shown flowing into the module. Print Heading does, however, change the page number, so it also flows out of the module.

The program also counts the number of lines printed so that it knows when to start a new page. One way to accomplish this is to have the Print Detail Line activity add 1 to the line count every time it prints a line. Therefore, the program outline shows the line count to be increased by 1 going into Print Detail Line and the updated line count leaving. The Print Heading activity can reset the line count at the start of each page. You complete the revised program outline by showing the line count entering and leaving that activity.

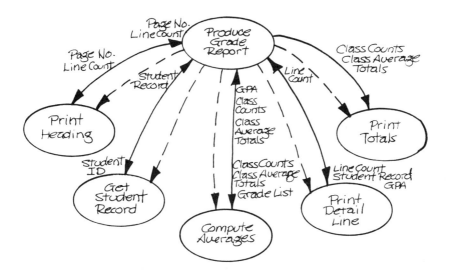

**Figure 5.1. Program outline for Produce Grade Report.**

In all, three activities are affected by the changes. The Print Heading module must set the line count to 0 and update the page number. The Print Detail Line module must update the line count. The top module is affected as well. Somewhere the program must check the line number to find out when to start a new page. Because the top activity coordinates the printing of both the detail line and the heading, it should determine when a new page begins. It also initializes the page number and line count.

## ADDING INDIVIDUAL UPDATES TO STORE STUDENT DATA

### Defining the function

The counselor wants to choose which fields in a student record he updates.  To plan this change to the Store Student Data program, you first inspect the original data flow diagram for that program in Figure 3.3 and modify it as necessary.

In the new program, the counselor continues to indicate the record he wants to update by entering a student ID number, but he must also tell the program which field he wants to change.  For this purpose, you introduce a new incoming data flow to identify that field, labeled Update Command in Figure 5.2.  This is the only necessary change to the diagram.

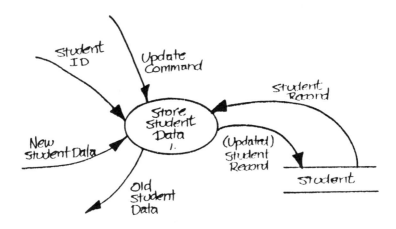

**Figure 5.2. Revised data flow diagram for Store Student Data.**

### Defining the data

To update the data dictionary, you must change the new data flow and the format of New Student Data to indicate that the user now chooses the data items instead of entering all of them.  You simply put square brackets around the definition and straight lines between the data items to show that the data can be any of four choices.  Because New Student Data is now defined differently from Old Student Data, you remove the parentheses from *Old* and *New*.

New Student Data is further modified in that the period during which the course is now held accompanies each grade.  By entering the class period along with the grade, the counselor tells the program which grade to change.  The grades are listed in the student record in order by period.  Entering period 1 places the grade in the first position; entering period 6 places the grade in the last.  The course to which a grade is assigned may be scheduled for any one of six periods in the day.

To select one data item for updating, the user types a number between 1 and 4 as defined by the Update Command entry. The user enters 1 to change the student's first name, 2 for his last name, 3 for his class, and 4 to change one grade. The user enters END when he completes all updates to a record.

---

## DATA DICTIONARY

New Student Data = [ First Name | Last Name | Class | Period + Grade ]

Period = Integer between 1 and 6

Update Command = [ 1 | 2 | 3 | 4 | END ]

---

**Table 5.3. Revised data definitions.**

**Estimating the size of the change**

You begin estimating by counting changes to the data flow diagram. Because Update Command is a new data flow and New Student Data is changed, count each as one token.

Now, look at the new data dictionary entries. First, you add one to the token count for the set of brackets in Update Command. Next, you must decide if the change to New Student Data deserves a token count. It contains the same data items, which are entered by the user and manipulated by the program in the same way. Now, however, rather than getting the student data items in order, the function must decide which data item to get from the user. The new set of brackets around New Student Data tells you that the code that works with this data item will be more complex. Therefore, the new set of brackets counts as one token, bringing the total to four.

**Identifying the test cases**

To be sure that the Store Student Data program still works as expected, you use the test cases from Chapter 3 to check the program's results; they test each field identifier — that is, the four numbers in the Update Command data flow. The program should, of course, store the record properly after all changes have been made. This is checked by reentering the student ID to see the displayed data.

You should also verify that the counselor can update any grade in the grade list. As you know, many programming errors occur as a program works on the first or last piece of data. Because the grade from one of six periods can be updated, you should build test cases to update the first- and sixth-period grades. In addition, the program should report as an error any field identifier in the Update Command that is not between 1 and 4. Table 5.4 contains the new test cases for adding individual updates.

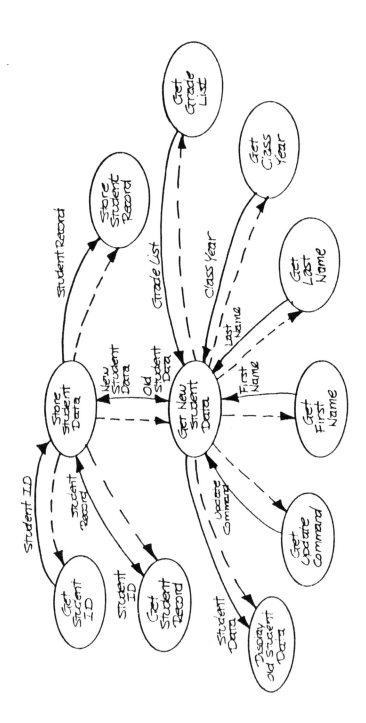

**Figure 5.3. Program outline for Store Student Data.**

TEST CASE LOG

| Test Data: | | Result: |
|---|---|---|
| Update Command | Data | Class Averages Printed |
| 5 | | Error message |
| 0 | | Error message |
| 1 | John | Updates first name |
| 2 | Smith | Updates last name |
| 3 | FR | Updates class code |
| 4 | 1A | Updates first grade |
| 4 | 6F | Updates sixth grade |
| END | | Stores data on file |

**Table 5.4. Test case log.**

## Building the program outline

To update the program outline in Figure 3.8, first add an activity that gets the new data flow, the user's Update Command. Like all activities that get data from the outside world, it asks the user for the data, gets the input, makes sure it is valid, and returns the data to whichever module invoked them. Which module, however, should invoke the Get Update Command activity?

You determine the new activity's placement on the program outline by asking which activity needs the information retrieved by it. Store Student Record, Get Student Record, Display Old Student Data, and Get Student ID do not use field IDs. The top module does not need the Update Command, since it is concerned only with complete sets of Student Data. On the other hand, the Get New Student Data module does need the Update Command to find out which piece of data the user is entering. Therefore, the new module is placed under Get New Student Data.

You should have the program display the student data to the user each time he enters a new field. That way, the user always has a complete, up-to-date display of student data on the screen, including new data just entered for a field in that record. Only the Get New Student Data module can invoke Display Old Student Data each time a new field is entered, so the display module goes under Get New Student Data.

## DELETING A STUDENT RECORD

### Defining the function

The counselor needs to delete a student's record when that student leaves the school. While his other requests are changes to functions that already exist, deleting a student record is a new function. This function is discussed in section 5B, because it becomes part of the Store Student Data program. This will not become apparent until you've planned the program, so proceed at first as you would for any new function. You begin by building a data flow diagram, treating Delete Student Record as a separate program.

An initial model is shown in Figure 5.4. As the model indicates, you !elete a record by replacing it with a blank record. This process is similar to updating a record, except that you place blanks instead of real data in the fields.

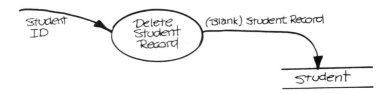

**Figure 5.4. Data flow diagram for Delete Student Record.**

Deleting all data on a record can be dangerous. If the user enters the wrong student ID, the wrong data is deleted. Therefore, you should put some type of edit or confirmation in the function to prevent this from happening. One option is to display the data for the entered student ID so that the user can review it before telling the program to delete the record. Figure 5.5 shows a revised data flow diagram with the outgoing student data and the incoming confirmation.

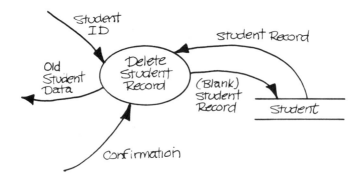

**Figure 5.5. Revised data flow diagram for Delete Student Record.**

## Defining the data

You have the data dictionary entries for all data flows in Figure 5.5 except Confirmation. The others — Student ID, Old Student Data, and Student Record — were defined in Chapter 3. The Confirmation data flow tells the program whether the student data being displayed are what the user wants to delete. Confirmation will either be YES, delete the record, or NO, do not delete the record.

Notice that Grade List has been removed from this version of the data dictionary. It is no longer needed because its definition has been placed instead into the definitions of Old Student Data and Student Record. Either way of defining the list of grades is fine; the choice is yours.

---

### DATA DICTIONARY

Confirmation = [ Yes | No ]

Old Student Data = Student Name + Class Year + 6 {Grade}6

Student ID = Integer between 1 and 100

Student Record = Student ID + Student Name + Class Year + 6 {Grade}6

---

**Table 5.5. Data dictionary for Delete Student Record.**

## Estimating the size of the change

Count the data flows around the function to arrive at an initial token count of five. Add one to the token count for the set of brackets in Confirmation. Since the function also refers directly to the data in the grade list in Old Student Data, add one more to the token count for a total count of seven.

---

### PERFORMANCE LOG

| Function | Token Count | Estimate | Actual Time | Rate Token/Time |
|---|---|---|---|---|
| Change 1 | 2 | | | |
| Change 2 | 4 | | | |
| Change 3 | 7 | | | |
| TOTAL | 13 | | | |

---

**Table 5.6. Performance log.**

**Identifying the test cases**

Think back to the test cases for the original Store Student Data function in Chapter 3. They verified that the function updates records 1 and 100 on the file as intended and not records 0 and 101. You run the same tests for the Delete Student Record function to verify that the first and last records on the file are correctly deleted and that attempts to delete nonexistent records are reported as errors.

You should also check what happens when the user decides not to delete the record for the student number he has entered. This test checks that a confirmation of NO does not change the record.

---

## TEST CASE LOG

| Test Case | Result |
| --- | --- |
| Delete ID Number | |
| 1 | Record 1 is made blank |
| 100 | Record 100 is made blank |
| 0 | Error message |
| 101 | Error message |
| 5 with confirmation = NO | No change to record 5 |

---

**Table 5.7. Test case log.**

**Building the program outline**

To build the program outline, you identify the necessary activities for performing the delete function. The first two activities get the student ID from the user and the student record from the student file. The third activity displays data from the record. Next, the program gets the delete confirmation. If the confirmation is positive, a blank record is built. The last activity stores the blank student record on the student file.

Notice the similarity between Figures 5.6 and 5.3. The Get Student ID, Get Student Record, Display Old Student Data, and Store Student Record modules are identical in both figures. Get Delete Confirmation in Figure 5.6 and Get Update Command in Figure 5.3 are similar, since they both ask the user for a command, and that command tells the program whether to alter the student data.

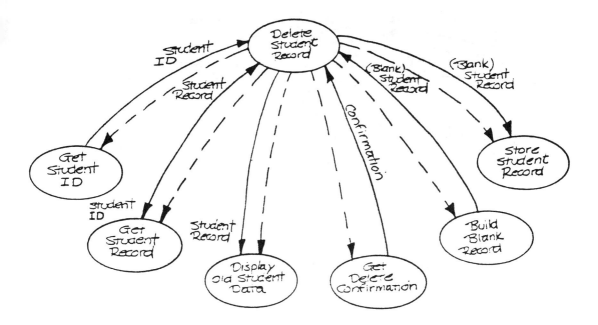

**Figure 5.6. Program outline for Delete Student Record.**

The number of similar activities found in the two functions indicates that they can be combined into one function. You simply expand the Get Update Command and add the Build Blank Record activity to the Store Student Data program. The delete function can be included in Figure 5.3 by changing the definition of Update Command to include a delete command.

Now that Get New Student Data has seven subordinate modules, they are difficult to fit on one page. For that reason, several modules under Get New Student Data have been stacked one on top of the other to make the program outline easier to read. Get New Student Data can invoke any one of the stacked modules, and it receives in return the corresponding field in Student Data. For example, if Get Last Name is performed, the returning data flow contains Last Name.

After combining two program outlines, you must revise your previous work. You change the name of the function in the data flow diagram in Figure 5.2 to Update Student Data, as shown in Figure 5.7. Otherwise, the diagram remains the same. (Updated) Student Record can now be blank, and Update Command now includes a delete option, but the latter is indicated by the revised data definition in Table 5.9 and the former requires no change in the model. The data definition of Student Record is the same whether the record contains blanks or data.

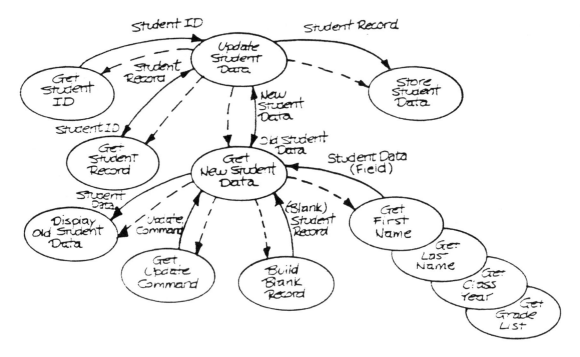

**Figure 5.7. Program outline for Update Student Data.**

The module Get New Student Data can decide to invoke a module either to get a new piece of data or to delete the student data. To describe more accurately the work the function now performs, its name is changed to Update Student Data. In addition to storing Student Data, the function now performs a variety of updates to Student Data and deletes old records.

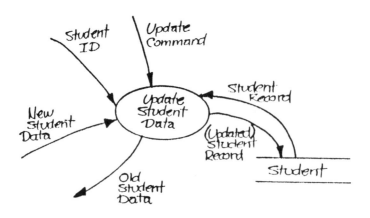

**Figure 5.8. Data flow diagram for Update Student Data.**

The test cases for the delete function are still valid, but the estimate must be changed. With the combined function you change only the update command; you do not build a new program. All other data definitions remain the same. Since only one data flow is changed, the token count for this task is one.

PERFORMANCE LOG

| Function | Token Count | Estimate | Actual Time | Rate Token/Time |
|----------|-------------|----------|-------------|-----------------|
| Change 1 | 2 | | | |
| Change 2 | 4 | | | |
| Change 3 | 1 | | | |
| TOTAL | 7 | | | |

**Table 5.8. Performance log.**

Why not consider the delete function as part of the Store Student Data function from the very beginning? There are two reasons: First, when you start, you don't know that the two functions have so many activities in common. You don't want to build one model before knowing for sure that the two functions are part of the same process. If you later found that the two processes had few activities in common, you would have to waste time separating them into their own programs. A better idea is to define one function at a time and then look for similarities.

Second, you want to be sure the delete function is defined completely and correctly before you try to integrate it with other parts of the system. It is much easier to spot flaws when looking at the model of a small function than at a large one. For example, if you combine the delete and update functions in the same bubble from the start, you might miss the importance of the user reviewing the student's data before the command to delete is entered.

DATA DICTIONARY

New Student Data = [ First Name | Last Name | Class | Period + Grade ]

Period = Integer between 1 and 6

Update Command = [ 1 | 2 | 3 | 4 | DELETE | END ]

**Table 5.9. Data dictionary revisions for Update Student Data.**

As you have seen in this section, modeling methods for both changes to functions and new functions are the same. You modify the data flow diagrams to define the change, and create new or changed data dictionary definitions. You compute an estimate based on the changed data flows and definitions, and build test cases to verify your work. Finally, you update the program outlines.

# 5B. Building the BASIC Program

In this section, you will learn how to code changes in your BASIC programs following a modified program outline. Section 5A showed you that the Produce Grade Report program must be changed to include a page number and headings on every page; it also demonstrated that the Update Student Data program must be changed to include a delete function and to allow updates to individual fields. Having updated the models, you are now ready to complete these examples.

### MODIFYING PRODUCE GRADE REPORT

For the first change, you expanded the program outline for Produce Grade Report to include Page Number and Line Count. The code must now be changed in every activity that uses or updates these new data items. Figure 5.9 repeats the program outline for Produce Grade Report, showing each module's starting line number. Page Number and Line Count — either one or both — flow through Produce Grade Report, Print Heading, and Print Detail Line, so the code for these three modules must be modified.

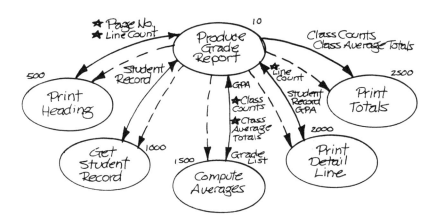

**Figure 5.9. Program outline for Produce Grade Report.**

A *star* in front of a data name indicates the data item flowing into and out of a module. This in turn implies that the data item is changed by the subordinate module. You can use this notation rather than write the data name at both ends of the data flow as in Figure 5.1.

As your final step before coding, you must assign a BASIC data name to Page Number and Line Count.

---

## DATA DICTIONARY

Line Count = Integer between 1 and 66
         L%

Page Number = Integer greater than 0
         P%

---

**Table 5.10. Data dictionary with BASIC data names.**

The code for the top module appears below. It must initialize the page number and line count and check when a new page is started. Lines 27, 57, and 62 have been added, allowing the module to perform its new tasks.

```
10 REM ----- PRODUCE STUDENT GRADE REPORT --------------------
11 REM
15 OPEN "R",#1,"STUDENT"
20 FIELD #1, 2 AS F1$,20 AS F2$,10 AS F3$,2 AS F4$,6 AS F5$,1 AS FX$
25 DIM GR$(5)
27 P%=1: L%=66
30 GOSUB 500
35 FR%=0: SO%=0: JR%=0: SR%=0
40 FR!=0: SO!=0: JR!=0: SR!=0
45 FOR ID%=1 TO 100
50   GOSUB 1000
55   IF AX$="A" THEN GOSUB 1500: GOSUB 2000
57   IF L%>54 THEN GOSUB 500
60 NEXT ID%
62 IF L%>50 THEN GOSUB 500
65 GOSUB 2500
70 CLOSE #1
75 END
76 REM - END PRODUCE STUDENT GRADE REPORT --------------------
77 REM
```

Line 27 sets the page number to 1 in preparation for printing the first page. It also sets the line count to 66. Why L% is set to that number will be explained when you review the Print Heading module.

Line 57 has been added to check the line count. In section 5A, you determined that there are 50 detail lines per page and that the heading uses 4 lines. After 54 lines have been printed, the program knows the next page is beginning, so it calls the Print Heading module.

Line 62 checks that all class averages are printed on the same page. Because the averages require 5 lines (1 blank line and 1 printed line for each of the 4 classes), they must begin no lower than line 50. If the Line Count is over 50 when the averages are ready to be printed, the program skips to the top of the next page.

Now that the Print Heading module puts a heading on every page, it must place the heading at the correct spot on the next page. Depending on whether the program calls the module from line 57 or line 60, the line count is either 54 or 50. Since the printer remains at the bottom of the page, the module must first skip a certain number of lines until the printer is positioned correctly.

Assume that the user mounts the paper in the printer so that the first line printed is 1" (6 lines) from the top of the paper. This way, after it prints 66 lines the printer is positioned at the sixth line of the next page. Therefore, if the Print Heading module skips lines until it reaches line 66, the printer is positioned 1" from the top of the next page, ready to print the heading. This is accomplished by the counting loop at lines 507 through 509. This loop starts with the current value of Line Count (L%) and prints blank lines until Line Count reaches 66.

```
500 REM ----- PRINT HEADING -------------------
502 REM       ASSUMES L% LESS THAN OR EQUAL TO 66
503 REM            P% IS GREATER THAN 0
504 REM       PROMISES 1 IS ADDED TO P% AND L% EQUALS 5
505 REM
507 FOR L%=L% TO 66
508   LPRINT
509 NEXT L%
510 LPRINT SPACES$(25); "STUDENT GRADE REPORT       PAGE";P%
515 LPRINT
520 LPRINT "STUDENT ID   FIRST AND LAST NAME        CLASS";
525 LPRINT "  GRADES    GPA"
530 LPRINT
532 P% = P% + 1
533 L% = 5
535 RETURN
536 REM - END PRINT HEADING -------------------
537 REM
```

It is now clear why the top module must initialize Page Number and Line Count in line 27; that line guarantees that the first time Print Heading is invoked, the report starts at the top of the first page, page 1. If Line Count equals 66, the counting loop starting at line 507 prints no blank lines and the module prints the heading at page 1.

Line 532 has been added to increase the page number, line 533 to initialize the line count. The line count is set to 5 in line 533 to account for the 4 lines used by the heading. Print line 5 contains the first detail line on the page. Notice that the remarks at the top of Print Heading have been changed to reflect the data flows going into the module.

Print Detail Line is the only other activity that must be modified. Each time the module is invoked, the program must add 1 to Line Count. This is accomplished by adding line 2057 to the module.

```
2000 REM ----- PRINT DETAIL LINE -------------------
2005 REM      ASSUMES STUDENT RECORD, A! AND L%
2010 REM
2015 LPRINT USING "#####"; ID%;
2020 LPRINT "      "; NF$;
2025 LPRINT " "; NL$;
2030 LPRINT " "; CL$;
2035 LPRINT "    ";
2040 FOR C%=0 TO 5
2045   LPRINT GR$(C%); " ";
2050 NEXT C%
2055 LPRINT USING "##.##"; A!
2057 L% = L% + 1
2060 RETURN
2061 REM - END PRINT DETAIL LINE -------------------
2062 REM
```

With these changes, the Produce Grade Report program should meet the user's requirements.  The test cases developed in section 5A must be run to verify that there are no errors.


## MODIFYING UPDATE STUDENT DATA

When you have verified that the report program is working properly, you can move on to the Update Student Data program.  You must change this program to include the new functions defined in section 5A.  These functions allow the user to delete a student record and to change individual data items on the record.  Because both changes affect the same program, you code them together.

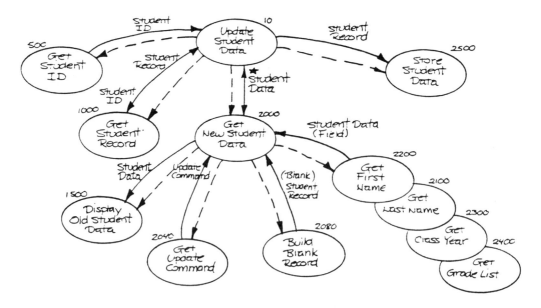

**Figure 5.10. Program outline for Update Student Data.**

By comparing the program outline in Figure 5.10 to that in Figure 3.8, you can see the required changes. Display Old Student Data has been moved, so the GOSUB 1500 statement too is moved from the top module to the Get New Student Data module. Also, two new modules are needed: Get Update Command and Build Blank Record.

As you look at the code for the update program, the counselor telephones to tell you he needs an additional modification. The program is set up so that each time it is executed the counselor can update only one student record, which means that if he needs to update several records, the program must be executed repeatedly. The counselor wants to update any number of records with only one program execution.

It often happens that you think of a new improvement while in the middle of writing code. In that case, you simply update your model to account for the new change, adjust your estimate, and return to building the code.

If the counselor updates several records during one program run, he must have some way of telling the program when he is finished updating. A good place for the user to indicate this is at the beginning of a new cycle, when the computer asks for a new student ID. If the counselor enters a piece of data equal to END, the program stops executing; otherwise, it allows the user to update the record and loops back for another student ID. Therefore, Student ID must be defined as either a number between 1 and 100 or the literal END.

Table 5.11 contains definitions of data whose BASIC names are new to the Update Student Data program. The data dictionary entry for Student ID includes two BASIC data names. If Student ID is an integer, its BASIC name must end with a percent sign (ID%). Since a piece of data going into the function can also be the word END, the program must also be able to accept this as a character string (ID$).

---

### DATA DICTIONARY

Student ID = [ Integer between 1 and 100 | END ]
      ID$ / ID%

Update Command = [ 1 | 2 | 3 | 4 | DELETE | END ]
      UC$

---

**Table 5.11. Data dictionary with BASIC data names.**

Note that the new data definition of Student ID contains a set of brackets. According to the guidelines for estimating, you add one to the previous token count. The token count for changes to Update Student Data is now six.

The top module of the Update Student Data program invokes the same modules as did the Store Student Data program in Chapter 3, except that it no longer invokes Display Old Student Data. The main difference between the two is that Update Student Data needs a loop to continue updating the new record until the counselor is done.

The top module first gets a student ID (GOSUB 500). If the data item ID$ does not equal END, the program enters the loop between lines 102 and 123. Inside the loop, the program gets the student record (GOSUB 1000), gets the new student data (GOSUB 2000), stores the record back onto the student file (GOSUB 2500), and gets another student ID (GOSUB 500). If the data entered by the user (ID$) equals END, the program exits from the loop, closes the student file, and ends.

```
10 REM ----- UPDATE STUDENT DATA -------------------
11 REM
15 OPEN "R",#1,"STUDENT"
20 FIELD #1, 2 AS F1$,20 AS F2$,10 AS F3$,2 AS F4$,6 AS F5$,1 AS FX$
25 DIM GR$(5)
100 GOSUB 500
102 WHILE ID$<>"END"
105   GOSUB 1000
115   GOSUB 2000
120   GOSUB 2500
122   GOSUB 500
123 WEND
125 CLOSE #1
130 END
131 REM - END UPDATE STUDENT DATA -------------------
132 REM

500 REM ----- GET STUDENT ID -------------------
505 REM       PROMISES STUDENT ID% BETWEEN 1 AND 100
507 REM            OR ID$ = "END"
510 REM
512 PRINT CHR$(26);
515 E%=1
520 WHILE E%=1
525   INPUT "ENTER STUDENT ID OR END";ID$
527   IF ID$="END" THEN ID%=1 ELSE ID%=VAL(ID$)
530   IF (ID%<1) OR (ID%>100) THEN PRINT "BETWEEN 1 AND 100" ELSE E%=0
535 WEND
540 RETURN
541 REM - END GET STUDENT ID -------------------
542 REM
```

The code in the Get Student ID module must now accept the three-character END as well as a number between 1 and 100. The BASIC name for the piece of data entered is changed from ID% to ID$ so that it can accept letters as well as numbers. If the user does not enter END, the module converts the piece of data to an integer in line 527 using the VAL function. The loop is set up as it was in Chapter 3: It exits only when ID% contains a valid student number. Therefore, if the user enters END, the module places a valid number in ID% to exit the loop. If the user does not enter a valid student number or END, the module displays an error message and again asks for data.

The statement on line 512 (PRINT CHR$(26);) erases all characters on the screen, removing anything that might be confused with the student data. Many BASIC interpreters have a specific command to clear the screen (often CLS). If your BASIC does not have such a command, use PRINT CHR$(26);.

The Get Student Record module is unchanged from Chapter 3, so you move on to the next module, Get New Student Data, which needs heavy revision since it now receives the update command and updates certain fields only.

The first major change involves adding a loop. The Get New Student Data module must now continue to ask for update commands and get the new data until the user enters an update command of END. Line 2012 has the module perform these tasks as long as UC$, which contains the update command, does not equal END.

```
2000 REM ----- GET NEW STUDENT DATA --------------------
2005 REM       ASSUMES VALID STUDENT DATA
2007 REM       PROMISES VALID VALUES IN STUDENT DATA
2010 REM
2011 UC$=""
2012 WHILE UC$<>"END"
2013   GOSUB 1500: GOSUB 2040
2015   IF UC$="1" THEN GOSUB 2200
2020   IF UC$="2" THEN GOSUB 2100
2025   IF UC$="3" THEN GOSUB 2300
2030   IF UC$="4" THEN GOSUB 2400
2032   IF UC$="DELETE" THEN GOSUB 2080
2033 WEND
2035 RETURN
2036 REM - END GET NEW STUDENT DATA --------------------
2037 REM
```

The data name UC$ is set to an empty string in line 2011 to ensure that the program enters the WHILE loop and executes it at least once.

According to the program outline, Get New Student Data now invokes the module Display Student Data from Chapter 3 and the new module Get Update Command. Line 2013 sends the program to these two modules each time the loop is executed. The value of UC$ determines which module is invoked. For example, if Update Command equals 1, the Get First Name module at 2200 is invoked. If Update Command equals 2, the Get Last Name module is invoked. If Update Command equals DELETE, the Build Blank Record module is executed.

Get Update Command is a typical input module: It gets the input from the user and checks that the input is valid. If the input is not valid, the module displays an error message and asks the user to reenter the data. The data dictionary indicates that the user has six possible update commands to enter. Because the user probably won't remember them all, this module lists the options before the user enters any.

```
2040 REM ----- GET UPDATE COMMAND(UC$) --------------------
2042 REM
2044 E%=1
2046 WHILE E%=1
2048   PRINT "ENTER UPDATE COMMAND:"
2050   PRINT "  1 - FIRST NAME"
2052   PRINT "  2 - LAST NAME"
2054   PRINT "  3 - CLASS"
2056   PRINT "  4 - GRADE LIST"
2058   PRINT "  DELETE - BLANK RECORD"
2060   PRINT "  END - TO END UPDATING"
2062   INPUT UC$
2064   IF UC$="1" OR UC$="2" OR UC$="3" OR UC$="4" THEN E%=0
2066   IF UC$="END" OR UC$="DELETE" THEN E%=0
```

```
2068   IF E%=1 THEN PRINT "UNRECOGNIZED COMMAND, REENTER"
2070 WEND
2072 RETURN
2073 REM - END GET UPDATE COMMAND -------------------
2074 REM
```

The Build Blank Record module is the same module used in the Create Student File program, except for one minor change. In the earlier version, the instructions to put blanks in NL$ and NF$ used blank spaces between quotation marks, just as lines 2088 and 2092 still do. The danger is that you can easily lose count when spacing ten or twenty times. The SPACE$ command used in the following code accomplishes the same thing without the possibility of error.

```
2080 REM ----- BUILD BLANK RECORD -------------------
2082 REM
2084 NL$=SPACE$(20)
2086 NF$=SPACE$(10)
2088 CL$="  "
2090 FOR C%=0 TO 5
2092   GR$(C%)="  "
2094 NEXT C%
2096 AX$="X"
2097 RETURN
2098 REM - END BUILD BLANK RECORD -------------------
2099 REM
```

In Chapter 3, the Get Grade activity asks the user to enter exactly six grades. Now it must ask the user for one period and one grade at a time. The code below sets up a new loop that gets the period and checks that it is valid.

```
2400 REM ----- GET GRADE LIST -------------------
2401 REM        PROMISES TO UPDATE GR$() WITH ONE GRADE
2402 REM
2403 F%=1
2404 WHILE F%=1
2405   INPUT "ENTER PERIOD 1-6: ",C%
2410   IF C%>0 AND C%<7 THEN F%=0
2412   IF F%=1 THEN PRINT "PERIOD MUST BE 1,2,3,4,5,OR 6"
2413 WEND
2415 E%=0
2420 WHILE E%=0
2425   INPUT "GRADE";G$
2430   IF G$="A" THEN E%=1
2435   IF G$="B" THEN E%=1
2440   IF G$="C" THEN E%=1
2445   IF G$="D" THEN E%=1
2450   IF G$="F" THEN E%=1
2455   IF G$="W" THEN E%=1
2460   IF E%=0 THEN PRINT "UNRECOGNIZED GRADE.  REENTER."
2465 WEND
2470 GR$(C%-1)=G$
2480 RETURN
2481 REM - END GET GRADE LIST -------------------
2482 REM
```

If the period is valid, a grade is retrieved from the loop starting at line 2420. That grade is then placed in the grade array in line 2470. Note that the period (C%) determines the grade's position in the array. The grade for period 1 goes into GR$(0) and the grade for period 6 goes into GR$(5). The module subtracts 1 from the period before using C% as the array subscript, since arrays in BASIC start with 0.

One last change is needed to make the program work properly. In its previous version, the Store Student Record module set the status field to *A* for active. Although the user could only update active records when that module was first written, the user now has the option of deleting a record. If Store Student Record was unchanged, it would mark a deleted record incorrectly as active when putting the record back on the file. For this reason, the instruction to set the status flag to *A* is removed from Store Student Record.

At some point, however, the flag should be set to *A* to signify an active record. Which module should perform that task? In the code below, the Get Last Name module has been changed to mark the record being updated as active. A record without the student's last name would be meaningless, so a student record is not marked active until the user enters the last name. If the user does not enter a last name for a record, that record remains inactive and is not reported. Only active records are reported on the student grade report.

```
2100 REM ----- GET LAST NAME(NL$) --------------------
2102 REM
2103 AX$="A"
2105 E%=1
2110 WHILE E%=1
2115   INPUT "ENTER STUDENT'S LAST NAME ",NL$
2120   IF LEN(NL$)>20 THEN PRINT "ONLY 20 CHARACTERS" ELSE E%=0
2125 WEND
2130 RETURN
2131 REM - END GET LAST NAME --------------------
2132 REM

2500 REM ----- STORE STUDENT RECORD --------------------
2505 REM        ASSUMES VALID STUDENT DATA, ID% BETWEEN 1 AND 100
2510 REM             STUDENT FILE OPEN
2515 REM        PROMISES TO STORE STUDENT DATA ON RECORD ID%
2520 REM
2525 LSET F1$=MKI$(ID%)
2530 LSET F2$=NL$
2535 LSET F3$=NF$
2540 LSET F4$=CL$
2545 G$=""
2550 FOR C%=0 TO 5
2555   G$=G$+GR$(C%)
2560 NEXT C%
2565 LSET F5$=G$
2570 LSET FX$=AX$
2575 PUT #1,ID%
2580 RETURN
2581 REM - END STORE STUDENT RECORD --------------------
2582 REM
```

No other modules need modification. Get Student Record, Display Old Student Data, Get First Name, and Get Class Year are unchanged from Chapter 3. The last step is to run the test cases developed in section 5A against the new versions of the programs. Once you are satisfied that the programs work correctly, you can turn them over to the user.

The software you build is always subject to change. In this section, you have seen how the models are used to define requested changes and how the code is then altered to implement the change.

## EXERCISE V

The last production by the community theater was a huge success. The patron sales report proved to be very helpful because it provided a neat, orderly record of ticket sales. There were a few minor problems, however. A detail line on the sales report was difficult to read because it was printed on the perforation between pages. Also, two people canceled their ticket reservations and several changed their reservations, causing some confusion.

The president and the ticket seller recently reviewed the changes needed in the programs you wrote. The list follows:

- add a function to delete a sales record, making it easier to cancel a patron's ticket request

- allow the ticket seller to change individual fields on the sales record so changes to ticket reservations are easier to enter

- change the Produce Sales Report function so that it skips to the top of a new page; this eliminates the problem of a detail line being printed on the perforation between pages

To implement the above changes, do the following:

1.   update the data flow diagrams in your portfolio to show any changes in the data flows

2.   update the data dictionary to reflect changed data definitions

3.   estimate the extent of these changes

4.   build at least four new test cases for each program

5.   using your program outlines, determine which activities need to be changed and which new activities need to be added; be sure all data flows between activities are accurate and up-to-date

6.   change the BASIC programs to reflect the changes in the program outlines

# Adding a Transaction Center

## 6A. Building the Model

The examples and exercises in the previous chapters are *stand-alone* programs. A different program must be executed for each function the user wants to perform. This becomes time-consuming when the user has a large amount of work to do at one time. A more convenient method is to combine these programs as functions into one large program; the user can then execute one program and tell it which function he wants. After each function is completed, the program asks the user which function should be performed next.

A program can act as a center through which the user can initiate any number of transactions in any combination. This section will demonstrate how to build a master program, or *transaction center,* that can invoke other programs.

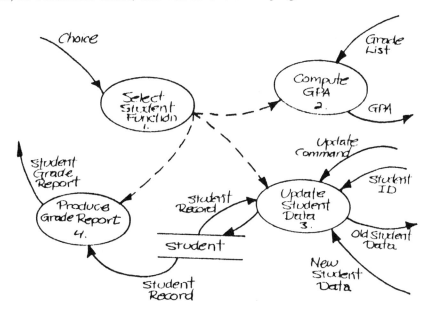

**Figure 6.1. Transaction center for student programs.**

## Defining the function

The bubble Select Student Function ties together the three programs built in previous chapters. It allows the user to select among the available programs, and it initiates the desired program when the user enters his choice. The old programs are not changed.

The dotted lines in the data flow diagram from function 1 to the other functions are a new symbol, but they have the same meaning as a dotted line on the program outline: They indicate that the Select Student Function bubble initiates one of the three functions. The diagram shows no data flow arrows between function 1 and the other functions because no data flows from function 1 to the others. Their only relation to function 1 is that it initiates them.

## Defining the data

The data flow Choice going into Select Student Function is the only new data flow in the diagram. This data flow contains the counselor's four options, to activate one of the three programs or to end the session. The following data dictionary entry shows that the counselor chooses any of three functions by entering 1, 2, or 3. To end the session, he enters 0.

---

### DATA DICTIONARY

Choice = [ 1 | 2 | 3 | 0 ]
    1 - Compute GPA
    2 - Update Student Record
    3 - Produce Grade Report
    0 - End

---

**Table 6.1. Data dictionary.**

## Estimating the size of the program

Only data flows are counted in the estimate, so the dotted lines are not included in the token count. The data flow Choice going into the new bubble gives you an initial token count of one.

The data definition of Choice shows a set of data items enclosed in brackets. The function refers to the data inside the brackets, so the set of data is counted as one more token, giving a total of two. The performance log is presented below, including this time the rate computed from earlier programs and the final estimate.

PERFORMANCE LOG

| Function | Token Count | Estimate | Actual Time | Rate Token/Time |
|----------|-------------|----------|-------------|-----------------|
|          |             |          |             | 1.25 token/hr.  |
| 1        | 2           | 1.6      |             |                 |

Table 6.2. Performance log.

### Identifying the test cases

To test the transaction center, you need a test case for each valid value of Choice. These test cases verify that the correct program is invoked when the user selects a function. If the user enters an invalid choice, the program should produce an error message. For this reason, one invalid choice is included in the test. The test case log for validating Select Student Function is presented below.

TEST CASE LOG

| Test Case | Result |
|-----------|--------|
| Choice    |        |
| 1         | Compute GPA executes |
| 2         | Update Student Data executes |
| 3         | Produce Grade Report executes |
| 0         | Transaction center ends |
| 4         | Error message |

Table 6.3. Test case log.

### Building the program outline

Remember that you build the program outline by identifying the activities that perform the function. As its first activity, the transaction center gets data from the outside world — namely, the counselor's choice of program to run. It then invokes the appropriate program.

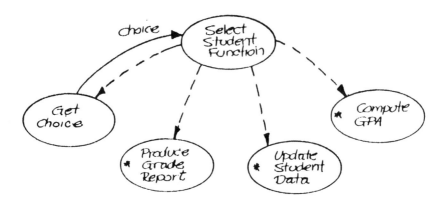

**Figure 6.2. Program outline for Select Student Function.**

An *asterisk* next to the module name means that the module is further broken down on another page. Since you have already outlined the subordinate activities for each function called by the transaction center, there is no need to draw these lower-level activities again in this figure.

Notice that the program Create Student File is not included in the transaction center. Although invoking this program could have been a fourth choice, you should not allow this function to be invoked easily. When the Create Student File program is run, all data on the file are erased. If you include the function in the transaction center, Create Student File may be initiated by mistake. By leaving Create Student File as a separate program that must be directly executed, you reduce the risk of erasing the file accidentally.

Adding a transaction center to the system gives the counselor a convenient way to work with his programs. Rather than executing each program separately, he can simply enter a number to perform any of the functions in any combination. Rather than three stand-alone programs, you now have a set of programs that work together as a system.

Your portfolio represents tangible evidence of the work done to build the system. Periodically, you should review the portfolio to see how the system has grown and changed as well as how the models help define and organize the software development process.

The following pages show how the portfolio might look at this point in the system's development.

* * * * * * * * *

* * *

## DATA FLOW DIAGRAM

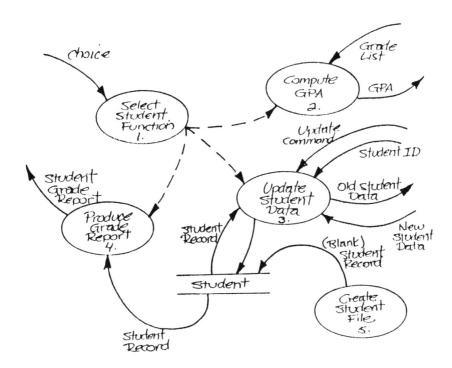

**Figure 6.3. Data flow diagram for student system.**

* * *

## DATA DICTIONARY

---

Choice = [ 1 | 2 | 3 | 0 ]
    1 - Compute GPA
    2 - Update Student Record
    3 - Produce Grade Report
    0 - End

Class Year = [ FR | SO | JR | SR ]

Class Averages = FR Average + SO Average + JR Average + SR Average

Detail Line = Student ID + Student Name + Class + Grade List +
      Grade Average

First Name = Maximum length of 10 characters

Grade = [ A | B | C | D | F | W ]

Grade List = 6 {Grade} 6

Grade Point Average = Real number between 0.0 and 4.0

Last Name = Maximum length of 20 characters

New Student Data = [ First Name | Last Name | Class | Period + Grade ]

Old Student Data = Student Name + Class + {Grade} 6

Page = Page Number + {Detail Line} 50

Page Number = Integer greater than 0

Period = Integer between 1 and 6

Student File = 100 {Student Record} 100

Student Grade Report = 1 {Page} + Class Averages

Student ID = Integer between 1 and 100

Student Name = First Name + Last Name

Student Record = Student ID + Student Name + Class + Grade List

Update Command = [ 1 | 2 | 3 | 4 | DELETE | END ]

---

* * *

# PROGRAM OUTLINES

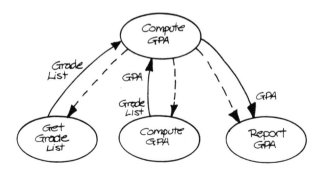

Figure 2.2. Program outline for Compute GPA.

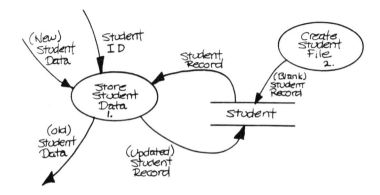

Figure 3.3. Program outline for Create Student File.

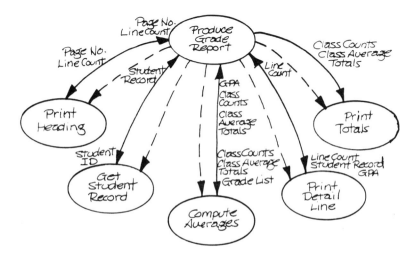

Figure 5.1. Program outline for Produce Grade Report.

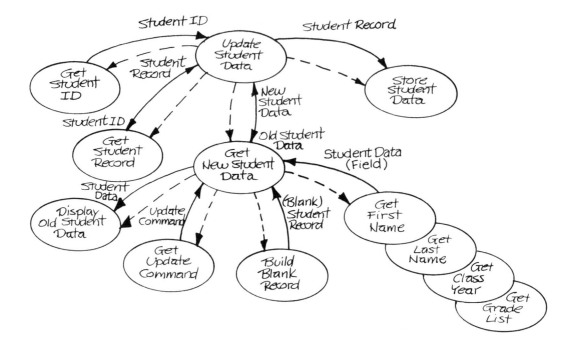

**Figure 5.7. Program outline for Update Student Data.**

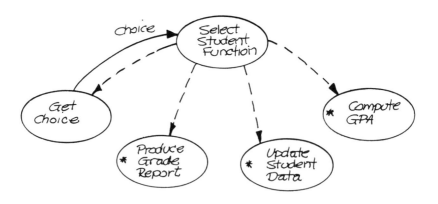

**Figure 6.2. Program outline for Select Student Function.**

* * *

## PERFORMANCE LOG

| Function | Token Count | Estimate | Actual Time | Rate Token/Time |
|---|---|---|---|---|
| 1 | 4 | | 5 hrs. | 0.8 |
| 3 (initial) | 9 | | 10 hrs. | 0.9 |
| 5 | 1 | | 1.5 hrs. | 0.7 |
| 4 (initial) | 5 | 7 hrs. | 7 hrs. | 0.7 |
| 4 (change) | 2 | 2.5 hrs. | 3 hrs. | 0.7 |
| 3 (changes) | 5 | 6.5 hrs. | 5 hrs. | 1.0 |

* * *

## TEST CASE LOG

| Test Case | Result |
|---|---|
| Function No. 2 | |
| A A A A A A | 4.0 |
| B B B B B B | 3.0 |
| C C C C C C | 2.0 |
| D D D D D D | 1.0 |
| F F F F F F | 0.0 |
| W W W W W W | 0.0 |
| A A A F F F | 2.0 |
| A A A W A A | 4.0 |
| X | Error message |

\* \* \*

**Test Case:**                                                  **Result:**

| Student ID | Characters Last and First Name | | Class Year | Grade List | | | | | | Result |
|---|---|---|---|---|---|---|---|---|---|---|
| **Function No. 3** | | | | | | | | | | |
| 0 | | | | | | | | | | Error message |
| 101 | | | | | | | | | | Error message |
| | 21 | | | | | | | | | Error message |
| | | 11 | | | | | | | | Error message |
| | | | FX | | | | | | | Error message |
| | | | | X | | | | | | Error message |
| 1 | Smith | John | FR | A | A | A | A | A | A | Updates record 1 |
| 100 | Jones | Mary | SO | B | B | B | B | B | B | Updates record 100 |
| 10 | Peters | Jon | JR | C | C | C | C | C | C | Updates record 10 |
| 11 | Pike | Sue | SR | D | D | D | D | D | D | Updates record 11 |
| 2 | Adams | Al | FR | F | F | F | F | F | F | Updates record 2 |
| 3 | Baker | Wes | SR | W | W | W | W | W | W | Updates record 3 |

\* \* \*

| | Record | Class Year | Grade List | | | | | | GPA | Class Average |
|---|---|---|---|---|---|---|---|---|---|---|
| **Function No.4** | | | | | | | | | | |
| no records on file | | | no detail lines and 0 averages | | | | | | | |
| add records | 1 | FR | A | A | A | A | A | A | 4.0 | |
| 1 and 100 | 100 | FR | B | B | B | B | B | B | 3.0 | FR avg. = 3.5 all others 0 |
| add records | 2 | JR | C | C | C | C | C | C | 2.0 | |
| 2 and 99 | 99 | JR | D | D | D | D | D | D | 1.0 | JR avg. = 1.5 |
| add records | 3 | SR | A | A | A | A | A | A | 4.0 | |
| 3 and 98 | 98 | SR | W | W | W | B | B | B | 3.0 | SR avg. = 3.5 |
| add records | 4 | SO | A | A | A | B | B | B | 3.5 | |
| 4 and 97 | 97 | SO | B | B | B | C | C | C | 2.5 | SO avg. = 3.0 |

* * *

| Test Case: | | Result: |
|---|---|---|
| File | No. of Pages | Class Averages |
| 50 records on file | 2 | on second page |
| 51 records on file | 2 | on second page |
| 47 records on file | 2 | on second page |

* * *

| | Data | |
|---|---|---|

Function No. 3 after changes

Update Command

| | | |
|---|---|---|
| 5 | | Error message |
| 0 | | Error message |
| 1 | John | Updates first name |
| 2 | Smith | Updates last name |
| 3 | FR | Updates class code |
| 4 | 1A | Updates first grade |
| 4 | 6F | Updates sixth grade |

Delete Student ID

| | | |
|---|---|---|
| 1 | | Record 1 is blanked |
| 0 | | Record 100 is blanked |
| 0 | | Error message |
| 1 | | Error message |

# 6B. Building the BASIC Program

The transaction center just modeled allows the user to invoke any program by entering a number. You will now build the code for the transaction center, which accepts a program request from the user and invokes the correct function. Since you have already written the code for the three programs to be invoked, you code only two of the modules in the outline: Select Student Function and Get Choice. As usual, on the outline the starting line numbers appear next to these modules.

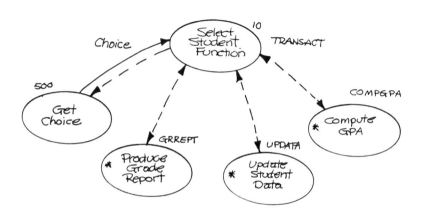

**Figure 6.4. Program outline for Select Student Function.**

The words above Produce Grade Report, Update Student Data, and Compute GPA are program names. Every file and program has a name by which the computer identifies it. You tell the computer a program's name when you type in its code. Usually, these names are no more than eight characters in length. For example, the student file in the counselor's system is named STUDENT; in the suggested answers for the theater exercises, the name SALES identifies the patron sales file.

Choose program names that can be recognized. The program that computes a student's grade point average is labeled COMPGPA, which stands for COMPute GPA. UPDATA stands for UPdate Student DATA, and GRREPT stands for produce GRade REPorT. The name of the TRANSACTion center program is TRANSACT. Keep in mind also that coming up with meaningful names is not always easy.

Before beginning to code, you have one last task: You must record the BASIC data name for Choice in the data dictionary; you decide to call it CH$.

---

## DATA DICTIONARY

Choice = [ 1 | 2 | 3 | 0 ]
  CH$   1 - Compute GPA
        2 - Update Student Record
        3 - Produce Grade Report
        0 - End

---

**Table 6.4. Data dictionary with BASIC data name.**

For the transaction center program to invoke a program, it needs a special BASIC command that allows one program to execute another. Although some versions use the command RUN, in most versions of BASIC this command is CHAIN. In the program TRANSACT, the statement below causes the computer to stop processing the current program and start processing the program named COMPGPA. COMPGPA starts running as if the user had executed it from the keyboard.

1020 CHAIN "COMPGPA"

The CHAIN command may seem similar to the GOSUB command, but there are important differences between the two. CHAIN allows one program to initiate another program, while GOSUB allows one module to initiate another module when both are part of the same program. When a module executes a GOSUB, the subordinate module performs its function and the upper module automatically continues to the next statement. When you use the CHAIN command, however, the program TRANSACT does not start processing after COMPGPA ends. COMPGPA must execute a CHAIN statement as well. The computer will not return to the statement following the CHAIN command, but will start the TRANSACT program from the beginning.

The two-way dotted lines in the program outline show that Select Student Function invokes the other programs (GRREPT, UPDATE, and COMPGPA) and that they in turn invoke Select Student Function. Consequently, all four programs must have CHAIN statements.

The new modules, Select Student Function and Get Choice, do not contain much code, yet this small amount greatly improves the system's ease of use.

The top module has no files to declare or arrays to define. As the code below shows, it first invokes Get Choice by means of the GOSUB statement, checks which choice has been entered, and uses the CHAIN command to execute the appropriate program.

```
10 REM ----- SELECT STUDENT FUNCTION TRANSACTION CENTER -------------------
11 REM
15 GOSUB 500
20 IF CH$="1" THEN CHAIN "COMPGPA"
25 IF CH$="2" THEN CHAIN "UPDATA"
30 IF CH$="3" THEN CHAIN "GRREPT"
35 END
36 REM - END SELECT STUDENT FUNCTION -------------------
37 REM
```

The top module does not verify that the user's choice is valid; that is the task of the lower module, Get Choice.

The Get Choice module has two tasks. It first displays the options that are available to the user; that is, it displays the programs the user can request and also gives the user the option of saying he is finished. Get Choice must also check that the user has selected a valid choice.

```
500 REM ----- GET CHOICE --------------------
505 REM       PROMISES CHOICE (CH$) BETWEEN 0 AND 3
510 REM
515 PRINT CHR$(26);
520 PRINT SPACE$(15);"STUDENT TRANSACTION CENTER"
525 PRINT
530 PRINT SPACE$(15);"1 - COMPUTE GPA"
535 PRINT SPACE$(15);"2 - UPDATE STUDENT RECORD"
540 PRINT SPACE$(15);"3 - PRODUCE GRADE REPORT"
545 PRINT SPACE$(15);"0 - TO END"
550 E%=1
555 WHILE E%=1
560   PRINT SPACE$(15);
565   INPUT CH$
570   IF CH$="1" OR CH$="2" OR CH$="3" OR CH$="0" THEN E%=0
575   IF E%=1 THEN PRINT "ENTER 1, 2, 3, OR 0"
580 WEND
585 RETURN
586 REM - END GET CHOICE --------------------
587 REM
```

Notice that line 515 first clears the screen. This prevents displays from previous transactions from being confused with the current display.

After clearing the screen, the program displays the menu of options to the user. This task requires a series of PRINT statements that give the number code and the program that corresponds to it or, in the case of the code 0, the opportunity to end the transaction center program altogether. The program then enters a loop looking for a valid choice. If the user does not enter an invalid code, an error message is printed and the program continues to loop. The program sets E% to 1 before entering the loop so that the message "ENTER 1, 2, 3, or 0" appears to cue the user.

The programs COMPGPA, UPDATA, and GRREPT must be changed so that, instead of simply ending, they execute TRANSACT when they are finished. If the computer returns to the transaction center, the user can easily invoke another function when one finishes.

The code listed below is the new top module for the Compute GPA program. If you compare it with the original version in Chapter 2, you see that several changes have been made: The CHAIN command has replaced the END statement, and a loop has been added that allows the user to do more than one GPA calculation before returning to the transaction center.

```
5 REM ----- COMPUTE STUDENT GPA --------------------
6 REM
10 DIM GR$(5)
```

```
100 REM ** COMPUTE STUDENT GPA **
101 E%=1
102 WHILE E%=1
105   GOSUB 500
110   GOSUB 1000
115   GOSUB 1500
116   INPUT "DO YOU WANT TO COMPUTE GPA";A$
117   IF MID$(A$,1,1)<>"Y" THEN E%=0
118 WEND
120 CHAIN "TRANSACT"
121 REM - END COMPUTE STUDENT GPA -------------------
122 REM
```

The code for the modified Update Student Data and Produce Grade Report program is not shown because these two programs remain essentially the same. The only difference between their new version and the old is that the CHAIN "TRANSACT" statement replaces the END statement in the top module.

You have seen that implementing a transaction center is not a large task. The transaction center itself is only one small program, and after building it you simply add a CHAIN statement to the other programs. As a result of this, the user has a convenient way of working with the system of programs you have built.

**EXERCISE VI**

The programs you have written for the theater are being used heavily. The ticket seller uses the Calculate Ticket Charge and Update Ticket Sales programs daily, and the president often asks for a sales report. Because the ticket seller now finds it awkward to execute the programs repeatedly, he asks you to build a transaction center.

1.  build a data flow diagram to show the transaction center
    and its data flow

2.  define the choices the user enters to initiate a function in
    the data dictionary

3.  estimate the size of the job and project the time it will
    take to deliver an error-free transaction center

4.  build at least four test cases to verify the program

5.  build a program outline by identifying the activities
    necessary to perform the function of the transaction center

6.  write the BASIC code, using the program outline as a guide

Review the portfolio you have been building through the text. Your data flow diagrams should now start to resemble a complete system. Instead of separate programs, you now have a group of interrelated functions that work together to perform useful work for the community theater.

# 7

# Changing File Contents

## 7A. Building the Model

In Chapter 5, you saw how changes to the function of a system are modeled and implemented. In this chapter, you will follow a similar procedure to model and code a change to the content of a file.

Although in one sense file content is changed every time you update a record, this section discusses a broader type of change which alters the structure of a file: It may add to a record a field for a new data item, delete a field, change the number of characters in a field, redefine the valid data for a field, or change the number of records on a file. The examples in this section concentrate on adding new data items to a record, more records to a file, and a new valid data item to an already existing field, but you will find it easy to apply what you learn here to any change in file content.

Programmers often face the problem of changing data storage content after the user has started to work with the system. They must define a new record format and convert the records on the current file to the new format. The data already entered on the file must be correctly transcribed to the new file.

After working with the computer system for a while, the guidance counselor decides that the address of each student should be stored on the student record, which would allow him to find a student's address easily when mailing a letter to the student's home. The counselor also wants to record a student's courses along with the grades. The three-character course codes are entered at the beginning of each semester, but the grades for the courses are not awarded until the end of the semester. To indicate that the course is in progress, the counselor wants to enter a grade of I to stand for incomplete. The function should treat I exactly as it treats W. The counselor also wants the file expanded to hold records for 200 students.

You may wonder why the address and course code were not included in the first version of the student file. They should have been included, but you are seldom able to define all a system's functions correctly the first time. Although you should try to define all components of the system as accurately as possible, you should always be prepared to make changes to the system as new features are needed.

### Defining the function

In Chapter 2, the program Create Student File initialized the Student File with 100 blank records before any data were stored on the file. The new file must contain 200 student records, including the records on the old file. The new program must first transfer the active records from the old student file to a file that can hold 200 records.

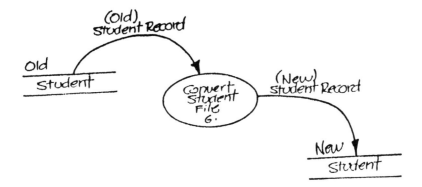

**Figure 7.1. Beginning data flow diagram for Convert Student File.**

The adjectives *Old* and *New* are used on the data flow diagram to distinguish between the two files during the conversion process. After the conversion is completed, the New Student File will be called simply the Student File and the difference between old and new will be unimportant.

After the New Student File is built, every function that accesses the Student File must be changed so that it can use the New Student File. Looking back at the data flow diagram in Figure 6.3, you see that Update Student Data and Produce Grade Report use the Student File, so they need to be changed.

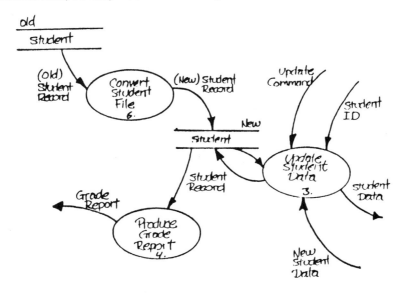

**Figure 7.2. Data flow diagram for Convert Student File.**

## Defining the data

Definitions of the new data items for the Student Record go into the data dictionary. The field for the new data item Course Code contains three characters, and the other new data item, Address, is spread among four fields, Street, City, State, and Zip. The State field contains a two-character state code, and Zip contains a five-digit postal code. The lengths of the Street and City fields are the estimated maximum size of each piece of data.

---

## DATA DICTIONARY

City = Maximum length of 15 characters

Course Code = 3 characters

Period = Integer between 1 and 6

State = 2 characters

Street = Maximum length of 20 characters

Student Data = First Name + Last Name + Street + City + State + Zip
   + Class + {Course Code + Grade}6

Update Command = [ 1 | 2 | 3 | 4 | 5 | 6 | 7 | 8 | END | DELETE ]

Zip = 5 digits

---

**Table 7.1. Data dictionary.**

These new data items will be part of New Student Data, so its definition must be revised to show eight different data items instead of the original four. Another revision concerns the course codes. Now that the courses are included in New Student Data, you no longer need the class period. You will identify each grade by its course, not by its period. Thus, Period is replaced by Course Code in the definition of Student Data, and its definition is deleted.

Now inspect the data flow diagram in Figure 7.2. for any more data flows needing revision. You will find that Update Command must change to allow the user to enter the new data items and store them on the file.

The data flow definition of Student Grade Report does not change unless the user asks that some of the new data be included. The Produce Grade Report function is included in Figure 7.2 because the program will read a different record format. The (New) Student Record holds the data in different locations from those in the (Old) Student Record. For example, the third data item of the new Record is Street, while the third data item of the old Record is Class. If Produce Grade Report is not changed, it will list the first part of the Street field as the Class code.

## Estimating the size of the program

As you know, you base the time estimate for changing the file content on the number of new and changed data flows. Function 6 (Convert Student File) works with two data flows and so has an initial token count of two. You do not add to the count for the brackets and braces in the dictionary definitions because when the bubble retrieves an (Old) Student Record or stores a new one, it treats the record as a single piece of data.

Five out of six data flows around Update Student Data (bubble 3) have changed — only Student ID remains the same: therefore, the initial token count for this function is five. Look at the data definitions for more additions to the token count. New Student Data has more data items than before, but the structure of the data has not changed. That is, you have not added or removed sets of braces or brackets. Since you increase the token count only when the structure of the data has changed, the token count for this function remains at five.

The only data flow that changes in the Produce Grade Report function is Student Record, so this function has a token count of one. Had the counselor requested a change to the content of the Student Grade Report, the token count would have been higher.

PERFORMANCE LOG

| Function | Token Count | Estimate | Actual Time | Rate Token/Time |
|----------|-------------|----------|-------------|-----------------|
|          |             |          |             | 1.2 token/hr.   |
| 6        | 2           |          |             |                 |
| 3        | 5           |          |             |                 |
| 4        | 1           |          |             |                 |
| TOTAL    | 8           | < 7 hr.  |             |                 |

**Table 7.2. Performance log.**

## Identifying the test cases

You can easily introduce errors into a program when adding new features. Therefore, you should have especially thorough test cases. Two sets are needed: Test cases from Chapter 6 verify that the unchanged data items are still processed correctly, and new test cases verify that new items are also processed correctly.

In order to test the Convert Student File program, you must first finish modifying the Update Student Data program. You can then check the contents of the New Student File. If you find that the data were incorrectly copied from the old file to the new one, you correct the Convert Student File program and again check the data through the Update Student Data program. This means that the Old Student File must not be destroyed until you are sure the new file is valid. You should make a backup copy of the Student File before running the conversion program. This way, if an error in Convert Student File destroys any data stored on the Student File, you can recover them by using the backup copy.

---

### TEST CASE LOG

| Test Case | Result |
| --- | --- |

Test function 6 by checking Student Data on new file:

Student ID

| | |
| --- | --- |
| 1 | Records 1 and 100 contain |
| 100 | data from the old file. |
| 101 | Records 101 and 200 |
| 200 | are blank. |

Test function 3:

Update Command

| | |
| --- | --- |
| 3 Street > 20 characters | Error message |
| 4 City > 15 characters | Error message |
| 5 State > 2 characters | Error message |
| 6 Zip > 5 digits | Error message |
| 6 Zip nonnumeric | Error message |
| 8 Course > 3 characters | Error message |
| 8 1 course and grade I | Record updated with course and grade |
| 8 6 courses and 6 grades | Record updated with courses and grades |

Test function 4:

| | |
| --- | --- |
| Run the report program | Report identical to old report |
| Add record 200 with grade I | Report reflects additional record |

---

**Table 7.3. Test case log.**

## Building the program outline

The conversion program has four activities in the program outline: It gets data from the Old Student File; manipulates data by converting the (Old) Student Record into the (New) Student Record; manipulates data by creating a (Blank) Student Record; and stores that (New) Student Record on the New Student File.

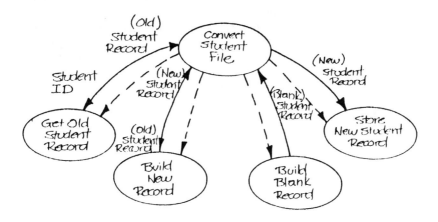

**Figure 7.3. Program outline for Convert Student File.**

The program outline for Update Student Data now includes activities to get the new data items: Get Street, Get City, Get State, and Get Zip.

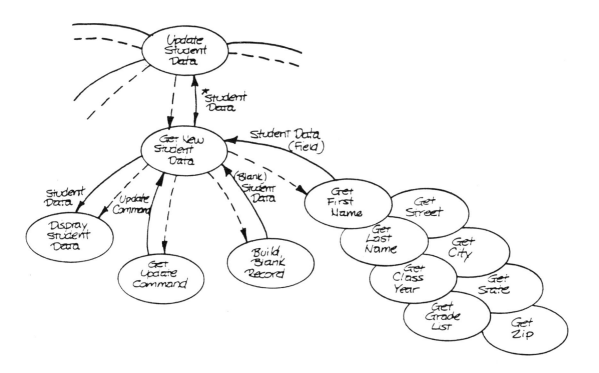

**Figure 7.4. Program outline for Update Student Data.**

Although the program outline for Produce Grade Report remains the same, the data it uses do not. The Get Student Record activity now gets the (New) Student Record and the top activity must now process 200 records instead of 100. Since none of this new information shows up on the program outline, there is no need to reproduce it here.

Your model now defines the system where the Student File contains more information. In this section, you have responded to a request to change the file's content by defining the change on the data flow diagram and data dictionary, estimating the size of the task, preparing test cases, and altering the program outline to reflect the new activities.

# 7B. Building the BASIC Program

This section contains methods of changing a BASIC program's file definitions when expanding a file to include additional data. The models built in section 7A define a program that converts the Student File to a new format. It accomplishes the conversion by taking the information from the Old Student File and placing it on a New Student File. As the program outline in Figure 7.5 shows, the program transforms each old record into a record fitting the new format, then builds a blank record to fill unused space on the new file. Finally, both new records and blank records are stored on the New Student File.

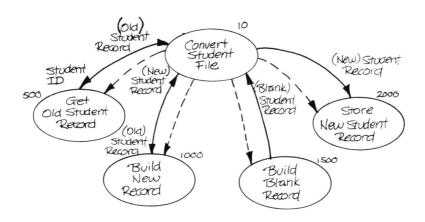

**Figure 7.5. Program outline for Convert Student File.**

First, you assign the BASIC names to be used in the data code. Recall that BASIC requires names for all data items listed in a FIELD statement, one name for the field and another name to be used for editing the data or doing calculations. To distinguish between old and new data, field names beginning with X have been given to the old record, and field names beginning with F have been given to the new record.

---

### DATA DICTIONARY

City = Maximum length of 15 characters
    CI$ or F5$

Course Code = 3 characters
    C$

Grade = [ A | B | C | D | F | I | W ]
    G$

New Grade List = 6{Course Code + Grade}6
    F9$    CR$()    GR$()

New Student Data = [ Last Name | First Name | Street | City
        | State | Zip | Class | Period + Course Code + Grade ]
New Student File = 200{New Student Record}200
    STUDENT2

New Student Record = Student ID + Student Name + Street + City
        + State + Zip + Class Year + New Grade List

Old Grade List = 6{Grade}6
    X5$

Old Student File = 100{Old Student Record}100
    STUDENT

Old Student Record = Student ID + Student Name + Class Year + Grade List
    X1$   X2$ and X3$   X4$

Period = Integer between 1 and 6

State = 2 characters
    ST$ or F6$

Street = Up to 20 characters
    RD$ or F4$

Student Data = First Name + Last Name + Street + City + State + Zip
        + Class + {Course Code + Grade}6

Update Command = [ 1 | 2 | 3 | 4 | 5 | 6 | 7 | 8 | END | DELETE ]
    UC$

Zip = 5 digits
    ZP$ or F7$

---

**Table 7.4. Data dictionary with BASIC data names.**

The top module of this program must declare the two student files and assign each one a name. Most computer systems allow you to create a new file with the same name as an existing file. When the new file is closed, however, it takes the place of the old file. If the Convert Student File program uses the same name for both the New and Old Student File (STUDENT), the old file will be removed when the new one is built. If the program contains an error, the data on the Old Student File is lost.

In the code shown below, the top module of Convert Student File assigns the name STUDENT2 to the new file. If the program should fail to transfer the student data correctly, the old file remains.

Modifying the field statement for the new record is simple. The first three lines are unchanged. After those, you insert the four fields making up the address, giving each the length already noted in the data dictionary. The class code is next, its name changed from X4$ to F8$. The field holding the grades and course codes must be 24 characters long because there are six periods in the day, the course code is three characters long, and the grade has a length of one character. As before, the field finishes with a one-character status flag.

```
5 REM ----- CONVERT STUDENT FILE --------------------
6 REM
10 OPEN "R",#1,"STUDENT"
15 FIELD #1, 2 AS X1$,20 AS X2$,10 AS X3$,2 AS X4$,6 AS X5$,1 AS XX$
20 OPEN "R",#2,"STUDENT2"
25 FIELD #2, 2 AS F1$,20 AS F2$,10 AS F3$,20 AS F4$,15 AS F5$,2 AS F6$,
     5 AS F7$,2 AS F8$,24 AS F9$,1 AS FX$
30 DIM GR$(6)
35 PRINT "TRANSFERRING OLD STUDENT RECORDS"
40 FOR ID%=1 TO 100
45   GOSUB 500
50   GOSUB 1000
55   GOSUB 2000
60 NEXT ID%
65 CLOSE #1
70 PRINT "OLD STUDENT FILE CLOSED"
75 PRINT "EXTENDING SIZE OF NEW FILE"
80 GOSUB 1500
85 FOR ID%=101 TO 200
90   GOSUB 2000
95 NEXT ID%
100 CLOSE #2
105 PRINT "CONVERSION COMPLETE"
110 END
111 REM - END CONVERT STUDENT FILE --------------------
112 REM
```

The loop in lines 40 through 60 invokes the three modules that get an old record, reformat it into a new record, and store the record on the New Student File. The Old Student File is then closed. Next, the program builds a blank record (GOSUB 1500) and executes a second loop that stores the blank record in the last 100 positions of the file. The PRINT statements in lines 35, 70, 75, and 105 tell the user what the program is doing. A program that leaves the screen blank is often unnerving to the user because he cannot see what the program is doing, if anything. You therefore display messages that describe the process being performed.

The code for Get Old Student Record and Build New Record appears below.  The first module reads a record from the Old Student File.  Build New Record moves the data from the old record to the new format.

```
500 REM ----- GET OLD STUDENT RECORD -------------------
505 REM      ASSUMES ID% BETWEEN 1 AND 100
510 REM      PROMISES STUDENT RECORD FOR ID% IN BUFFER
515 REM
520 GET #1,ID%
525 RETURN
526 REM - END GET OLD STUDENT RECORD -------------------
527 REM
```

```
1000 REM ----- BUILD NEW RECORD -------------------------
1005 REM      ASSUMES OLD STUDENT DATA IN BUFFER
1010 REM      PROMISES NEW STUDENT RECORD WITH OLD STUDENT DATA
1015 REM
1020 LSET F1$=X1$
1025 LSET F2$=X2$
1030 LSET F3$=X3$
1035 LSET F4$=SPACE$(20)
1040 LSET F5$=SPACE$(15)
1045 LSET F6$="  "
1050 LSET F7$="   "
1055 LSET F8$=X4$
1060 FOR C%=0 TO 5
1065    GR$(C%)=MID$(X5$,C%+1,1)
1070 NEXT C%
1075 G$=""
1080 FOR C%=0 TO 5
1085    G$=G$+"   "+GR$(C%)
1090 NEXT C%
1095 LSET F9$=G$
1100 LSET FX$=XX$
1105 RETURN
1106 REM - END BUILD NEW RECORD -------------------
1107 REM
```

The field F9$ contains six grades, each one preceded by three blank spaces for the course code.  The counting loop in lines 1060 through 1070 builds an array of grades from the old Student Record.  You have seen the same loop before in the program.  A new field containing the grades and room for the course code is built in the counting loop from lines 1080 through 1090.  Every fourth character contains a grade from the old Student Record.  The following example shows the format of the grade list in field X5$ of the old record to the 24-character field F9$ of the new record.

Field X5$:      BBCABA

   period:      1    6

Field F9$:    __B __B __C __A __B __A

   period:      1    2    3    4    5    6

The Build Blank Record module moves spaces into all fields of the new record except for the first and last fields, which contain 0 and X, respectively.  To write the code for this module, you can use the Build Blank Record module from Chapter 3 by adding lines 1530 through 1545 for the new fields and changing line 1555 to hold 24 spaces.

```
1500 REM ----- BUILD BLANK RECORD --------------------
1505 REM        PROMISES BLANK DATA IN THE NEW STUDENT RECORD
1510 REM
1515 LSET F1$=MKI$(0)
1520 LSET F2$=SPACE$(20)
1525 LSET F3$=SPACE$(10)
1530 LSET F4$=SPACE$(20)
1535 LSET F5$=SPACE$(15)
1540 LSET F6$=" "
1545 LSET F7$="   "
1550 LSET F8$=" "
1555 LSET F9$=SPACE$(24)
1560 LSET FX$="X"
1565 RETURN
1566 REM - END BUILD BLANK RECORD --------------------
1567 REM
```

The module Store New Student Record below writes the (New) Student Record onto the New Student File.  This simple instruction finishes the Convert Student File program.  Running this program gives you a 200-record file with the old records in the first 100 records and blank records in the second 100 records.

```
2000 REM ----- STORE NEW STUDENT RECORD --------------------
2005 REM       ASSUMES NEW FILE IS OPEN
2010 REM               STUDENT DATA IS IN BUFFER
2015 REM
2020 PUT #2,ID%
2025 RETURN
2026 REM - END STORE NEW STUDENT RECORD --------------------
2027 REM
```

Although the order is not important, the Update Student Data program is changed first to update new data items as well as the old.  Figure 7.6 shows Update Student Data's program outline along with the starting line numbers for each module.  Almost every module on this outline needs to be modified, yet these modifications are simple.

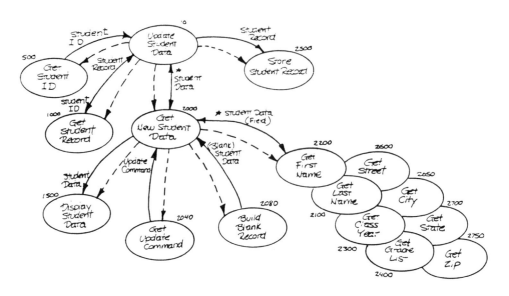

**Figure 7.6. Program outline for Update Student Data.**

On the top module, change the name of Student File to STUDENT2; also change the FIELD statement to match that in the Convert Student File program. Including a second array in the DIM statement at line 25 finishes this module. The new array holds the course codes. After a later module retrieves a student record from the file, the course code for period 1 will be in CR$(0) and the grade for that course will be in GR$(0).

```
10 REM ----- UPDATE STUDENT DATA --------------------
11 REM
15 OPEN "R",#1,"STUDENT2"
20 FIELD #1, 2 AS F1$,20 AS F2$,10 AS F3$,20 AS F4$,15 AS F5$,2 AS F6$,
     5 AS F7$,2 AS F8$,24 AS F9$,1 AS FX$
25 DIM GR$(5),CR$(5)
100 GOSUB 500
102 WHILE ID$<>"END"
105   GOSUB 1000
115   GOSUB 2000
120   GOSUB 2500
122   GOSUB 500
123 WEND
125 CLOSE #1
130 CHAIN "TRANSACT"
131 REM - END UPDATE STUDENT DATA --------------------
132 REM
```

The Get Student ID module must now accept ID numbers up to 200. To change the highest ID number accepted by the program, you change the condition of the IF statement in line 530.

The next module, Get Student Record, first retrieves a record from the file (line 1025) and then prepares all new data for processing by assigning the data in fields to their BASIC data name. You must remember to place the six course codes and letter grades from Field F9$ into two separate arrays, built from the statements in lines 1046 and 1050. The first course code starts in position 1, and the second starts in position 5: There is a four-character gap between them. To find the correct starting position of each array element, the program must skip over four characters, and it does that by multiplying the counter by 4 (C% * 4). Because C% starts off as 0 and the positions begin with 1, the program must add 1 to (C% * 4) to find the starting position of the course codes. The first time through the counting loop, C% will equal 0 and the equation *C% * 4 + 1* will equal 1. The second time through, C% will equal 1 and the equation will equal 5.

The same principle is used to find the starting position for each grade, except that you add 4 to (C% * 4) because the first grade does not come until the fourth position.

```
500 REM ----- GET STUDENT ID NUMBER -------------------
505 REM        PROMISES STUDENT ID% BETWEEN 1 AND 200
510 REM
512 PRINT CHR$(26);
515 E%=1
520 WHILE E%=1
525   INPUT "ENTER STUDENT ID OR 'END'";ID$
527   IF ID$="END" THEN ID%=1 ELSE ID%=VAL(ID$)
530   IF (ID%<1) OR (ID%>200) THEN PRINT "BETWEEN 1 AND 200" ELSE E%=0
535 WEND
540 RETURN
541 REM - END GET STUDENT ID NUMBER -------------------
542 REM


1000 REM ----- GET STUDENT RECORD -------------------
1002 REM        RECEIVES ID% BETWEEN 1 AND 200
1005 REM             STUDENT FILE IS OPEN
1010 REM        PROMISES NF$, NL$, RD$, CI$, ST$, ZP$, CL$, CR$(),
1015 REM         GR$(), AND AX$ FILLED WITH DATA FROM STUDENT RECORD ID%
1020 REM
1025 GET #1,ID%
1030 NL$=F2$
1035 NF$=F3$
1036 RD$=F4$
1037 CI$=F5$
1038 ST$=F6$
1039 ZP$=F7$
1040 CL$=F8$
1045 FOR C%=0 TO 5
1046   CR$(C%)=MID$(F9$,C%*4+1,3)
1050   GR$(C%)=MID$(F9$,C%*4+4,1)
1055 NEXT C%
1060 AX$=FX$
1065 RETURN
1066 REM - END GET STUDENT RECORD -------------------
1067 REM
```

Display Student Data must be changed to display all data now stored on the Student Record. This requires adding lines 1526 through 1529 and line 1541 to print the address and course codes.

```
1500 REM ----- DISPLAY OLD STUDENT DATA --------------------
1505 REM        ASSUMES STUDENT DATA NF$, NL$, RD$, CI$, ST$, ZP$,
1510 REM              CL$, CR$(), GR$(), AX$, ID%
1511 REM
1512 PRINT CHR$(26);
1515 PRINT "DATA FOR STUDENT ID ";ID%
1520 PRINT "LAST NAME ",NL$
1525 PRINT "FIRST NAME",NF$
1526 PRINT "STREET    ",RD$
1527 PRINT "CITY      ",CI$
1528 PRINT "STATE     ",ST$
1529 PRINT "ZIP       ",ZP$
1530 PRINT "CLASS     ",CL$
1535 PRINT "GRADE LIST    ",
1540 FOR C%=0 TO 5
1541   PRINT CR$(C%);" ";
1545   PRINT GR$(C%);" ";
1550 NEXT C%
1555 PRINT
1560 PRINT "STATUS    ",AX$
1565 PRINT
1570 PRINT "-----------------------------------------"
1575 PRINT
1580 RETURN
1581 REM - END DISPLAY OLD STUDENT DATA --------------------
1582 REM
```

You now expand the Get New Student Data activity to recognize the new pieces of data. This activity needs the new modules Get Street, Get City, Get State, and Get Zip, which ask the user for elements of the address and check that they are valid. The addition of the lines calling for those modules is the only change to the top module of Get New Student Data which is needed. As the line numbers after the GOSUB command in lines 2021 through 2024 indicate, these modules are added to the end of the program. Insufficient space prevents you from placing the new modules between lines 2495 (the end of the Get Grade List module) and 2500 (the beginning of the Store Student Record module).

```
2000 REM ----- GET NEW STUDENT DATA --------------------
2005 REM        ASSUMES VALID STUDENT DATA
2007 REM        PROMISES VALID VALUES IN STUDENT DATA
2010 REM
2011 UC$=""
2012 WHILE UC$<>"END"
2013   GOSUB 1500: GOSUB 2040
2015   IF UC$="1" THEN GOSUB 2200
2020   IF UC$="2" THEN GOSUB 2100
2021   IF UC$="3" THEN GOSUB 2600
2022   IF UC$="4" THEN GOSUB 2650
2023   IF UC$="5" THEN GOSUB 2700
2024   IF UC$="6" THEN GOSUB 2750
2025   IF UC$="7" THEN GOSUB 2300
2030   IF UC$="8" THEN GOSUB 2400
2032   IF UC$="DELETE" THEN GOSUB 2080
2033 WEND
2035 RETURN
2036 REM - END GET NEW STUDENT DATA --------------------
2037 REM
```

Now that the module Get Update Command displays four new update commands, the number of lines necessary to show the choices on the screen has grown from 9 to 13. If you listed all command choices one under the other, and added a line asking the user to enter his choice, you would have at least 25 lines of display. Since most screens contain only 24 lines, the choices must be listed in two columns.

```
2040 REM ----- GET UPDATE COMMAND(UC$) -------------------
2042 REM
2044 E%=1
2046 WHILE E%=1
2048   PRINT "ENTER UPDATE COMMAND:"
2050   PRINT "  1 - FIRST NAME"," 5 - STATE"
2052   PRINT "  2 - LAST NAME "," 6 - ZIP"
2054   PRINT "  3 - STREET    "," 7 - CLASS"
2056   PRINT "  4 - CITY      "," 8 - GRADES"
2058   PRINT "  DELETE - BLANK RECORD"
2060   PRINT "  END - TO END UPDATING"
2062   INPUT UC$
2064   IF UC$="1" OR UC$="2" OR UC$="3" OR UC$="4" THEN E%=0
2065   IF UC$="5" OR UC$="6" OR UC$="7" OR UC$="8" THEN E%=0
2066   IF UC$="END" OR UC$="DELETE" THEN E%=0
2068   IF E%=1 THEN PRINT "UNRECOGNIZED COMMAND, REENTER"
2070 WEND
2072 RETURN
2073 REM - END GET UPDATE COMMAND -------------------
2074 REM
```

The remaining modules for the update program are listed below. Build Blank Record must be expanded to initialize the new data fields. The Get Grade List module must now ask for the course code along with the grade. Statements have been added to Store Student Record which place the new student data onto the Student Record.

```
2080 REM ----- BUILD BLANK RECORD -------------------
2082 REM
2083 NL$=SPACE$(20)
2084 NF$=SPACE$(10)
2085 RD$=SPACE$(20)
2086 CI$=SPACE$(15)
2087 ST$=" "
2088 ZP$="    "
2089 CL$=" "
2090 FOR C%=0 TO 5
2091   CR$(C%)="  "
2092   GR$(C%)=" "
2094 NEXT C%
2096 AX$="X"
2097 RETURN
2098 REM - END BUILD BLANK RECORD -------------------
2099 REM

2357 REM
2400 REM ----- GET GRADE LIST -------------------
2401 REM      PROMISES TO UPDATE GR$() WITH ONE GRADE
2402 REM
```

```
2403 F%=1
2404 WHILE F%=1
2405   INPUT "ENTER PERIODS 1-6: ",C%
2410   IF C%>0 AND C%<7 THEN F%=0
2412   IF F%=1 THEN PRINT "PERIOD MUST BE 1,2,3,4,5,OR 6"
2413 WEND
2415 E%=0
2420 WHILE E%=0
2425   INPUT "GRADE";G$
2430   IF G$="A" THEN E%=1
2435   IF G$="B" THEN E%=1
2440   IF G$="C" THEN E%=1
2445   IF G$="D" THEN E%=1
2450   IF G$="F" THEN E%=1
2455   IF G$="W" THEN E%=1
2460   IF E%=0 THEN PRINT "UNRECOGNIZED GRADE.  REENTER."
2465 WEND
2470 E%=0
2475 WHILE E%=0
2480   INPUT "ENTER THREE-CHARACTER COURSE CODE: ",C$
2485   IF LEN(C$)<>3 THEN PRINT "MUST BE THREE CHARACTERS" ELSE E%=1
2490 WEND
2492 GR$(C%-1)=G$
2494 CR$(C%-1)=C$
2495 RETURN
2496 REM - END GET GRADE LIST --------------------
2497 REM

2500 REM ----- STORE STUDENT RECORD --------------------
2505 REM       ASSUMES VALID STUDENT DATA, ID% BETWEEN 1 AND 200
2510 REM               STUDENT FILE OPEN
2515 REM       PROMISES TO STORE STUDENT DATA ON RECORD ID%
2520 REM
2525 LSET F1$=MKI$(ID%)
2530 LSET F2$=NL$
2535 LSET F3$=NF$
2536 LSET F4$=RD$
2537 LSET F5$=CI$
2538 LSET F6$=ST$
2539 LSET F7$=ZP$
2540 LSET F8$=CL$
2545 G$=""
2550 FOR C%=0 TO 5
2555   G$=G$+CR$(C%)+GR$(C%)
2560 NEXT C%
2565 LSET F9$=G$
2570 LSET FX$=AX$
2575 PUT #1,ID%
2580 RETURN
2581 REM - END STORE STUDENT RECORD --------------------
2582 REM

2600 REM ----- GET STREET(RD$) --------------------
2605 REM
2610 E%=1
2615 WHILE E%=1
2620   LINE INPUT "ENTER STREET ADDRESS ",RD$
2625   IF LEN(RD$)>20 THEN PRINT "LESS THAN 20 CHARACTERS" ELSE E%=0
```

```
2630 WEND
2635 RETURN
2636 REM - END GET STREET -------------------
2637 REM

2650 REM ----- GET CITY(CI$) -------------------
2655 REM
2660 E%=1
2665 WHILE E%=1
2670   LINE INPUT "ENTER CITY NAME ",CI$
2675   IF LEN(CI$)>15 THEN PRINT "LESS THAN 15 CHARACTERS" ELSE E%=0
2680 WEND
2685 RETURN
2686 REM - END GET CITY -------------------
2687 REM

2700 REM ----- GET STATE(ST$) -------------------
2705 REM
2710 E%=1
2715 WHILE E%=1
2720   LINE INPUT "ENTER TWO-CHARACTER STATE CODE ",ST$
2725   IF LEN(ST$)<>2 THEN PRINT "MUST BE TWO CHARACTERS" ELSE E%=0
2730 WEND
2735 RETURN
2736 REM - END GET STATE -------------------
2737 REM

2750 REM ----- GET ZIP(ZP$) -------------------
2755 REM
2760 E%=1
2765 WHILE E%=1
2770   LINE INPUT "ENTER FIVE-DIGIT ZIP CODE ",ZP$
2775   IF LEN(ZP$)<>5 THEN PRINT "MUST BE FIVE DIGITS" ELSE E%=0
2780 WEND
2785 RETURN
2786 REM - END GET ZIP -------------------
2787 REM
```

Once these changes have been placed in Update Student Data, you can check in the New Student File that the data from the old file have been converted correctly. The test cases developed in section 7A also verify that the changes perform as planned.

If you get unexpected results during testing, look through the program outlines for the modules that may contain the error. For example, if the grade is placed in the wrong period, the error is probably in the Get Grade List module.

The last part of the conversion project alters the Produce Grade Report program to read the data on the New Student File correctly. Every module that works with the new data must be altered to reflect the new data definitions. The top module must declare the new file structure and Get Student Record must be changed for the new record format.

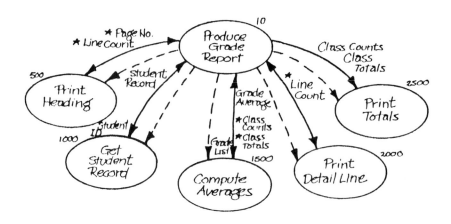

**Figure 7.7. Program outline for Produce Grade Report.**

The top module must use the new file name and FIELD statement.  In addition, as the file is twice as big as before, the top module must loop through all 200 records.

```
10 REM ----- PRODUCE STUDENT GRADE REPORT -------------------
11 REM
15 OPEN "R",#1,"STUDENT2"
20 FIELD #1, 2 AS F1$,20 AS F2$,10 AS F3$,20 AS F4$,15 AS F5$,2 AS F6$,
    5 AS F7$,2 AS F8$,24 AS F9$,1 AS FX$
25 DIM GR$(5),CR$(5)
27 P%=1: L%=66
30 GOSUB 500
35 FR%=0: SO%=0: JR%=0: SR%=0
40 FR!=0: SO!=0: JR!=0: SR!=0
45 FOR ID%=1 TO 200
50   GOSUB 1000
55   IF AX$="A" THEN GOSUB 1500: GOSUB 2000
57   IF L%>54 THEN GOSUB 500
60 NEXT ID%
62 IF L%>50 THEN GOSUB 500
65 GOSUB 2500
70 CLOSE #1
75 CHAIN "TRANSACT"
76 REM - END PRODUCE STUDENT GRADE REPORT -------------------
77 REM
```

The Get Student Record activity can be copied directly from the Update Student Data program which you just changed. As you recall, the other modules in the Produce Grade Report program are unaffected by the new record format.

Once the changes have been made, you can execute the program.  The report it produces should be identical to the report produced from the Old Student File.  Any differences indicate an error in the program.

You should review the code for the changes that the counselor requested and then look back at the models built in section 7A and review the relationship between the design and code. The data flow diagram, data dictionary, program outline, test cases, and code together form a complete model of the software system.

In this section, you have studied the process of modifying BASIC programs in order to change the data on a file. As Chapter 5 illustrated, you use the program outline and data dictionary to determine which modules of code are affected by a change.

### EXERCISE VII

The theater group is becoming increasingly popular; its last two plays were sold out. In response to the great demand for more productions, the board of directors has decided to schedule several performances of each show. The patrons have a choice of which date they wish to attend. Some days have two performances, one in the afternoon and the other in the evening.

The theater's president believes that the increase in patronage can increase donations. To help in fund raising, he has asked the ticket seller to record the patron's address when a ticket is sold. The theater can then send letters asking for support to those who attended a recent play.

As the software developer, you must change the theater's system to accommodate these requests. The Patron Sales File must be expanded to include the patron's name and address, and the date of the performance must also be stored on the sales record.

The ticket seller has asked that the date of the performance be added to the Patron Sales Report. Currently, the report lists only the seats sold to a particular person. Now, however, the same seat can be sold for different performances. To be useful, the report must list the date for which the seat is sold.

1. build a data flow diagram for the conversion function; update the data flow diagrams for the functions that use the sales file

2. update the data dictionary to define all new and changed data flows and files

3. estimate the time it will take to complete the conversion and deliver an error-free system to the theater group; record your size estimate in the performance log

4. define at least six new test cases to ensure that the changed system works as expected

5. build the program outline for the conversion function and update the program outlines for the changed functions

6. build the code for any new programs and modify existing programs to implement the requested changes

*8*

# Analyzing Data on a File

## 8A. Building the Model

Storing and retrieving data is not the only purpose of computer-based systems. Computers can derive valuable statistics from the data on their files. By combining different pieces of data and performing calculations with them, computers supply information that gives extra insights to users.

In this section, you will learn how to build a model of a function that analyzes data from a file. This function will accumulate statistics about the data and produce a summary report.

For an example of this type of analysis, you return to the counselor. He wants a report that summarizes data on the student file. In the summary, he needs the average grade for each course, the total number of students in each course, the grade average for each class year, and the total number of students in each class year.

| Course | CLASS | | | | | |
| | FR | SO | JR | SR | TOTAL | Course Average |
| --- | --- | --- | --- | --- | --- | --- |
| ALG | 1 | 6 | 1 | | 8 | 3.8 |
| GEM | 1 | 5 | | 6 | | 2.4 |
| GEO | | | 5 | 8 | 13 | 2.9 |
| SOC | | | | | | |
| GYM | | | | | | |
| . | | | | | | |
| . | | | | | | |
| TOTAL | 1 | 7 | 11 | 8 | 27 | |
| Class Average | 4.0 | 3.4 | 3.8 | 2.4 | | 3.4 |

Table 8.1. Sample student summary report.

To see how useful this information is, you have only to use your imagination. For example, the course average may indicate that a class is too easy or too difficult for its students. By looking at the total number of students in a class, the counselor can tell how popular it is.

None of the information on this report appears automatically on the student file. For example, to get the total number of students in each class year taking a course, the computer needs three pieces of information from the file — a student record, the course code, and class code. The computer then adds all student records containing the appropriate course and class code. To get the course average, the computer performs a more complicated calculation; it figures out individual GPAs, adds them, and divides the sum by the number of students in the class.

By contrast, the grade report in Chapter 4 simply lists data from the student file. While it also performs simple analysis, producing the individual and class averages, it is far less complex than the report in this chapter.

### Defining the function

All data on the sample report in Table 8.1 are derived from data on the student file, so the data flow diagram in Figure 8.1 must show a data flow from the file into the function. The Grade Analysis Report is the only piece of data you have been asked to produce, so it is shown as the one outgoing data flow.

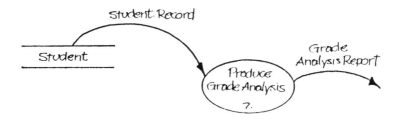

**Figure 8.1. Data flow diagram for Produce Grade Analysis.**

This function can be placed in the transaction center built in Chapter 6. Be sure to change the Select Student Function program to include this function.

### Defining the data

To define the data for the function Produce Grade Report, you begin by looking at the sample report. Every element in the report must appear in the data dictionary. As the definition of Grade Analysis Report in Table 8.2 shows, you divide the report into three parts: Course Array, Class Counts, and Class Averages.

The first part is a series of lines, each containing information about a particular course. Each line contains a course code, the number of students enrolled by class year, the total number of students enrolled, and the course average. You know to call this section of the report an array because it consists of many lines, each containing the same number and type of data items.

The last two lines of the report contain summary data listed according to class year. The next-to-last line is called Class Counts in the dictionary; it lists the total number of students in each class and in the school. The last line lists the average grade for the class and the school-wide grade point average. You will find its definition in Table 8.2 under Class Averages.

---

## DATA DICTIONARY

Class Averages = FR Average + SO Average + JR Average + SR Average
  + School Average

Class Counts = Total FR Count + Total SO Count + Total JR Count
  + Total SR Count + School Total

Course Array = { Course Code + Course Counts + Course Average }

Course Average = Real number between 0.0 and 4.0

Course Code = 3 characters

Course Counts = FR Count + SO Count + JR Count + SR Count + Course Count

Grade Analysis Report = Course Array + Class Counts + Class Averages

Grade List = 6{Course Code + Grade}6

Student File = 200{New Student Record}200

Student Record = Student ID + Student Name + Street + City + State
  + Zip + Grade List

---

**Table 8.2. Data dictionary for Produce Grade Analysis.**

Now that data flows around the function are defined, you can review the relationship between incoming and outgoing data to get a better understanding of the Produce Grade Analysis function. Each Student Record has up to six course codes, with a grade for each course. Each line in the Course Array, which is in the Grade Analysis Report, is a series of course codes with its own totals. Each course on the Student Record is used to update the data on a line of Course Array. You will achieve a better understanding of their relationship by working through an example as if you were doing the function manually.

Assume that the first student record lists a freshman who has two course codes and associated grades: ALG, A; GEO, B. You would write the course code ALG on a piece of paper, add 1 to a freshman count, and add 4.0 to the grade total for course ALG. Course GEO is added to the list in the same way. Next, assume that the second record is also for a freshman and has two course codes: ALG, B; SOC, C. You would take the first course (ALG), look down the list to find the course already recorded, and add 1 to the ALG freshman count and 3.0 to the grade total. The SOC course code is not on the page yet, so you update the list and begin a count and grade total for SOC. After all student records have been processed, you compute the averages by dividing the grade total by the student count.

Produce Grade Analysis's function is retrieving student records and producing the Grade Analysis Report. Reviewing the relationship between incoming and outgoing data flows helps to define the process.

## Estimating the size of the program

Since one data flow goes into the function and one leaves it, the initial token count is two. You increase this estimate by one to take into account the set of braces in the data dictionary definition of Grade Analysis Report. The Student Record also contains a set of braces that the function uses {Course and Grade}, so the estimate is now four tokens.

Next, review the data dictionary for an outgoing data item that is not built directly from an incoming one. Grade Analysis Report consists of three parts, Course Array, Class Counts, and Class Averages. Each part is updated by incoming student records. Add one token for each of these data items, making a total token count of seven.

You may be wondering why, if the transformation from Student Record to Grade Analysis Report is indirect, you don't add a token for each of the five component items of Class Counts or for each component of Class Averages and Course Arrays. You do not count Class Counts as five tokens because the individual student records will not update the five components separately. Each Student Record will update the set of data called Class Counts rather than an individual data item. The same is true of Class Averages and Course Array.

| | PERFORMANCE LOG | | | |
|---|---|---|---|---|
| Function | Token Count | Estimate | Actual Time | Rate Token/Time |
| 7 | 7 | < 8 hr. | | .9 token/hr. |

Table 8.3. Performance log for Produce Grade Analysis.

## Identifying the test cases

To construct test cases, you look at the definitions for data items enclosed in braces and build test cases for the first and last data items. For example, because Student File has 200 records, you should test that the function accesses the first and last records of the file. Since Produce Grade Analysis processes the grades from Student Record, test that both the first and last course and grade are processed by the program.

The braces around Course Array indicate that it repeats data as well, so the program must be able to handle both the least number of courses possible — which means a report with no courses — and the most. A report will have no courses when either no Student Record contains a course code or the Student File contains no active records.

The Class Averages computed by this program should be the same as those computed by Produce Grade Report, built in Chapter 4. Therefore, one way to test Analysis Grade Report is to run both programs with the same records. Any difference in results points to an error in one of the programs. The error will probably be in the newest program, because the older program has already been tested.

---

## TEST CASE LOG

| Test Case | Result |
|---|---|
| File with no records | 0 on the report |
| Add record 1 with one grade | |
| FR GEO A | GEO course average 4.0 |
| | FR average 4.0 |
| | GEO course count 1 |
| | |
| Add record 200 with six grades | |
| SR  GEO B | GEO course average 3.5 |
| ALG B | SR average 3.33 |
| GYM A | GEO course count 2 |
| SOC A | Other course counts 1 |
| SHP B | |
| HOM B | |
| | |
| Add record 2 with four grades | |
| JR  GEO D | GEO course average 2.67 |
| ALG D | JR average 1.0 |
| GYM D | GEO course count 3 |
| SOC D | ALG, GYM, SOC course count 2 |

---

Table 8.4. Test case log for Produce Grade Analysis.

**Building the program outline**

The program outline in Figure 8.2 shows the activities that perform the Produce Grade Analysis function. Each data flow around the function has an activity, one to get the Student Record from the Student File and a second activity called Print Arrays to print the Grade Analysis Report. The function also accumulates data in Course Array, Class Counts, and Class Averages.

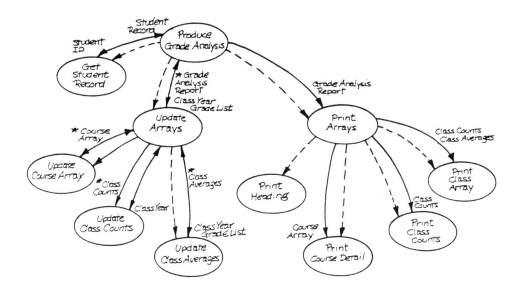

**Figure 8.2. Program outline for Produce Grade Analysis.**

Based on your experience so far, you can anticipate that the activity accumulating student data will be a large function with many parts. Remember that the Get Student Data module from the Update Student Data program in Chapter 3 dealt with so many different data items that you factored it into subordinate activities, each working on a different piece of data. The module that updates the Grade Analysis Report should also be factored into subordinate activities, each working on a separate part of the Grade Analysis Report. You add a subordinate module to the program outline for each of the report's three parts: Course Array, Class Counts, and Class Averages.

The program becomes easier to code as you subdivide the program outline. By factoring the activities into smaller, more detailed modules, you avoid having to work with large blocks of code that are difficult to conceptualize.

Notice that Print Arrays is factored into four activities. In factoring both Update Arrays and Print Arrays, you use the data definitions as a guide to choosing the lower-level modules. Except for Print Heading, each subordinate module is responsible for one component of the data item Grade Analysis Report.

This section has given you an example of how to model a program that analyzes and summarizes data. You have seen how the data dictionary plays an important part in building the test cases and program outline. With the program outline completed, you can now build the program that actually produces the summary report.

# 8B. Building the BASIC Program

In this section, you will expand your understanding of how arrays are used to accumulate data. The Produce Grade Analysis function contains data, namely the data in Course Array, that can be put into an array. Your program defines these data as three arrays that are updated by each Student Record. When all student records are processed, the program prints the data accumulated in the arrays.

Remember that BASIC requires you to declare arrays at the beginning of each program. This declaration is accomplished with the DIM statement, which specifies the size of each array. Since the data dictionary in section 8A does not specify an upper limit to the Course Array, you must estimate and declare a size large enough to hold all course codes. An estimate of 100 entries should be enough.

According to the data dictionary, each element in Course Array contains a course code, course counts, and a course average. The course code is a three-character string, the course counts are integers, and the course average is a real number. Since BASIC allows only one type of data in any single array, one array cannot hold data contained in Course Array. For this reason, the program requires three arrays: a string array to hold the course code, an integer array to hold the course counts, and an array of real numbers to hold the class averages. You can keep track of the corresponding elements on the three arrays because a subscript for an element in one array will be the subscript for the corresponding element in the others.

Course Counts contains five pieces of data, the four class counts and a school count. You could declare a separate array for each of the five counts, but a better solution is to declare one array that has two dimensions. A two-dimensional array has two subscripts: In this case, the first one indicates the course associated with the data item and the second points to one of the five totals.

| CA$(99) Course Code Array | CA%(99,4) Course Counts Array | | | | | CA!(99) Course Average Array |
|---|---|---|---|---|---|---|
| | FR | SO | JR | SR | TOTAL | |
| | 0 | 1 | 2 | 3 | 4 | |
| 0   SOC | 5 | 14 | 0 | 0 | 19 | 3.20 |
| 1   ALG | 0 | 0 | 18 | 0 | 18 | 2.95 |
| 2   TRI | 5 | 4 | 1 | 7 | 17 | 3.45 |
| 3   GYM | 11 | 6 | 0 | 0 | 17 | 2.90 |
| 99   PHY | 0 | 0 | 0 | 23 | 23 | 1.97 |

**Table 8.5. Course array organization.**

To find the number of freshmen with course code SOC, the program uses the reference CA%(0,0). In the same manner, CA%(99,4) refers to the number of seniors with course code PHY on their record.

Now you can determine how the program uses the array to update a course count. When the program reads a student record, it searches the Course Code array to find the position of the course code on that record. For example, if Student Record contains a course code of TRI, the program searches the Course Code array until it finds a matching course code and sets the first subscript to that position (2 in Table 8.5). Next, the second subscript is assigned based on the student's class code. If the student has a class code of SO, the program assigns 1 to the second subscript. The Course Count array is updated by adding 1 to CA%(2,1).

Class Counts and Class Averages can also be declared arrays. This makes updating them more convenient, since the program can use the subscript set with the student's class code to indicate which count or average should be increased.

---

## DATA DICTIONARY

Class Counts = Total FR Count + Total SO Count + Total JR Count
     + Total SR Count + School Total
     CC%()

Class Averages = FR Average + SO Average + JR Average + SR Average
     + School Average
     CC!()

Course Array = { Course Code + Course Counts + Course Average }
     CA\$(n)   CA%(n,m)   CA!(n)

Course Average = Real number between 0.0 and 4.0

Course Code = 3 characters

Course Counts = FR Count + SO Count + JR Count + SR Count + Course Count

Grade Analysis Report = Course Array + Class Counts + Class Averages

Grade List = 6{Course + Grade}6
     CR\$()  GR\$()

Student File = 200{New Student Record}200
     STUDENT2

Student Record = Student ID + Student Name + Street + City + State
     + Zip + Grade List

---

**Table 8.6. Data dictionary with BASIC data names.**

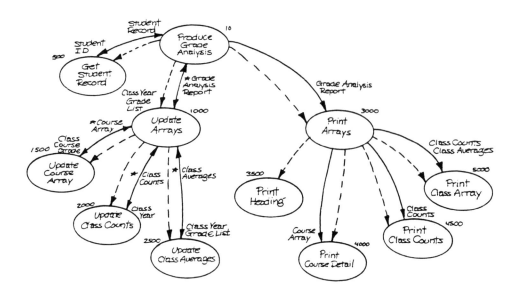

**Figure 8.3. Program outline for Produce Grade Analysis.**

The top module below declares the arrays in line 25.  It also declares the Student File with OPEN and FIELD statements.  It then invokes the Get Student Record and Update Arrays modules until all records have been processed.  Last, the arrays are printed by the Print Arrays module and the transaction center program is executed.

```
10 REM ----- PRODUCE GRADE ANALYSIS --------------------
11 REM
15 OPEN "R",#1,"STUDENT2"
20 FIELD #1, 2 AS F1$,20 AS F2$,10 AS F3$,20 AS F4$,15 AS F5$,2 AS F6$,
    5 AS F7$,2 AS F8$,24 AS F9$,1 AS FX$
25 DIM GR$(5), CR$(5), CA$(99), CA%(99,4), CA!(99), CC%(4), CC!(4)
30 FOR ID%=1 TO 200
35   GOSUB 500
40   IF AX$="A" THEN GOSUB 1000
45 NEXT ID%
50 CLOSE #1
55 GOSUB 3000
60 CHAIN "TRANSACT"
61 REM - END PRODUCE GRADE ANALYSIS --------------------
62 REM
```

The Get Student Record module is copied from the Update Student Data program; the only difference is that Get Student Record starts on line 500 in this program.

```
500 REM ----- GET STUDENT RECORD --------------------
505 REM       ASSUMES ID% TO BE BETWEEN 1 AND 200
510 REM            STUDENT FILE IS OPEN
515 REM       PROMISES NF$, NL$, AD$, CI$, ST$, ZP$, CL$, CR$(),
520 REM        GR$(), AND AX$ FILLED WITH DATA FROM STUDENT RECORD ID%
525 REM
530 GET #1,ID%
```

```
535 NL$=F2$
540 NF$=F3$
545 RD$=F4$
550 CI$=F5$
555 ST$=F6$
560 ZP$=F7&
565 CL$=F8$
570 FOR C% = 0 TO 5
575  CR$(C%)=MID$(F9$,C%*4+1,3)
580  GR$(C%)=MID$(F9$,C%*4+4,1)
585 NEXT C%
590 AX$=FX$
595 RETURN
596 REM - END GET STUDENT RECORD ----------------
597 REM
```

Each time the Update Arrays module is invoked, it knows that the student record is ready for processing. It first sets a subscript {M%} based on the student class code, and then invokes Update Course Array for each course code. After all course codes on the student record have been processed, Update Arrays invokes Update Class Counts and Update Class Averages.

```
1000 REM ----- UPDATE ARRAYS -------------------
1005 REM        ASSUMES VALID STUDENT DATA
1010 REM        PROMISES TO UPDATE GRADE ANALYSIS REPORT
1015 REM
1020 E%=0
1025 IF CL$="FR" THEN M%=0:E%=1
1030 IF CL$="SO" THEN M%=1:E%=1
1035 IF CL$="JR" THEN M%=2:E%=1
1040 IF CL$="SR" THEN M%=3:E%=1
```

There is a chance that the class code will be blank. The user may not have entered the class code when entering the student's data. If the student record does not have the class code, line 1045 displays a message and assumes the student is a freshman.

```
1045 IF E%=0 THEN PRINT "STUDENT " ID% " HAS NO CLASS":M%=0
1050 FOR G%=0 TO 5
1055  IF CR$(G%)<>"   " THEN C$=CR$(G%): G$=GR$(G%): GOSUB 1500
1060 NEXT G%
1065 GOSUB 2000
1070 GOSUB 2500
1075 RETURN
1076 REM - END UPDATE ARRAYS -------------------
1077 REM
```

The Update Course Array module must find the position of the course code in the array, update the course counts, and add the student's grade average to the course average. If, after searching the Course Code array, the module finds the course code in the twentieth position of the array, it sets the subscript N% to 20 and uses that subscript to locate the elements to update in the other arrays. If the course code is not found, the program places the code in the next available position of the Course Code array.

The first time Update Course Array is invoked, the Course Code array contains no course codes. Finding the first position empty, the module places the first course code on the record in position CA$(0). The program searches the array for the next course on the student record. If that course code is not already in the array, it is placed in CA$(1). If the Course Code array is full (the module tries to add course code 101), an error message is printed and the module gets out of the loop.

```
1500 REM ----- UPDATE COURSE ARRAY --------------------
1505 REM        ASSUMES COURSE ARRAY, G$ CONTAINS A GRADE
1510 REM            C$ CONTAINS COURSE CODE, M% BETWEEN 0 AND 3
1515 REM        PROMISES TO ADD COURSE CODE TO ARRAY AND ADJUST COURSE AMOUNTS
1520 REM
1525 E% = 1
1530 N% = 0
1535 WHILE E% = 1
1540    IF CA$(N%) = "" THEN CA$(N%) = C$
1545    IF C$ = CA$(N%) THEN GOSUB 1600: E% = 0
1550    N% = N% + 1
1555    IF N% > 99 THEN PRINT "COURSE ARRAY FULL - REPORT WILL BE ERRONEOUS":E% = 0
1560 WEND
1565 RETURN
1570 REM - END UPDATE COURSE ARRAY --------------------
1575 REM

1600 REM ----- ADD TO COURSE ARRAYS -------------------
1605 REM
1610 CA%(N%,M%) = CA%(N%,M%) + 1
1615 CA%(N%,4) = CA%(N%,4) + 1
1620 IF G$ = "A" THEN CA!(N%) = CA!(N%) + 4.0
1625 IF G$ = "B" THEN CA!(N%) = CA!(N%) + 3.0
1630 IF G$ = "C" THEN CA!(N%) = CA!(N%) + 2.0
1635 IF G$ = "D" THEN CA!(N%) = CA!(N%) + 1.0
1640 IF G$ = "F" THEN CA!(N%) = CA!(N%) + 0.0
1645 RETURN
1646 REM - END ADD TO COURSE ARRAYS --------------------
1647 REM
```

Notice that the code that adds 1 to the course counts and the grade value to the course average has been factored into its own module. The IF statement at line 1545 determines that the course code has been found on the Course Code array and that the arrays are therefore ready to be updated. However, so many statements are needed to perform the updates that they will not fit in the IF statement itself. So, the statements are coded as a separate submodule and invoked with the GOSUB command.

The Course Average array contains the sum of all completed grades awarded for a given course. The report prints the course average. It is possible that the grade for a course is I or W; in this case, the student is counted in the Course Counts array $CA\%(n,m)$, but the student should not be included in the calculation of the course average.

Now that you are at the coding level, you see that you will need to build another array containing all completed grades totaled in the Course Average array. The counts in this new array will be used to compute the average grade for each course. The array is not part of the function model built in section 8A because it does not appear on any data flow in the data flow diagram. The new code looks like this:

```
25 DIM GR$(5), CR$(5), CA$(99), CA%(99,4), CA!(99), CC%(4), CC!(4), CN%(99)
1600 REM ----- ADD TO COURSE ARRAYS --------------------
1605 REM
1610 CA%(N%,M%) = CA%(N%,M%) + 1
1615 CA%(N%,4) = CA%(N%,4) + 1
1620 IF G$ = "A" THEN CA!(N%) = CA!(N%) + 4.0: CN%(N%) = CN%(N%) + 1
1625 IF G$ = "B" THEN CA!(N%) = CA!(N%) + 3.0: CN%(N%) = CN%(N%) + 1
1630 IF G$ = "C" THEN CA!(N%) = CA!(N%) + 2.0: CN%(N%) = CN%(N%) + 1
1635 IF G$ = "D" THEN CA!(N%) = CA!(N%) + 1.0: CN%(N%) = CN%(N%) + 1
1640 IF G$ = "F" THEN CA!(N%) = CA!(N%) + 0.0: CN%(N%) = CN%(N%) + 1
1645 RETURN
1646 REM - END ADD TO COURSE ARRAYS --------------------
1647 REM
```

The Update Class Counts module accumulates the total number of students in each class. The subscript for the class code is assigned in lines 1025 through 1040 of the Update Arrays module.

```
2000 REM ----- UPDATE CLASS COUNTS --------------------
2002 REM        ASSUMES CLASS COUNTS AND M% BETWEEN 0 AND 3
2005 REM        PROMISES TO ADD TO CLASS COUNTS - CC%()
2010 REM
2015 CC%(M%) = CC%(M%) + 1
2020 CC%(4) = CC%(4) + 1
2025 RETURN
2026 REM - END UPDATE CLASS COUNTS --------------------
2027 REM
```

Update Class Averages computes the student's GPA and adds it to the Class Averages array.

```
2500 REM ----- UPDATE CLASS AVERAGES --------------------
2505 REM        ASSUMES GR$(),CC!(),AND M%
2510 REM        PROMISES TO UPDATE CC!() WILL STUDENT GPA
2515 REM
2520 C%=0
2525 A!=0
2530 FOR G%=0 TO 5
2535   IF GR$(G%) = "A" THEN A! = A! + 4.0: C% = C% + 1
2540   IF GR$(G%) = "B" THEN A! = A! + 3.0: C% = C% + 1
2545   IF GR$(G%) = "C" THEN A! = A! + 2.0: C% = C% + 1
2550   IF GR$(G%) = "D" THEN A! = A! + 1.0: C% = C% + 1
2555   IF GR$(G%) = "F" THEN A! = A! + 0.0: C% = C% + 1
2560 NEXT G%
2565 IF C% > 0 THEN A! = A! / C%
2570 CC!(M%) = CC!(M%) + A!
2575 CC!(4) = CC!(4) + A!
2580 RETURN
2581 REM - END UPDATE CLASS AVERAGES --------------------
2582 REM
```

As shown in the program outline, the next step in the program is to print the arrays that make up Grade Analysis Report. The coordinate module, Print Arrays, steps through the printing sequence by invoking its subordinate modules.

```
3000 REM ----- PRINT ARRAYS -------------------
3005 REM      ASSUMES GRADE ANALYSIS ARRAYS
3010 REM
3015 GOSUB 3500
3020 GOSUB 4000
3025 GOSUB 4500
3030 GOSUB 5000
3035 RETURN
3036 REM - END PRINT ARRAYS -------------------
3037 REM


3500 REM ----- PRINT HEADING -------------------
3505 REM
3510 LPRINT SPACE$(25);"GRADE ANALYSIS REPORT"
3515 LPRINT
3520 LPRINT "               - - - - CLASS - - - -"
3525 LPRINT "      COURSE   FR  SO  JR  SR  TOTAL   COURSE GPA"
3530 LPRINT
3535 RETURN
3536 REM - END PRINT HEADING -------------------
3537 REM
```

The Print Course Detail module must step through the Course Code array and print the course code, course counts, and course average for each entry. In the code shown below, notice that the block of code to print one row of data has been factored into its own module.

```
4000 REM ----- PRINT COURSE DETAIL -------------------
4005 REM      ASSUMES COURSE ARRAYS
4010 REM
4015 E%=1
4020 N%=0
4025 WHILE E%=1
4030   IF CA$(N%)<>"" THEN GOSUB 4100 ELSE E%=0
4035   N%=N%+1
4040   IF N%>99 THEN E%=0
4045 WEND
4050 LPRINT
4055 RETURN
4056 REM - END PRINT COURSE DETAIL -------------------
4057 REM


4100 REM ----- PRINT COURSE ROW -------------------
4102 REM
4105 A!=0
4110 IF CN%(N%) > 0 THEN A! = CA!(N%) / CN%(N%)
4115 LPRINT "      ";CA$(N%);"  ";
4120 FOR M%=0 TO 4
4125   LPRINT USING "#####";CA%(N%,M%);
4130 NEXT M%
4135 LPRINT "     ";
4140 LPRINT USING "#.##";A!
4145 RETURN
4146 REM - END PRINT COURSE ROW -------------------
4147 REM
```

The code for Print Class Counts and Print Class Array is shown below. Their task is to format the data in the Class Counts and Class Averages arrays and print them at the bottom of the report.

```
4500 REM ----- PRINT CLASS COUNTS -------------------
4505 REM      ASSUMES CLASS COUNTS - CC%()
4510 REM
4515 LPRINT "      TOTAL   ";
4520 FOR M%=0 TO 4
4525  LPRINT USING "#####";CC%(M%);
4530 NEXT M%
4535 LPRINT
4540 RETURN
4541 REM - END PRINT CLASS COUNTS -------------------
4542 REM

5000 REM ----- PRINT CLASS ARRAY -------------------
5005 REM      ASSUMES CC%() AND CC!()
5010 REM
5015 LPRINT "      AVERAGE ";
5020 FOR M%=0 TO 4
5025  A!=0
5030  IF CC%(M%) > 0 THEN A! = CC!(M%) / CC%(M%)
5035  LPRINT USING "##.##";A!;
5040 NEXT M%
5045 RETURN
5046 REM - END PRINT CLASS ARRAY -------------------
5047 REM
```

The code in this section shows how arrays are used to organize and collect data. This example also illustrates how large amounts of data stored on a file can be summarized into a small, usable report.

## EXERCISE VIII

The community theater has a source of data about its patrons, and the members are beginning to ask questions. How many tickets are sold to people who live in town? How many special tickets are sold? What percentage of the total sale was special tickets? The president of the theater has asked you to build a program to report some of these statistics. He has prepared a sample report to illustrate what he wants.

### AREA ANALYSIS REPORT

| Zip | # of Reg. | % of Area | # of Spec. | % of Area | Total | % of Total |
|-----|-----------|-----------|------------|-----------|-------|------------|
| 83810 | 5 | 71.4 | 2 | 28.6 | 7 | 5.7 |
| 83814 | 84 | 84.0 | 16 | 16.0 | 100 | 81.3 |
| 83837 | 16 | 100.0 | 0 | 0.0 | 16 | 13.0 |
| TOTAL | 105 | 85.4 | 18 | 14.6 | 123 | |

The report summarizes the data by zip code. The user wants the following data listed for each zip code:

• the number of regular tickets sold in the area and their percentage of area sales

• the number of special tickets sold in the area and their percentage of area sales

• the total number of tickets sold in the area

• the percentage of total ticket sales sold in the area

The report ends with a summary line listing the total number of regular tickets sold, their percentage of total sales, the total number of special tickets, their percentage of total sales, and the total number of tickets sold.

1. draw a data flow diagram for the function

2. define data flows in the data dictionary

3. compute a size estimate and record it in the performance log

4. build at least four test cases

5. build the program outline by identifying the activities performed by the function; factor any activities that deal with large groups of data

6. write the BASIC code using the program outline as a guide

# Building an Index to the File

*9*

## 9A. Building the Model

Up until now, the programs in this book have located a record by using a number, the student ID, corresponding to the record's position on the file. At times, however, you must find a particular record when you don't know its position on the file, but you do know a piece of data on the record. In this section, you will learn how to build an index for a file that allows you to access the file by entering a certain data item from the record you want.

As the guidance counselor's system now works, the counselor must enter the student's ID number before getting a record from the file. Students, however, also request information without knowing their ID number, so the counselor must first find the correct number before he can retrieve the student's record. This process is time consuming, and it would be more convenient if the counselor could locate a record by using the student's last name.

In Chapter 8, the Produce Grade Analysis function applied an index to locate the correct course counts and course average in the Course Array. It used the course code, not the position number on the student record. The function found the code in the Course Code array and then updated the corresponding course totals.

You can use the same method to find student records with the student's name. To accomplish this task, you must create an array of 200 elements that holds each student's last name. The position of each student's name in the array will correspond to the position of that student's record on the file. For example, the last name from the first student record on the file is recorded in the first element of the array, while the last name from record 200 is placed in the 200th element. The program reads every last name in the array until it finds the one requested, then uses the subscript for that position as it would the ID number to locate the record. Each time the user adds a new record, the last name of the student is placed in the array's corresponding position. Each time the user deletes a student record, the corresponding position on the array is made blank.

Another method using the last name to access a student record involves reading every record on the file. However, since reading the entire file takes several seconds, the counselor will have to wait during each inquiry. As the file gets larger, the waiting increases. Storing the last names on an array speeds the search process by reducing the data the program must read.

Several problems created by using an index need to be resolved. The possibility exists that the file contains two students with the same last name. If the program pulls out only one of those records, it may be the wrong one. Including the student's first name in the array would not eliminate the possibility of duplicates, because two students named JOHN SMITH, for example, could be stored on the file.

A better solution is to search the entire array for all entries that match the user's request. If the program finds more than one match, it provides a numbered list of the duplicate names. The user chooses the student's record from this list by entering its number. Using this approach, the user and the program interact like this:

- the user enters the name JONES

- the program searches for JONES and finds three in the array

- the program retrieves the records from the student file and
  displays the first and last names along with the student's class

  1 JONES, BOBBY FR
  2 JONES, SALLY SR
  3 JONES, SUE  SR

- the user enters the number (1, 2, or 3) that identifies
  which JONES he wants

Another problem involved with using the student's name to access the student file is that the user may not know the correct spelling. For instance, the counselor may enter the name WELSBURY when the name in the index is spelled WELLSBURY; the program will report that it cannot find the record. The program can minimize the chance of error by limiting the index to the first three letters of the last name. With this approach, the counselor enters the first three characters and the program list all names that start with those letters. If the counselor isn't sure of the correct spelling, he now has a list of possible names from which to choose. Also, the user saves time by entering three characters instead of the whole name.

This method may result in an extra step for the counselor. For instance, if the counselor enters the last name WELSBURY, he might receive the following list of names from the program:

1 WELLINGTON, JOHN SO
2 WELSBURY, STAN  FR
3 WELLS, LEONARD  JR
4 WELSLEY, MARY   JR
5 WELLS, SUSAN    SR

The counselor's extra step is to enter 2, telling the program he wants to look at Stan Welsbury's record. Adding this procedure is preferable to storing the entire last name and dealing with the possibility of misspellings.

### Defining the function

The above discussion refers to four different pieces of data: the name entered by the counselor, the list of duplicate names, the duplicate choice made by the counselor, and the index record or array. These data flows must be added to the data flow diagram for the Update Student Data function. Because the user has the choice of entering either the student ID or the last name, the data flows for both are combined into one, called Student Reference.

To build an index for the Student File, you define a function called Build Student Index, which creates the array containing the first three characters of the last name. This function reads each student record and puts the last name into the array. The array is then stored on a Student Index File, so two data flows are needed: one for the Student Record being read, and one for the completed Index Record being stored.

In Figure 9.1, the function Update Student Data has so many data flows that it is difficult to read and understand. You resolve this problem by building a data flow diagram showing the component functions of Update Student Data. By representing the function as several bubbles, you provide a more detailed view of the subfunctions performed inside Update Student Data.

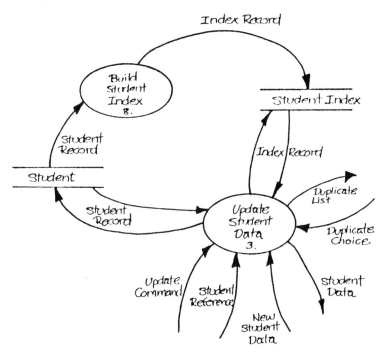

**Figure 9.1. Data flow diagram for functions using Student Index.**

The subfunctions shown in Figure 9.2 are determined by following the first data flow entered by the user through the function and identifying the processes it undergoes. The Student Reference data flow is first used to search the Student Index for the desired Student Record. This process may involve displaying a list of duplicates and accepting the user's choice. The first subfunction, therefore, is Find Student Record.

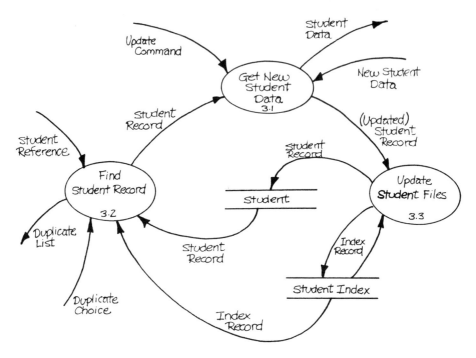

**Figure 9.2. Second-level data flow diagram for Update Student Data.**

You now follow the Student Record through the Update Student Data process. The Student Record flows to a function that accepts changes to it, creating an (Updated) Student Record. This is the second subfunction, Get New Student Data. Its output, the updated record, flows to a process that stores the record on the Student File and updates the Student Index.

**Defining the data**

The Build Student Index function creates a Student Index File, an array containing 200 abbreviated last names. You could store the entire array on one 600-character record (200 x 3 characters). However, all computers limit record size, so refer to your computer manual to determine the maximum. In the data dictionary in Table 9.1, the Student Index File is divided into five records, each containing 40 abbreviated last names.

You now inspect the Update Student Data program for new data flows. When this function finds duplicate names, a numbered list — the Duplicate List — containing the first and last name and class code is displayed. The user then chooses the student record he wants by entering the student number shown in the list. This number is called the Duplicate Choice.

---

### DATA DICTIONARY

Abbreviated Last Name = 3 characters

Duplicate Choice = Integer

Duplicate List = 2{Last Name + First Name + Class}

Index Record = 40{Abbreviated Last Name}40

Student Index = 5{Index Record}5

Student Reference = [ Student ID | Last Name ]

---

**Table 9.1. Data dictionary for Build Student Index.**

Now that you have set up the structure of the Student Index, you can see the relationship between each abbreviated last name in the array and its corresponding record. The top of Table 9.2 shows several last names from the first two records on the index file. Each name is matched to its position on the record. The first index record corresponds to the first 40 records of the student file. The second record corresponds to the next 40 student records (41 through 80). The student file below contains the records listed according to ID number, which matches their position on the file.

---

Student Index:

```
1   2   3   4   5   6   ... 40
SMI DAV ___ ___ PET ___ ... WEL
JON ___ SAM STU ___ ___ ... SHE
```

Student File:

```
001 SMITH  JOHN   FR ...
002 DAVIS  SALLY  JR ...
003 ___
004 ___
005 PETERS SAM    SR ...
006 ___
  .
  .
040 WELLS   ARTHUR SR ...
041 JONES   PETER  FR ...
042 ___
043 SAMUELS JONIE  JR ...
044 STUART  SCOTT  SR ...
045 ___
046 ___
  .
  .
080 SHERMAN JOY   SO ...
```

---

**Table 9.2. Relationship between Student Index and Student File.**

## Estimating the size of the program

Since Build Student Index has two data flows in the data flow diagram, the initial token count is two. One token is added for the set of braces in the data definition of Index Record, making a total estimate of three tokens for that function.

When a function has a lower level, as does Update Student Data, you compute a separate token count for each subfunction. Begin by counting the number of changed data flows around each function. No data flows around Get New Student Data (function 3.1) have changed. The function still gets the student record and updates it with new data entered by the user, so the token count for function 3.1 is zero.

Because Find Student Record (function 3.2) has four new or changed data flows, it has an initial token count of four. Adding one for the brackets in Student Reference and one for the braces in Duplicate List brings the total to six. The Index Record contains an array of Abbreviated Last Names, so you add one for this set of braces. The final token count for Find Student Record is seven.

Update Student Files works with two new data flows, the incoming and outgoing Index Record, so its initial token count is two. You add one to the token count for the braces in the outgoing Index Record's definition; the function updates the Abbreviated Last Names array when it places the new name into the outgoing Index Record. You do not, however, count the set of braces in the incoming Index Record. The function does not refer to this array when the Index Record is read from the Student Index File. This subfunction has a token count of three.

## PERFORMANCE LOG

| Function | Token Count | Estimate | Actual Time | Rate Token/Time |
|----------|-------------|----------|-------------|-----------------|
|          |             |          |             | 1.2 token/hr.   |
| 8        | 3           |          |             |                 |
| 3.1      | 0           |          |             |                 |
| 3.2      | 7           |          |             |                 |
| 3.3      | 3           |          |             |                 |
| TOTAL    | 13          | < 11 hrs.|             |                 |

**Table 9.3. Performance log.**

## Identifying the test cases

One test case should check that an error message results when the user enters a name that does not exist on the file. This is the purpose of the first test case in Table 9.4. The second and third cases test that you can access students that are already on the Student Index File. If the first record of the Student File is for SAM SMITH, you must be able to access his record by entering a Student Reference of SMI. The last record on the Student File must also be tested. You should also define two test cases that make sure the correct record is accessed after the names on the first and last student records have been changed.

The final test case checks that the program handles duplicate names correctly. When the user enters a Student Reference for a name that appears twice on the file, the program should display a Duplicate List containing two entries. This test case also tests Duplicate Choice. If a Duplicate List containing two names is displayed and the user enters a Duplicate Choice of three, an error message should result.

## TEST CASE LOG

| Test Case | Result |
|---|---|
| Student Reference— | |
| JON when there is no <br> JON on file | Error message |
| SMI when SMITH is the first <br> record on file | Display the SMITH record |
| Change name on first record to <br> THOMAS and enter THO | Display the first record |
| WEL when WELLS is the 200th <br> record on file | Display the WELLS record |
| Change name on 200th record to <br> PETERS and enter PET | Display the 200th record |
| DAV when DAVID appears twice <br> on file <br> Enter choice 3 <br> Enter choice 1 | Display Duplicate List <br> with two names <br> Error message <br> Display correct record |

**Table 9.4. Test case log.**

**Building the program outline**

The program outline for Build Student Index is fairly simple. It must include an activity that gets each Student Record and an activity that stores each completed Index Record. The program does manipulate data by adding the student's last name to Index Record, so Update Index Record is the third activity.

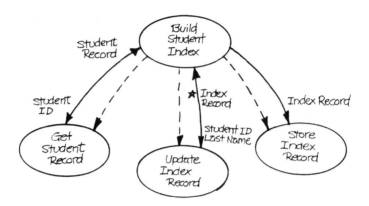

**Figure 9.3. Program outline for Build Student Index.**

The new program outline for Update Student Data is based on the lower-level data flow diagram of the function. The three functions on that data flow diagram become activities on the program outline under the Update Student Data module.

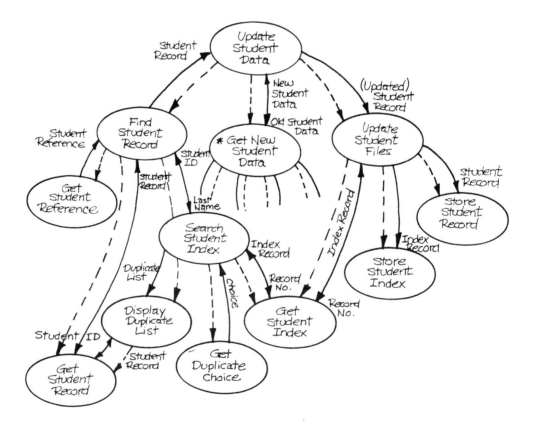

**Figure 9.4. Program outline for Update Student Data.**

For Find Student Record and Update Student Files, you complete the program outline by drawing an activity for each incoming and outgoing data flow. The Find Student Record function gets the Student Reference, searches the index and resolves any duplicates, and retrieves the Student Record. The function needs one activity that gets the Student Reference and another that searches the Student Index and determines which record the user wants. The last activity retrieves the Student Record from the Student File.

Update Student Files gets the Index Record, stores the Student Index File, and then stores the Student Record on the Student File. Therefore, Update Student Files requires three activities: Store Student Record, Get Index Record, and Store Index Record. The (Updated) Student Record flows to the module from the top module.

Get New Student Data receives the Student Record and updates it with New Student Data as it did in Chapter 7. This portion of the program outline, therefore, remains unchanged. You do not have to show the lower-level modules under Get New Student Data on the outline because they have not changed. The asterisk next to the function name tells you that the module is shown in more detail in another figure (see Figure 7.4).

After studying this section, you have an understanding of how an index can be used to access records stored on a file. By building an array that summarizes data on the file, a program can find a record by searching through the array and then using that position to read the full record from the file.

# 9B. Building the BASIC Program

In section 9A, you built a model that shows how an index of last names is used to access records on a file. In this section, you will write the code that creates the index and learn how your previously built BASIC programs are affected by the addition of an index.

To the BASIC program, the Student Index File is just another file. It is created in the same way as New Student File: The program retrieves data from one file, reformats them, and stores them on a new file.

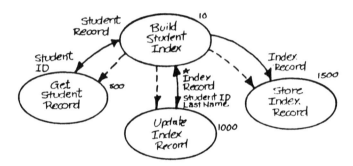

**Figure 9.5. Program outline for Build Student Index.**

As soon as you have added the BASIC data names to the data dictionary, you are ready to begin coding.

---

### DATA DICTIONARY

Student Index = 5{Index Record}5
        STINDEX

Student Reference = [ Student ID | Last Name ]
        ID%    ID$

Index Record = 40{Abbreviated Last Name}40
        IX$ or SX$()

Abbreviated Last Name = 3 characters

Duplicate List = 2{Last Name + First Name + Class}
        DL%()

Duplicate Choice = Integer
        ID%

---

**Table 9.5. Data dictionary with BASIC data names.**

# The Build Student Index program

The top module must declare the Student File and Student Index File. Notice that the FIELD statement for the Student Index File is defined as one field of 120 characters rather than forty fields with 3 characters each. Instead of referring to forty different data fields, the program refers to different positions within one data field. Each position, and therefore each last name, is an element in the array SX$. This array is declared in the DIM statement, along with the grade and course arrays.

This program does not produce any output on the screen, so lines 40 and 85 are included to inform the user that the program is running and to indicate when it is finished.

Next, the top module goes on to its main task, coordinating the lower-level modules. In lines 55 and 60, it invokes Get Student Record to retrieve each Student Record, and Update Index Record to place an abbreviated last name onto the Index Record. When the Index Record is full, the top module invokes Store Index Record to place the record on the Student Index File. The top module knows when the Index Record is full by looking at the current subscript of the array SX$. When the fortieth position has been filled (subscript 39), the record is ready to be stored.

```
10 REM ----- BUILD STUDENT INDEX -------------------------
11 REM
15 OEN "R",#1,"STUDENT2"
20 FIELD #1, 2 AS F1$,20 AS F2$,10 AS F3$,20 AS F4$,15 AS F5$,
   2 S F6$,5 AS F7$,2 AS F8$,24 AS F9$,1 AS FX$
25 OPEN "R",#2,"STINDEX"
30 FIELD #2, 120 AS IX$
35 DIM GR$(5),CR$(5),SX$(39)
40 PRINT "BUILDING STUDENT INDEX"
45 IR%=1
50 FOR ID%=1 TO 200
55   GOSUB 500
60   GOSUB 1000
65   IF P%=39 THEN GOSUB 1500:IR%=IR%+1
70 NEXT ID%
75 CLOSE #1
80 CLOSE #2
85 PRINT "STUDENT INDEX COMPLETE"
90 END
91 REM - END BUILD STUDENT INDEX --------------------
92 REM
```

The Get Student Record module is a much smaller version of the one used in Update Student Data. That module retrieved the record using a GET statement and then assigned the data item from each field to a BASIC name. Build Student Index, however, needs only one data item, the last name (NL$). You do not need to format all data from the student record.

```
500 REM ----- GET STUDENT RECORD = STUDENT REFERENCE -------------------
505 REM      ASSUMES ID% TO BE BETWEEN 1 AND 200
510 REM               STUDENT FILE IS OPEN
```

```
515 REM      PROMISES NL$ FROM STUDENT RECORD ID%
520 REM
525 GET #1,ID%
530 NL$=F2$
535 RETURN
536 REM - END GET STUDENT RECORD --------------------
537 REM
```

The Update Index Record activity first determines where in the index array the abbreviated last name is stored. If the student ID is 1, the name goes into the first position, SX$(0). If the student ID is 40, the name is placed in the last position of the array, SX$(39). When all 40 positions on the array are filled, its contents are stored on a record on the Student Index File. At this point, the program can start refilling the array. Thus, the name for ID number 41 will be stored in the first position of the array.

In the program below, the subscript P% indicates a name's position in the SX$ array. To determine the subscript for a particular name, you must know how many sets of 40 student records have been processed. That number is assigned the BASIC name X%. Once you know X%, you can use it and the ID number to determine your position in the current set of 40.

```
1000 REM ----- UPDATE INDEX RECORD --------------------
1005 REM      ASSUMES ID%, NL$
1010 REM      PROMISES TO UPDATE INDEX ARRAY-SX$() AND P%
1015 REM
1016 REM ----- POINTER INTO ARRAY - P%
1020 X% = INT( (ID% - 1) / 40)
1025 P% = ID% - (X% * 40) - 1
1030 SX$(P%) = LEFT$(NL$,3)
1035 RETURN
1036 REM - END UPDATE INDEX RECORD --------------------
1037 REM
```

The statement on line 1020 assigns to X% the integer portion of the equation *(ID%-1) / 40*. Any decimal portion of the result is removed. So, X% equals 0 for ID numbers between 1 and 40 because the result of the equation will always be less than 1. Since X% represents the number of sets of 40 records processed so far, when X% equals 0 you know that the program is working on its first set of 40 records. These student names will become the first record on the index file. For ID numbers beween 41 and 80, X% will equal 1. The program will store this set of student names in the second index record. This pattern continues through all 200 ID numbers and 5 index records.

Line 1025 computes the subscript for the Index array. It subtracts 40 once from the student ID for each set of 40 records the program has already processed (X% * 40). The result is the student ID's position in the current Index array. This line also subtracts 1 because BASIC starts numbering its arrays with 0. Line 1030 places the first three characters of the last name into the array. The final module, Store Index Record, is invoked when the top module knows that the fortieth element of the array {SX$(39)} has been filled.

```
1500 REM ----- STORE INDEX RECORD --------------------
1505 REM      ASSUMES SX$()
1510 REM
```

```
1515 X$ = ""
1520 FOR P% = 0 TO 39
1525   X$ = X$ + SX$(P%)
1530 NEXT P%
1535 LSET IX$ = X$
1540 PUT #2,IR%
1545 RETURN
1546 REM - END STORE INDEX RECORD -------------------
1547 REM
```

## Modifying the Update Student Data program

Now that you have a program that builds the Student Index File, you must modify the Update Student Data program so that it uses the index. Obviously, you must add statements to the top module that open and close the new file, Student Index, or STINDEX in BASIC. These statements and the FIELD statement for that file are the same as those in the Build Student Index program. You also remember to declare any new arrays in the DIM statement.

Turn to the main body of the module, the loop that calls the lower-level activities. For each record that the counselor wants to update, the interior of the loop gets the record, makes the changes, and stores it. Note the important changes between the program outline in Figure 9.6 and the previous version of the program in Figure 7.6.

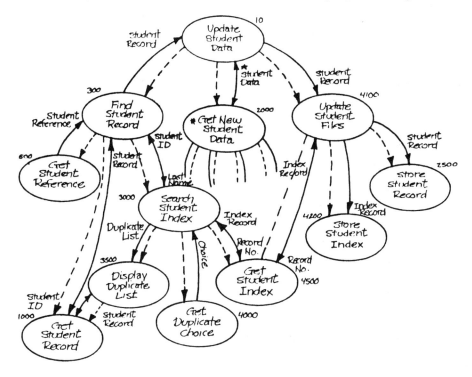

**Figure 9.6. Program outline for Update Student Data.**

The loop now invokes the new module Find Student Record (GOSUB 300). This new, intermediate-level module calls modules 500 and 1000, so the GOSUB commands are deleted. Similarly, Update Student Files (GOSUB 4100) is now above the old Store Student Record and is called instead.

The exit condition of the loop must also be changed. In the previous version of Update Student Data, the top module invoked Get Student ID and resulted in either a valid student ID or the literal END. According to the current program outline, when Find Student Record is invoked, the result is a student record. The literal END does not flow back to the top module to indicate that the user has no more records to update. In the code listed below, the top module asks the user if he wants to continue. If the answer is NO, the loop exits and the program ends.

```
10 REM ----- UPDATE STUDENT DATA -------------------
11 REM
15 OPEN "R",#1,"STUDENT2"
20 FIELD #1, 2 AS F1$,20 AS F2$,10 AS F3$,20 AS F4$,15 AS F5$,
    2 AS F6$,5 AS F7$,2 AS F8$,24 AS F9$,1 AS FX$
22 OPEN "R",#2,"STINDEX"
23 FIELD #2, 120 AS IX$
25 DIM GR$(5), CR$(5), SX$(39), DL%(19)
100 E$="YES"
102 WHILE E$="YES"
105   GOSUB 300
115   GOSUB 2000
120   GOSUB 4100
121   INPUT "DO YOU WANT TO LOOK AT ANOTHER RECORD";E$
122   IF LEFT$(E$,1)="Y" THEN E$="YES" ELSE E$="NO"
123 WEND
125 CLOSE #1
126 CLOSE #2
130 CHAIN "TRANSACT"
131 REM - END UPDATE STUDENT DATA -------------------
132 REM
```

Find Student Record invokes Get Student Reference. If the user inputs a number, it invokes Get Student Record to read the Student File. Get Student Record is the same as shown in Chapter 7. If the user enters something other than a number, the program assumes the piece of data is a name and initializes the Search Student Index activity. To indicate that the user did not enter an ID number, module 300 sets ID$ to blanks; this is why the module at line 330 checks the content of ID$ to determine whether the index file must be searched.

If Search Student Index locates the correct student ID, ID% is between 1 and 200. If Search Student Index cannot find the correct student ID, ID% is 0. In that case, Find Student Record continues to loop until ID% is valid.

```
300 REM ----- FIND STUDENT RECORD -------------------
305 REM       PROMISES A VALID STUDENT RECORD
310 REM
315 ID%=0
320 WHILE ID%=0
325   GOSUB 500
330   IF ID$<>"  " THEN GOSUB 3000
```

```
335 WEND
340 GOSUB 1000
345 RETURN
346 REM - END FIND STUDENT RECORD --------------------
347 REM
```

The Get Student Reference module gets ID$ from the user. If the first character of ID$ is a number, the module assumes the user is entering a student ID, converts the string ID$ into an integer ID%, and edits to be sure the number is valid. If the first character of ID$ is not a number, the submodule at line 560 formats ID$ into a field exactly three characters long. Line 562 adds blanks to the end of ID$ to guarantee at least three characters in the string.

```
500 REM ----- GET STUDENT REFERENCE --------------------
501 REM      PROMISES STUDENT ID% BETWEEN 1 AND 200 AND ID$="   "
502 REM         OR  ID%=0 AND ID$ WITH ABBREVIATED LAST NAME
505 REM
510 PRINT CHR$(26);
515 E%=1
520 WHILE E%=1
525   INPUT "ENTER STUDENT ID OR LAST NAME";ID$
526   X$=LEFT$(ID$,1)
527   IF X$>="0" AND X$<="9" THEN GOSUB 550 ELSE GOSUB 560
530 WEND
535 RETURN
536 REM - END GET STUDENT REFERENCE --------------------
537 REM

550 REM ----- EDIT STUDENT ID --------------------
551 REM
552 ID%=VAL(ID$)
554 ID$="   "
556 IF (ID%<1) OR (ID%>200) THEN PRINT "BETWEEN 1 AND 200" ELSE E%=0
557 RETURN
558 REM - END EDIT STUDENT ID --------------------
559 REM

560 REM ----- EDIT ABBREVIATED LAST NAME --------------------
561 REM
562 ID$=ID$+"   "
564 ID$=LEFT$(ID$,3)
566 ID%=0
568 E%=0
570 RETURN
571 REM - END EDIT ABBREVIATED LAST NAME --------------------
572 REM
```

When the user enters a student's name, the activity Search Student Index produces that student's ID number. First, it gets all records on the Student Index File by invoking Get Student Index in the loop between lines 3030 and 3055. Get Student Index retrieves the next record from the Index File and puts the last names into the Index array SX(). Lines 3040 through 3050 scan the Index array looking for entries that match the abbreviated student name.

Line 3045 stores the record number of each matching entry and places it into the Duplicate List (DL%). The equation in line 3045, $P\% + (IR\% * 40 - 40) + 1$, computes the record number. If the module scans the second index record (IR% equals 2), you know that the index record represents student records 41 through 80. $(IR\% * 40 - 40) + 1$ gives the first ID number of that particular set of 40, 41 in the case of the second index record. The 1 is added to allow for the array starting with subscript 0. The position in the array (P%) tells you which of the 40 records you are addressing. Adding it to $(IR\% * 40 - 40) + 1$ determines the ID number for that record.

As the module searches the Student Index File, the data item D% records the number of duplicates found (line 3045). When the search is completed, D% equals 0 if no match was found. In that case, line 3060 causes the computer to print that the record cannot be found. If D% equals 1, only one match was found on the index. If five duplicates were found, D% equals 5. If the value of D% is greater than 1, the list of duplicates is displayed to the user by the module Display Duplicate List (GOSUB 3500). The user then enters his choice at the request of line 4025 in Get Duplicate Choice (GOSUB 4000). In line 4040, the module assigns his choice to the ID number.

```
3000 REM ----- SEARCH STUDENT INDEX --------------------
3005 REM      ASSUMES ID$ WITH ABBREVIATED LAST NAME
3010 REM      PROMISES ID% BETWEEN 1 AND 200 IF RECORD FOUND
3015 REM          OR ID%=0 IF NO RECORD FOUND
3020 REM
3025 D%=0
3030 FOR IR%=1 TO 5
3035   GOSUB 4500
3040   FOR P%=0 TO 39
3045     IF SX$(P%)=ID$ THEN DL%(D%)= P% + (IR% * 40 - 40) + 1: D%=D%+1
3050   NEXT P%
3055 NEXT IR%
3060 IF D%=0 THEN PRINT "CANNOT FIND STUDENT RECORD":ID%=0
3065 IF D%=1 THEN ID%=DL%(0)
3070 IF D%>1 THEN GOSUB 3500: GOSUB 4000
3075 RETURN
3076 REM - END SEARCH STUDENT INDEX --------------------
3077 REM


3500 REM ----- DISPLAY DUPLICATE LIST --------------------
3505 REM      ASSUMES DL$() WITH D% ENTRIES
3510 REM
3515 PRINT CHR$(26);
3520 PRINT "STUDENTS WITH SIMILAR NAMES."
3525 PRINT
3530 FOR L%=0 TO D%-1
3535   ID%=DL%(L%)
3540   GOSUB 1000
3545   PRINT L%+1;NL$;NF$;CL$
3550 NEXT L%
3555 PRINT
3560 RETURN
3561 REM - END DISPLAY DUPLICATE LIST --------------------
3562 REM
```

```
4000 REM ----- GET DUPLICATE CHOICE --------------------
4005 REM        PROMISES USER'S CHOICE OF DL%() IN ID%
4010 REM
4015 E%=1
4020 WHILE E%=1
4025  INPUT "ENTER NUMBER OF CHOICE: ",C%
4030  IF C%<1 OR C%>D% THEN PRINT "MUST BE 1 TO ";D% ELSE E%=0
4035 WEND
4040 ID%=DL%(C%-1)
4045 RETURN
4046 REM - END GET DUPLICATE CHOICE --------------------
4047 REM


4500 REM ----- GET STUDENT INDEX --------------------
4505 REM        ASSUME IR% BETWEEN 1 AND 5
4510 REM        PROMISES SX$() CONTAINING INDEX RECORD
4515 REM
4520 GET #2,IR%
4525 FOR I%=0 TO 39
4530   SX$(I%)=MID$(IX$,I%*3+1,3)
4535 NEXT I%
4540 RETURN
4541 REM - END GET STUDENT INDEX --------------------
4542 REM
```

Since the code under Get New Student Data performs exactly as it did in the previous version of Update Student Data, you can ignore those modules and begin work on Update Student Files.

The process of storing the Student Record on the Student File has changed because the Student Index File is updated with each Student Record. Update Student Files finds the correct Index Record by invoking Get Student Index, enters the abbreviated last name into the array, writes the Index Record back to the Index File using Store Student Index, and stores the Student Record on the Student File by invoking Store Student Record.

```
4100 REM ----- UPDATE STUDENT FILES --------------------
4105 REM        ASSUMES STUDENT DATA
4110 REM        PROMISES TO STORE STUDENT DATA AND UPDATE STUDENT INDEX
4115 REM
4120 GOSUB 2500
4125 X%=INT((ID%-1)/40)
4130 IR%=X%+1
4135 P%=ID%-(X%*40)-1
4140 GOSUB 4500
4145 NL$=NL$+" "
4150 SX$(P%)=LEFT$(NL$,3)
4155 GOSUB 4200
4160 RETURN
4161 REM - END UPDATE STUDENT FILES --------------------
4162 REM
```

The equations in lines 4125 and 4135 are taken from the Build Student Index program. They determine which Index Record to read and where to place the abbreviated last name on the Index Record. Store Student Record is copied from the previous version of Update Student Data in Chapter 7. Store Student Index is copied from the Build Student Index program.

After you have entered the Build Student Index program and the changes to Update Student Data, run the test cases built in section 9A to verify that the programs work correctly.

```
2500 REM ----- STORE STUDENT RECORD --------------------
2505 REM       ASSUMES VALID STUDENT DATA, ID% BETWEEN 1 AND 200
2510 REM             STUDENT FILE OPEN
2515 REM       PROMISES TO STORE STUDENT DATA ON RECORD ID%
2520 REM
2525 LSET F1$=MKI$(ID%)
2530 LSET F2$=NL$
2535 LSET F3$=NF$
2536 LSET F4$=RD$
2537 LSET F5$=CI$
2538 LSET F6$=ST$
2539 LSET F7$=ZP$
2540 LSET F8$=CL$
2545 G$=""
2550 FOR C%=0 TO 5
2555  G$=G$+CR$(C%)+GR$(C%)
2560 NEXT C%
2565 LSET F9$=G$
2570 LSET FX$=AX$
2575 PUT #1,ID%
2580 RETURN
2581 REM - END STORE STUDENT RECORD ----------------------
2582 REM

4200 REM ----- STORE STUDENT INDEX --------------------
4205 REM       ASSUMES SX$(), IR%
4210 REM
4215 X$=""
4220 FOR P%=0 TO 39
4225  X$=X$+SX$(P%)
4230 NEXT P%
4235 LSET IX$=X$
4240 PUT #2,IR%
4245 RETURN
4246 REM - END STORE STUDENT INDEX ------------------------
4247 REM
```

Lines 4220 through 4230 of Store Student Index take the Index array, SC$(), and build a single, 120-character string. The string is then placed in the field IX$ (line 4235) and the record is stored on the Student Index File.

Now that the Student Index File has been added to the system, the counselor has the flexibility to retrieve Student Record by either the student ID or the student's name. In this section, you have seen how a program uses two related files to provide a convenient way of accessing stored data.

## EXERCISE IX

In this exercise, you are to build an index for the Patron Sales File. The theater group wants to retrieve a sales record using the patron's last name.

1. build the data flow diagrams showing the functions necessary to create and use a patron index

2. update your data dictionary with new and changed data definitions

3. estimate the size of the job and compute the time it will take

4. define at least six new test cases to verify the program

5. build a program outline for the function that creates the patron index; modify the program outline of the function that updates sales data

6. build the program that creates the patron index; using the program outline as a guide, expand the program that updates sales data

As you build the model of this function, consider the issues covered in this section. How do you want to handle duplicates? Will spelling the last names be a problem? How many index entries should be on an index record? Your answers to these questions may not be the same as those in this section, but do use the data flow diagrams and data dictionary to evaluate different options.

*10*

# Building a Related File

## 10A. Building the Model

Most computer systems store data that describe objects, people, or events. For example, a library system records data such as title, author, and publisher that describe the books in its inventory. Book is the object described by the data in the book file. The system would also have a file that stores data about patrons, such as their names, addresses, and types of library privileges. Patron is the object described by the data in the patron file.

As you develop software systems, each file you build contains data describing a different object, but you must also take into account the relationships between objects (files). When a patron checks out a book in a library system, a relationship is set up between the two: That patron now has possession of the book for a certain period of time. The system must record this relationship, or the librarian will not know whether the book has been lost or borrowed; nor will he be able to fine the patron for not returning the book.

To record relationships between files, you store in one record a piece of data that refers to a record in another file. The patron record would have fields containing the book numbers of borrowed books, and the book record would have a field to record the patron's library card number. This way, the book record shows which patron has checked out the book, and the patron record shows all books borrowed.

In this chapter, you will build a new file for the high school counselor's system, one related to the already established student file. Building a related file is no different from building an unrelated file. For that reason, this chapter will be mostly review. It will prepare you for the next chapters, where you will see ways to use related files together.

You will expand the school counselor's system to include another file that records information about the courses taught at the school. The relationship between the student file and the new course file exists since a student is enrolled in a course and a course contains certain students. The files will help the guidance counselor arrange students into courses. He can review both the students enrolled in a particular course and the courses a particular student is taking.

## Defining the function

The guidance counselor has asked you to add a file containing information about courses taught at the school. Each course is identified by the same three-character code used by the Student File. For each of the almost 90 courses taught in the school, the counselor wants to record the teacher's last name, the period, and the classroom number. The classroom numbers are three characters long and contain both letters and numbers. The counselor wants to retrieve the information on the file by entering the course code. The system must record the students that are enrolled in each course; the counselor says that no class should have more than 25 students.

The data flow diagram is built according to the description given to you by the counselor. You must define a function that creates a Course File and another that updates it. Figure 10.1 shows a data flow diagram with one function creating the Course File and another getting the course code and update command from the user, displaying the old course data, accepting new course data, and storing the course record back on the file.

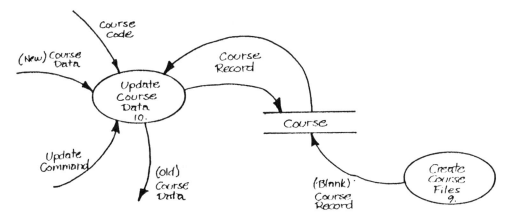

**Figure 10.1. Data flow diagram for Course File functions.**

The counselor wants to access the Course File by entering the course code. As you know from working with the Student File, however, records are retrieved from files with a record number that corresponds to a record's position on the file. Update Course Data must find the number of the record that contains that course code.

To provide access to the Course File using a course code, you use the same method used in Chapter 9. You build an index file of course codes. Update Course Data finds the correct course code in the index, whose position tells the function which record to retrieve from the Course File. The expanded data flow diagram in Figure 10.2 shows the references to the new Course Index Record. Notice that the functions Create Course Files and Create Course Index have been combined into one function. You do not need to build two separate programs for a file and its index when they are created at the same time.

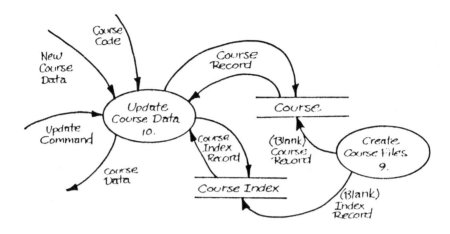

**Figure 10.2. Expanded data flow diagram for Course File functions.**

Because Update Course Data uses so many data flows, the data flow diagram is cluttered and difficult to interpret. To define the function more clearly, you must build a lower-level data flow diagram showing the breakdown of Update Course Data into smaller, less complex subfunctions.

As in Chapter 9, the lower-level data flow diagram is built by grouping together related data flows. The Course Code, access to the Course Index, and access to the Course File result in the Course Record. New data are added to the Course Record to produce the updated Course Record. Finally, the Course Index and Course File are updated.

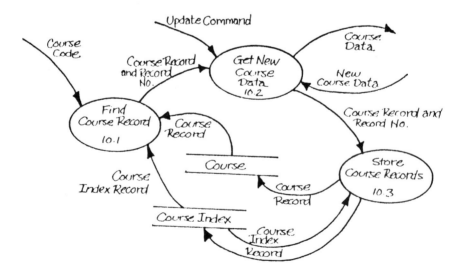

**Figure 10.3. Detailed data flow diagram for Update Course Data.**

As soon as you finish the data flow diagram, you should run through the system by yourself or with the user, if there is one. Use sample incoming data flows and work your way through the diagram, following the data flows to see if the system behaves properly. If you find mistakes or think of improvements, you can incorporate them into the model. Your conception of the system will be sharpened, and you will find it easier to define data and build a program outline.

In order to run through the Update Course Data function, you first set up part of a sample record. Assume that the first record of the Course Index File contains the following:

1  2  3  4  5  . . .  25

INDEX RECORD:   GYM __ ALG __ ENG . . . SHP

You begin the run-through by imagining the user entering course code ENG. Find Course Record searches the index and finds that the fifth record contains the data for that course. Get New Course Data allows the user to update this record. After all updates are entered, Store Course Records places the updated record back on the Course File, and the course code is recorded on the Course Index File.

If the user enters TRI and that code does not exist on the file, Find Course Record must find a blank record to which TRI can be added. Since the second entry in the above index is the first open position, TRI's data will be stored on the second record of the Course File. Get New Course Data accepts New Course Data, and Store Course Records places the course code in the second position of the index and stores the course record on the second record of the Course File.

If the counselor decides to delete the course record indexed by TRI, he enters TRI as usual and Find Course Record searches the index and retrieves the second record on the Course File. The user then enters the update command DELETE. Get New Course Data puts blanks into the course record, and last, Store Course Records places the blank course code into the second position of the Course Index File and the blank course record into the second record of the Course File.

## Defining the data

You get the data dictionary definitions of data flows and data stores from the user's description of his requirements.

The number of records on the Course File is based on the number of courses the school offers. According to the counselor there are almost 90, but you should allow for a possible increase in the number of courses. If the Course File contains 100 records, the Course Index File must contain 100 entries. You decide to divide the Course Index File into 4 records, each record containing 25 course codes.

Each course record contains room for 30 student IDs. The user may want to add or delete a student ID from the course record, so the student update of New Course Data must indicate whether the ID number is to be added or deleted. That is the purpose of the option between A and D in the Student Update data item.

---

## DATA DICTIONARY

Classroom = 3 Characters

Course Code = 3 Characters

Course Data = Course Code + Teacher + Classroom + Period + {Student ID}30

Course File = 100 {Course Record}100

Course Index File = 4 {Course Index Record}4

Course Index Record = 25 {Course Code}25

Course Record = Course Code + Teacher + Classroom + Period
    + 30 {Student ID}30

New Course Data = [ Course Code | Teacher | Classroom | Period |
    Student Update ]

Period = Integer between 1 and 6

Record Number = Integer between 1 and 100

Student ID = Integer between 1 and 200

Student Update = [ A | D ] + Student ID

Teacher = Maximum length of 20 characters

Update Command = [ 1 | 2 | 3 | 4 | 5 | END | DELETE ]
    1 - Course Code
    2 - Teacher
    3 - Classroom
    4 - Period
    5 - Student Update

---

**Table 10.1. Data dictionary for Course File functions.**

**Estimating the size of the program**

When you have more than one level of data flow diagrams, you base your estimate on the most detailed level, computing a token count for each detailed function. The sum of the token counts is the size estimate for the entire function.

Find Course Record has four data flows around it. The Course Index Record must look at the course code within braces in Course Index Record to find the right course code, so its total token count is five. Store Course Records also has a token count of five. When it must store a new or blank code on the Course Index, the function refers to the course codes within braces in the outgoing Course Index Record.

The Get New Course Data function has an initial count of five tokens. You add one token for the brackets in Update Command and one for the braces in Course Data. New Course Data has two sets of brackets, one around the data items and one within Student Update. Each counts as an additional token, making a total token count of nine. The data items inside Update Command and New Course Data indicate which data to add to the new file.

The token count for the Create Course Files function is two, one token for each data flow. The braces and brackets inside Course Record and Course Index Record are not counted because the function is placing only blank records on the file.

PERFORMANCE LOG

| Function | Token Count | Estimate | Actual Time | Rate Token/Time |
|----------|-------------|----------|-------------|-----------------|
| | | | | 1.3 token/hr. |
| 9 | 2 | | | |
| 10.1 | 5 | | | |
| 10.2 | 9 | | | |
| 10.3 | 5 | | | |
| TOTAL | 21 | 16 hrs. | | |

**Table 10.2. Performance log for Course File functions.**

### Identifying the test cases

You now read through the data dictionary to identify the test cases. The first test case in Table 10.3 tests valid data for most data items in Update Command and New Course Data. That first group of six lines is actually one large test case that combines smaller ones. For example, it tests that the first course code entered will be placed in the first position of the Course Index and that each valid Update Command updates the correct field.

The next group of test cases makes sure that invalid data are rejected. It checks that classrooms and course codes longer than three characters are reported as errors, as well as a teacher's name with over twenty characters or a period not between 1 and 6. A student ID must be between 1 and 200, so a test case with the student ID equal to 0 or 201 should result in an error message. The Course Record can hold up to 30 student IDs. If an extra student ID is entered, the user should be informed by an error message. If an invalid Update Command is entered, an error message should also appear.

Check that the first and last records on the Course File are updated and deleted correctly. An attempt to add Course Record 101 should result in an error message.

Since the definition of Course Index Record shows a series of course codes, test cases should be built for the first element in the Course Index Record as well as for a few in the middle. As before, each test case is checked by reentering the course code and reviewing the display for accurate updates.

---

## TEST CASE LOG

| Test Case | Result |
| --- | --- |
| Enter first course SOC | Blank record displayed |
| Update Command 2, SMITH | Updates teacher name |
| Update Command 3, 123 | Updates classroom |
| Update Command 4, 1 | Updates period |
| Update Command 5, A 001 | Adds student ID |
| Update Command END | Stores data on files |
| Enter second course GYM | Blank record displayed |
| Command 0 | Error message |
| Command 2 | |
| Fernando K. Harrington > 20 characters | Error message |
| Command 3, A 3051 > 3 characters | Error message |
| Command 4, 7 | Error message |
| Command 5, A 201 | Error message |
| Command 5, A 000 | Error message |
| Add 30 valid student IDs, | |
| then enter student ID #31 | Error message |
| Command 5, D student ID #1 | First student ID deleted |
| Command 5, D student ID #30 | Last student ID deleted |
| Fill the file with valid | |
| course records | Check course records #25 and #26 |
| Check course record #100 | |
| Enter course record #101 | Error message |
| Enter SOC | SOC data displayed |
| Command 1, SCI | Course Code updated |
| Command END | Stores data on files |
| Enter SCI | TRI data displayed |
| Command DELETE | Blank data |
| Command END | Stores blank data |

---

**Table 10.3. Test case log for Course File functions.**

### Building the program outline

The Create Course Files program needs four activities. The program must build a blank course record and store 100 blank course records on the Course File. Similarly, to create the Course Index it must build a blank course index record and store four blank course index records on the Course Index File.

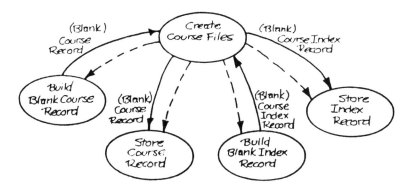

**Figure 10.4. Program outline for Create Course Files.**

The first step in building a program outline for Update Course Data is to place the three lower-level functions under the control of a coordinating module. Figure 10.5 shows the model after performing this first step. The top module invokes Find Course Record, which retrieves the Course Record requested by the user. Next, Get New Course Data is called so that it can accept New Course Data. Last, Store Course Records places the Course Record on the Course File and updates the Course Index File, if necessary.

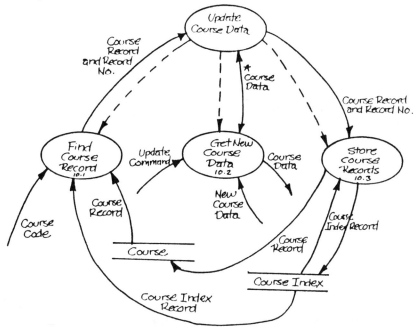

**Figure 10.5. First step toward a program outline for Update Course Data.**

Now you identify lower-level activities for each of the three functions. Each remaining data flow going into or out of the function corresponds to a lower-level activity. Therefore, if you leave the data flows in the first-step outline, as in Figure 10.5, these activities are easier to see. The Find Course Record function must include activities that get the Course Code, search the Course Index, and get the Course Record from the Course File. Get New Course Data must get the Update Command, display the old Course Data, and get the various new data items. Store Course Records must store the Course Record with the new data in it and, in some cases, restore the Index Record.

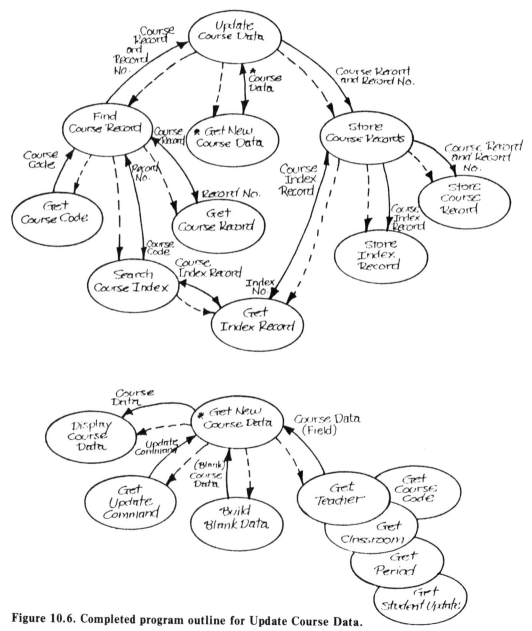

**Figure 10.6. Completed program outline for Update Course Data.**

In this section, you have applied to one function the file that handles techniques learned in Chapter 3, the record that updates techniques learned in Chapter 5, and the file index method learned in Chapter 9. After the code for this model is written, the counselor's system will contain two related files, one storing data about students and the other storing data about courses.

# 10B. Building the BASIC Program

In this section, you will expand the counselor's system by adding a related file to the Student File. In building the programs Create Course Files and Update Course Data, you will review most of the coding skills developed throughout the text. The programs create a file and its index, search and update arrays, and use factored modules. After they have been coded and tested, the counselor will be able to see which courses a student is taking and which students are enrolled in a given course.

The data dictionary in Table 10.4 contains the definitions of data used by Create Course Files and Update Course Data and supplies the BASIC data names used in those programs.

All data defined in Course Record must be declared in a FIELD statement, so each data item is given a field name. For instance, because Period is the fourth field in the record, it is called F4$ in the FIELD statement. The student IDs in Course Record, and course codes in Course Index Record, are placed in arrays and given names to be declared in the DIM statement.

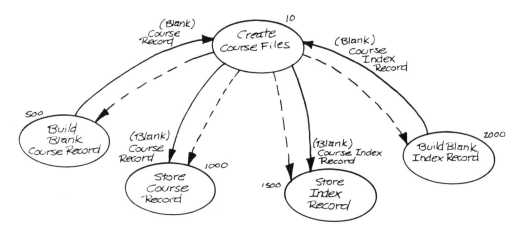

**Figure 10.7. Program outline for Create Course Files.**

## Create Course Files

As in all previous examples, the files and arrays used in a program are declared in the top module. In the code listed below, notice that the array of 30 student IDs is declared in the FIELD statement (line 20) as a 60-character field. Because BASIC needs 2 characters to store an integer on a record, 30 integers require 60 characters. Each Course Index Record has room for 75 characters, since 25 course codes multiplied by 3 characters for each code equals 75.

# DATA DICTIONARY

Classroom = 3 Characters
    F3$ and CR$

Course Code = 3 Characters
    F1$ and CC$

Course Data = Course Code + Teacher + Classroom + Period
    + {Student ID}30

Course File = 100 {Course Record}100
    COURSES

Course Index File = 4 {Course Index Record}4
    CRINDEX

Course Index Record = 25 {Course Code}25
    CX$        CI$()

Course Record = Course Code + Teacher + Classroom + Period
    + 30 {Student ID}30 + Status
    F5$ and ST%()   FX$ and AX$

New Course Data = [ Course Code | Teacher | Classroom | Period |
    Student Update ]

Period = Integer between 1 and 6
    F4$ and PR%

Record Number = Integer between 1 and 100
    RN%

Student ID = Integer between 1 and 200
    ID%

Student Update = [ A | D ] + Student ID

Teacher = Maximum length of 20 characters
    F2$ and TE$

Update Command = [ 1 | 2 | 3 | 4 | 5 | END | DELETE ]
    UC$  1 - Course Code
        2 - Teacher
        3 - Classroom
        4 - Period
        5 - Student Update

**Table 10.4. Data dictionary with BASIC data names.**

```
10 REM ----- CREATE COURSE FILES -------------------
11 REM
15 OPEN "R",#1,"COURSES"
20 FIELD #1,3 AS F1$,20 AS F2$,3 AS F3$,2 AS F4$,60 AS F5$,1 AS FX$
25 OPEN "R",#2,"CRINDEX"
30 FIELD #2,75 AS CX$
35 DIM CI$(24),ST%(29)
40 PRINT "CREATING COURSE FILE AND INDEX"
45 GOSUB 500
50 GOSUB 1000
55 GOSUB 2000
60 GOSUB 1500
65 CLOSE #1
70 CLOSE #2
75 PRINT "COURSE FILE AND INDEX INITIALIZED"
80 END
81 REM - END CREATE COURSE FILES -------------------
82 REM
```

The code for the four lower-level modules needs little explanation. It will be familiar to you from Chapter 3, where you created the Student File, and Chapter 9, where you created the Student Index File.

```
500 REM ----- BUILD BLANK COURSE RECORD -------------------
505 REM       PROMISES SPACES IN COURSE RECORD
510 REM
515 LSET F1$=" "
520 LSET F2$=SPACE$(20)
525 LSET F3$=" "
530 LSET F4$=MKI$(0)
535 X$=""
540 FOR S%=1 TO 30
545   X$=X$+MKI$(0)
550 NEXT S%
555 LSET F5$=X$
560 LSET FX$="X"
565 RETURN
566 REM - END BUILD BLANK COURSE RECORD -------------------
567 REM

1000 REM ----- STORE COURSE RECORD -------------------
1005 REM       ASSUMES BLANK DATA IN THE COURSE RECORD
1010 REM
1015 FOR RN%=1 TO 100
1020   PUT #1,RN%
1025 NEXT RN%
1030 RETURN
1031 REM - END STORE COURSE RECORD -------------------
1032 REM

1500 REM ----- STORE INDEX RECORD -------------------
1505 REM       ASSUMES BLANK DATA IN COURSE INDEX RECORD
1510 REM
1515 FOR IR%=1 TO 4
1520   PUT #2,IR%
1525 NEXT IR%
```

```
1530 RETURN
1531 REM - END STORE INDEX RECORD --------------------
1532 REM

2000 REM ----- BUILD BLANK INDEX RECORD --------------------
2005 REM        PROMISES SPACES IN COURSE INDEX RECORD
2010 REM
2015 LSET CX$=SPACE$(75)
2020 RETURN
2021 REM - END BUILD BLANK INDEX RECORD --------------------
2022 REM
```

The Build Blank Index Record module is so small that you might decide to place the code for that activity in the top module. Because it has only one statement, moving that code to the upper module should not make the upper module too complex. The code below shows how Build Blank Index Record can be combined with the top module.

```
10 REM ----- CREATE COURSE FILES --------------------
11 REM
15 OPEN "R",#1,"COURSES"
20 FIELD #1,3 AS F1$,20 AS F2$,3 AS F3$,2 AS F4$,60 AS F5$,1 AS FX$
25 OPEN "R",#2,"CRINDEX"
30 FIELD #2,75 AS CX$
35 DIM CI$(24),ST%(29)
40 PRINT "CREATING COURSE FILE AND INDEX"
45 GOSUB 500
50 GOSUB 1000
53 REM ----- BUILD BLANK INDEX RECORD
54 REM
55 LSET CX$=SPACE$(75)
56 REM - END BUILD BLANK INDEX RECORD
57 REM
60 GOSUB 1500
65 CLOSE #1
70 CLOSE #2
75 PRINT "COURSE FILE AND INDEX INITIALIZED"
80 END
81 REM - END CREATE COURSE FILES --------------------
82 REM
```

## Update Course Data

The program outline for Update Course Data declares the eighteen modules that allow the user to add data to the Course File.

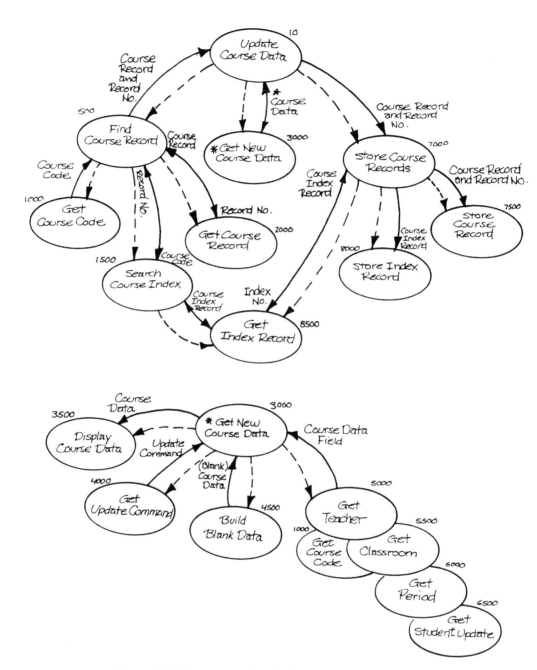

**Figure 10.8. Program outline for Update Course Data.**

Like the top module of Create Course Files, this top module also declares the Course File and Course Index File. It then steps through the lower-level activities, as shown in the code below. The code contains a loop that enables the counselor to continue adding data to different records.

```
10 REM ----- UPDATE COURSE DATA -------------------
11 REM
15 OPEN "R",#1,"COURSES"
20 FIELD #1,3 AS F1$,20 AS F2$,3 AS F3$,2 AS F4$,60 AS F5$,1 AS FX$
25 OPEN "R",#2,"CRINDEX"
30 FIELD #2,75 AS CX$
35 DIM CI$(24),ST%(29)
40 E$="YES"
45 WHILE E$="YES"
50   GOSUB 500
55   GOSUB 3000
60   GOSUB 7000
65   PRINT CHR$(26);
70   INPUT "DO YOU WANT TO LOOK AT ANOTHER COURSE";E$
75   IF LEFT$(E$,1)="Y" THEN E$="YES" ELSE E$="NO"
80 WEND
85 CLOSE #1
90 CLOSE #2
95 CHAIN "TRANSACT"
96 REM - END UPDATE COURSE DATA -------------------
97 REM
```

The Find Course Record module gets the Course Record requested by the user. It does its work solely by invoking other modules:  Get Course Code, Search Course Index, and Get Course Record.

```
500 REM ----- FIND COURSE RECORD -------------------
505 REM       PROMISES RECORD NUMBER AND COURSE DATA
510 REM
515 GOSUB 1000
520 GOSUB 1500
525 GOSUB 2000
530 RETURN
531 REM - END FIND COURSE RECORD -------------------
532 REM

1000 REM ----- GET COURSE CODE -------------------
1005 REM       PROMISES A THREE-CHARACTER COURSE CODE - CC$
1010 REM
1015 E%=1
1020 WHILE E%=1
1025   INPUT "ENTER THREE-CHARACTER COURSE CODE ",CC$
1030   IF LEN(CC$)=3 THEN E%=0 ELSE PRINT "MUST BE THREE CHARACTERS"
1035 WEND
1040 RETURN
1041 REM - END GET COURSE CODE -------------------
1042 REM

1500 REM ----- SEARCH COURSE INDEX -------------------
1505 REM       ASSUMES VALID COURSE CODE - CC$
1510 REM       PROMISES IF CC$ ON INDEX, RN% SET TO THAT RECORD
1515 REM               IF CC$ NOT ON INDEX, RN% SET TO FIRST BLANK RECORD
1516 REM
1520 IR%=1
1525 RN%=0
1530 E1%=1
```

```
1535 WHILE E1%=1
1540  GOSUB 8500
1545  P%=0
1550  E2%=1
1555  WHILE E2%=1
1560   IF CC$=CI$(P%) THEN E2%=0:E1%=0:RN%=P%+(IR%*25-25)+1
1565   IF CI$(P%)="  " AND RN%=0 THEN RN%=P%+(IR%*25-25)+1
1570   IF P%<24 THEN P%=P%+1 ELSE E2%=0
1575  WEND
1580  IF IR%<4 THEN IR%=IR%+1 ELSE E1%=0
1585 WEND
1590 IF RN%=0 THEN PRINT "COURSE FILE IS FULL":RN=100
1595 RETURN
1596 REM - END SEARCH COURSE INDEX -------------------
1597 REM
```

The code for Get Course Code is easily understood; Search Course Index, however, is more complex. It contains two loops, one inside the other. The first loop calls the Get Index module, which each time it is called takes the course codes from the next Course Index Record and puts them into the array CI$. The nested loop occurs between lines 1555 and 1575. For each index record, the loop searches the Course Codes array (CI$) for the code that matches what the user entered. If it finds this code, it computes the record number of the matching course record and assigns to it the BASIC name RN%.

If Search Course Index does not find the user's course code on the Course Index File, it returns the record number of the first blank record on the file. This is the purpose of line 1565, which says that if the position in the Course Index array is blank and Record Number (RN%) for the Course File is 0, then the record number is set to that position.

When you nest loops in this fashion, the code becomes harder to read and understand. Search Course Index has been rewritten using a smaller, more understandable block of code. The inner loop is factored into its own module starting at line 1600.

```
1500 REM ----- SEARCH COURSE INDEX -----------------
1505 REM      ASSUMES VALID COURSE CODE - CC$
1510 REM      PROMISES IF CC$ ON INDEX RN% SET TO THAT RECORD
1511 REM          IF CC$ NOT ON INDEX RN% SET TO FIRST BLANK RECORD
1515 REM
1520 IR%=1
1525 RN%=0
1530 E1%=1
1535 WHILE E1%=1
1540  GOSUB 8500
1545 REM ** SEARCH THE INDEX RECORD
1550  GOSUB 1600
1580   IF IR%<4 THEN IR%=IR%+1 ELSE E1%=0
1585 WEND
1590 IF RN%=0 THEN PRINT "COURSE FILE IS FULL":RN=100
1595 RETURN
1596 REM - END SEARCH COURSE INDEX -------------------
1597 REM
```

```
1600 REM ----- SEARCH 1 INDEX RECORD --------------------
1601 REM
1605 P%=0
1610 E2%=1
1615 WHILE E2%=1
1620   IF CC$=CI$(P%) THEN E2%=0:E1%=0:RN%=P%+(IR%*25-25)+1
1625   IF CI$(P%)="   " AND RN%=0 THEN RN%=P%+(IR%*25-25)+1
1630   IF P%<24 THEN P%=P%+1 ELSE E2%=0
1635 WEND
1640 RETURN
1641 REM - END SEARCH 1 INDEX RECORD --------------------
1642 REM


2000 REM ----- GET COURSE RECORD --------------------
2005 REM       ASSUMES RECORD NUMBER - RN% BETWEEN 1 AND 100
2010 REM       PROMISES RN% COURSE DATA CC$, TE$, CR$, PR%, ST%(), AX$
2015 REM
2020 GET #1,RN%
2025 CC$=F1$
2030 TE$=F2$
2035 CR$=F3$
2040 PR%=CVI(F4$)
2045 FOR S%=0 TO 29
2050   ST%(S%)=CVI(MID$(F5$,S%*2+1,2))
2055 NEXT S%
2060 AX$=FX$
2065 RETURN
2066 REM ----- GET COURSE RECORD --------------------
2067 REM
```

The entire section under the Get New Course Data module is a mirror image of the Update Student Data program: Both display the old course data, ask the user what update he wants to perform, and then invoke the requested module (Get Course Code, Get Teacher, Build Blank Data, etc.). The code for Get New Course Data and its subordinates is listed below.

```
3000 REM ----- GET NEW COURSE DATA --------------------
3005 REM       ASSUMES COURSE DATA CC$, TE$, CR$, PR%, ST%()
3010 REM       PROMISES VALID COURSE DATA
3015 REM
3020 UC$=""
3025 WHILE UC$<>"END"
3030   GOSUB 3500
3035   GOSUB 4000
3040   IF UC$="1" THEN GOSUB 1000: AX$="A"
3045   IF UC$="2" THEN GOSUB 5000
3050   IF UC$="3" THEN GOSUB 5500
3055   IF UC$="4" THEN GOSUB 6000
3060   IF UC$="5" THEN GOSUB 6500
3065   IF UC$="DELETE" THEN GOSUB 4500
3070 WEND
3075 RETURN
3076 REM - END GET NEW COURSE DATA --------------------
3077 REM
```

```
3500 REM ----- DISPLAY COURSE DATA -------------------
3505 REM       ASSUMES VALID COURSE DATA
3510 REM
3515 PRINT CHR$(26);
3520 PRINT "COURSE DATA FOR COURSE CODE: "CC$
3525 PRINT "TAUGHT BY:      "TE$
3530 PRINT "CLASSROOM:      "CR$
3535 PRINT "PERIOD:         "PR%
3540 PRINT "STUDENTS ENROLLED:";
3545 FOR S%=0 TO 14
3550   PRINT USING "####";ST%(S%);
3555 NEXT S%
3560 PRINT
3565 PRINT "              :";
3570 FOR S%=15 TO 29
3575   PRINT USING "####";ST%(S%);
3580 NEXT S%
3585 PRINT
3590 PRINT "STATUS:       :"AX$
3595 PRINT "--------------------------------------------"
3600 RETURN
3601 REM - END DISPLAY COURSE DATA -------------------
3602 REM


4000 REM ----- GET UPDATE COMMAND -------------------
4005 REM       PROMISES VALID UC$
4010 REM
4015 E%=1
4020 WHILE E%=1
4025   PRINT "  1 - COURSE CODE"
4030   PRINT "  2 - TEACHER"
4035   PRINT "  3 - CLASSROOM"
4040   PRINT "  4 - PERIOD"
4045   PRINT "  5 - STUDENT UPDATE"
4050   PRINT "  DELETE - BLANK RECORD"
4055   PRINT "  END - END UPDATES"
4060   INPUT "  ENTER CHOICE: ",UC$
4065   IF UC$="1" OR UC$="2" OR UC$="3" OR UC$="4" OR UC$="5" THEN E%=0
4070   IF UC$="DELETE" OR UC$="END" THEN E%=0
4075   IF E%=1 THEN PRINT "UNRECOGNIZED CHOICE - REENTER"
4080 WEND
4085 RETURN
4086 REM - END GET UPDATE COMMAND -------------------
4087 REM


4500 REM ----- BUILD BLANK DATA -------------------
4505 REM       PROMISES INITIAL VALUES IN COURSE DATA
4510 REM
4515 CC$="  "
4520 TE$=SPACE$(20)
4525 CR$="  "
4530 PR%=0
4535 FOR S%=0 TO 29
4540   ST%(S%)=0
4545 NEXT S%
4550 AX$="X"
4555 RETURN
4556 REM - END BUILD BLANK DATA -------------------
4557 REM
```

```
5000 REM ----- GET TEACHER -------------------
5005 REM        PROMISES VALID TE$
5010 REM
5015 E%=1
5020 WHILE E%=1
5025   LINE INPUT "ENTER TEACHER'S LAST NAME: ",TE$
5030   IF LEN(TE$)>20 THEN PRINT "NO MORE THAN 20 CHARACTERS" ELSE E%=0
5035 WEND
5040 RETURN
5041 REM - END GET TEACHER -------------------
5042 REM


5500 REM ----- GET CLASSROOM -------------------
5505 REM        PROMISES VALID CR$
5510 REM
5515 E%=1
5520 WHILE E%=1
5525   INPUT "ENTER THREE-CHARACTER CLASSROOM: ",CR$
5530   IF LEN(CR$)<>3 THEN PRINT "MUST BE THREE CHARACTERS" ELSE E%=0
5535 WEND
5540 RETURN
5541 REM - END GET CLASSROOM -------------------
5542 REM

6000 REM ----- GET PERIOD -------------------
6005 REM        PROMISES VALID PR%
6010 REM
6015 E%=1
6020 WHILE E%=1
6025   INPUT "ENTER PERIOD(1-6): ",PR%
6030   IF PR%<1 OR PR%>6 THEN PRINT "MUST BE 1 TO 6" ELSE E%=0
6035 WEND
6040 RETURN
6041 REM - END GET PERIOD -------------------
6042 REM
```

Get Student Update is responsible for getting a student ID from the user and updating the list of students enrolled in the course, ST%(). This activity is factored into two lower-level modules, one that adds a student ID to the array and another that removes one from the array.

Before the user adds a student ID, the module looks through the entire array to check whether the student is already enrolled. If the student ID is not found, the module places it in the first open position on the array.

```
6500 REM ----- GET STUDENT UPDATE -------------------
6505 REM        PROMISES TO UPDATE ST%() WITH STUDENT UPDATE
6510 REM
6515 E%=1
6520 WHILE E%=1
6525   INPUT "ARE YOU ADDING OR DELETING A STUDENT ID (A/D)";U$
6530   U$=LEFT$(U$,1)
6535   IF U$="A" THEN GOSUB 6600: E%=0
6540   IF U$="D" THEN GOSUB 6700: E%=0
6545   IF E%=1 THEN PRINT "ENTER A OR D"
6550 WEND
6555 RETURN
6556 REM - END GET STUDENT UPDATE -------------------
6557 REM
```

```
6600 REM ----- ADD STUDENT ID TO STUDENT ARRAY -------------------
6601 REM
6605 F%=1
6610 WHILE F%=1
6615   INPUT "WHICH ID IS TO BE ADDED";ID%
6620  IF ID%<1 OR ID%>200 THEN PRINT "MUST BE BETWEEN 1 AND 200" ELSE F%=0
6625 WEND
6630 S%=0
6635 SX%=-1
6640 FOR S%=0 TO 29
6645   IF ST%(S%)=ID% THEN PRINT "STUDENT ALREADY ENROLLED":SX%=S%
6650   IF ST%(S%)=0 AND SX%=-1 THEN SX%=S%
6655 NEXT S%
6660 IF SX%=-1 THEN PRINT "COURSE IS FULL" ELSE ST%(SX%)=ID%
6665 RETURN
6666 REM - END ADD STUDENT ID TO STUDENT ARRAY -------------------
6667 REM


6700 REM ----- DELETE STUDENT ID FROM STUDENT ARRAY -------------------
6701 REM
6705 F%=1
6710 WHILE F%=1
6715   INPUT "WHICH ID IS TO BE DELETED";ID%
6720   IF ID%<1 OR ID%>200 THEN PRINT "MUST BE BETWEEN 1 AND 200" ELSE F%=0
6725 WEND
6730 S%=0
6735 F%=1
6740 WHILE F%=1
6745   IF ST%(S%)=ID% THEN ST%(S%)=0: F%=0 ELSE S%=S%+1
6750   IF S%>29 THEN F%=0
6755 WEND
6760 IF S%=30 THEN PRINT "CANNOT FIND ID ";ID%
6765 RETURN
6766 REM - END DELETE STUDENT ID FROM STUDENT ARRAY -------------------
6767 REM
```

The section of the program outline under Store Course Records is shown below.

```
7000 REM ----- STORE COURSE RECORDS -------------------
7005 REM        ASSUMES COURSE DATA AND RN%
7010 REM        PROMISES TO STORE COURSE RECORD AND UPDATE COURSE INDEX
7015 REM
7020 GOSUB 7500
7025 X%=INT((RN%-1)/25)
7030 IR%=X%+1
7035 P%=RN%-(X%*25)-1
7040 GOSUB 8500
7045 CI$(P%)=CC$
7050 GOSUB 8000
7055 RETURN
7056 REM - END STORE COURSE RECORDS -------------------
7057 REM
```

```
7500 REM ----- STORE COURSE RECORD -------------------
7505 REM      ASSUMES VALID COURSE DATA AND RN% BETWEEN 1 AND 100
7510 REM
7515 LSET F1$=CC$
7520 LSET F2$=TE$
7525 LSET F3$=CR$
7530 LSET F4$=MKI$(PR%)
7535 X$=""
7540 FOR S%=0 TO 29
7545   X$=X$+MKI$(ST%(S%))
7550 NEXT S%
7555 LSET F5$=X$
7560 LSET FX$=AX$
7565 PUT #1,RN%
7570 RETURN
7571 REM - END STORE COURSE RECORD -------------------
7572 REM

8000 REM ----- STORE INDEX RECORD -------------------
8005 REM      ASSUMES INDEX ARRAY CI$() AND IR% BETWEEN 1 AND 4
8010 REM
8015 X$=""
8020 FOR I%=0 TO 24
8025   X$=X$+CI$(I%)
8030 NEXT I%
8035 LSET CX$=X$
8040 PUT #2, IR%
8045 RETURN
8046 REM - END STORE INDEX RECORD -------------------
8047 REM

8500 REM ----- GET INDEX RECORD -------------------
8505 REM      ASSUMES IR% BETWEEN 1 AND 4
8510 REM      PROMISES INDEX ARRAY CI$()
8515 REM
8520 GET #2,IR%
8525 FOR I%=0 TO 24
8530   CI$(I%)=MID$(CX$,I%*3+1,3)
8535 NEXT I%
8540 RETURN
8541 REM - END GET INDEX RECORD -------------------
8542 REM
```

By working through the example in this section, you have reviewed a wide variety of coding techniques. Now that the programs are completed, the counselor can store and review data about the courses offered and the students attending those courses.

## EXERCISE X

The community theater has decided to stage as many as fifteen performances of each play and to stage the show in different auditoriums on different nights. The theater can use five different auditoriums.

The theater's president wants his computer system to store data about these performances. The file must contain the date, location, seats sold, and the seats available for each performance. The auditoriums are approximately the same size, so the seating arrangement is the same in each, rows A through T and chairs 1 through 20.

You discuss the new function with the president, and he agrees that the performances should be identified by the date and time of performance, whether matinee or evening. The performance code will contain seven characters, a six-character date (MMDDYY) followed by the letter M or E. The ticket seller will enter 032485E to look at the data stored for the March 24, 1985 evening performance.

1.  build data flow diagrams to show the functions necessary to build and maintain the performance data

2.  build data dictionary entries to define all data flows shown on the data flow diagram

3.  compute a size and time estimate for completing the job

4.  build at least six test cases to verify that your programs function properly

5.  build the program outlines for the functions

6.  write the programs as declared on the program outlines

# 11

# Expanding the Update Functions

## 11A. Building the Model

In Chapter 10, you learned how to add a related file to a system. In this chapter, you will see how the system maintains consistency between the related files. Related files have certain items of data in common, and if the values of the data on one file don't match those on another file, the result is confusion and error for the user. For example, if the patron file of a library system shows that the patron has checked out a certain book, and the book file shows that the book has not been checked out, the librarian does not know if the book is with the patron or on the shelves.

In the system you have built for the counselor, one program allows him to update the Student File and another allows him to update the Course File. Each time the counselor updates one file, he must update both to remain consistent. This is more work for the counselor, and he may neglect to update one file. If the counselor enters a Student Record with course code ALG, there is no guarantee that a record on the Course File contains the code ALG. The counselor, however, may assume the code is there and not add it. Assuming that a Course Record containing ALG exists, the counselor could add the Student ID to the Course Record without realizing that the student is not recorded on the Student File.

In this section, you will expand both the Update Student Data and Update Course Data functions so that each one edits and updates both related files. When the counselor enters new data onto the Student File that include a course code, the program checks the Course Index File to verify that the course is recorded on the Course File. The student ID is then added to the Course Record.

When the counselor puts a student ID onto a Course Record, Update Course Data checks that an active Student Record exists for that ID number on the Student File. If so, the course code is placed on the Student Record.

**Defining the function**

When the user enters a course code and period into the Update Student Data program, his objective is checking that the Student File and Course File are updated consistently. To help define the new function, you identify the conditions it must check and the data to be used.

One condition the function must check is whether the given course code in the period is recorded on the Course File. If so, the course code is added to the Student Record and the student ID to the Course Record. The function uses the Course Index File and Course Record to determine if the course code and period are valid.

The second condition is whether the student has already enrolled in a course for that period. If yes, the student ID must be removed from the old Course Record. The function accesses the Student Record to check this condition.

Using the above description, you can build a data flow diagram of the new function which, using the course code and period, the Student Record, the Course Index File, and the Course Record, produces an updated Student Record and Course Record.

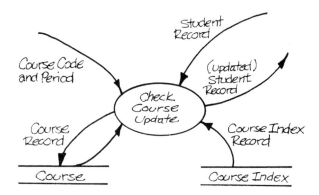

**Figure 11.1. Data flow diagram for Check Course Update.**

To determine how this function fits into the Update Student Data function, identify the source of Check Course Update's incoming data flows and destination of its outgoing data flows. Note the detailed data flow diagram for Update Student Data in Figure 9.2. Check Course Update uses the student record coming from Find Student Record as well as the course code and period from the user. The data dictionary states that Course Code, Period, and Grade are part of New Student Data. Part of the data flow New Student Data, therefore, must flow into Check Course Update; this appears in Figure 11.2 with the course code and period diverging from New Student Data.

Student Record is an outgoing data flow in the Check Course Update function. In Figure 9.2, Get New Student Data receives the Student Record. Since the Student Record can reach Get New Student Data directly from Find Student Record or Check Course Update, the data flow diagram in Figure 11.2 shows the data flows converging into Get New Student Data.

The Update Course Data program (see Figure 10.3) must have a similar check and update function to guarantee consistency between the Student File and Course File. When the counselor puts a Student Update into Update Course Data, the function checks that the student ID is recorded on the Student File. If the student ID is valid, the course code is entered onto the Student Record and the student is recorded on the Course Record.

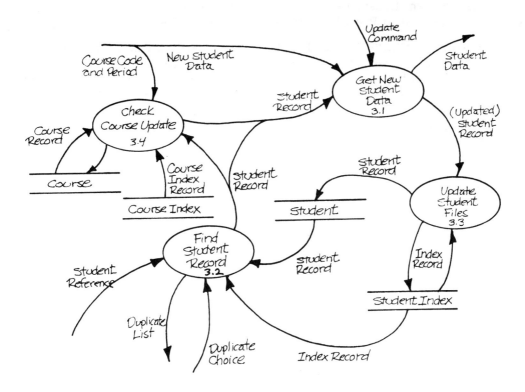

**Figure 11.2. Detailed data flow diagram for Update Student Data.**

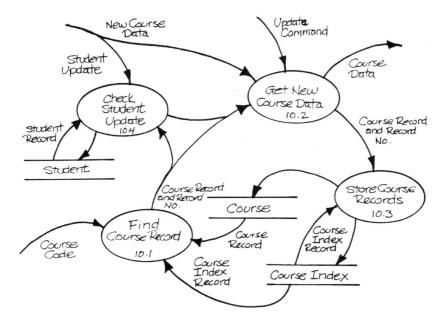

**Figure 11.3. Detailed data flow diagram for Update Course Data.**

Check Student Update does not need the Student Index File because the function can retrieve the Student Record directly from the Student File by using the Student ID.

Both Update Student Data and Update Course Data can delete a record from the file. If the record of a student enrolled in a course is deleted from the Student File, the Course Record will have an incorrect student ID. The delete activity in Update Student Data must be changed to prevent a Student Record with course codes from being deleted; so, too, Update Course Data must be changed to prevent the deletion of a Course Record containing student IDs.

## Defining the data

Based on the data flow diagram in Figure 11.2, the course code is entered separately from the grade. The definition of New Student Data below reflects this change.

---

## DATA DICTIONARY

Course Array = 6{Course Code + Grade}6

Course Data = Course Code + Teacher + Classroom + Period + Student Array

Course File = 100{Course Record}100

Course Index File = 4{Course Index Record}4

Course Index Record = 25{Course Code}25

Course Record = Course Code + Teacher + Classroom + Period
        + Student Array

New Course Data = [ Course Code | Teacher | Classroom | Period |
        Student Update ]

New Student Data = [ Last Name | First Name | Street | City | State |
        Zip | Class | Grade + Period | Course Code + Period ]

Student Array = 30{Student ID}30

Student Data = First Name + Last Name + Street + City + State + Zip
        + Class + Course Array

Student Record = Student ID + Student Name + Street + City + State
        + Zip + Class + Course Array

Student Update = [ A | D ] + Student ID

---

**Table 11.1. Data dictionary.**

### Estimating the size of the program

The initial token count for the Check Course Update function is six, one for each data flow. The function refers to the course codes inside the Course Index Record, so one token is added for the set of braces in Course Index Record's definition. The function also updates the Student Array from the Course Record, and the Course Array from the Student Record. These two sets of braces add two tokens to the code for a total size estimate of nine tokens.

The Check Student Update function has a size estimate of seven. Its initial token count is five, and one token is added for each of the two arrays updated by the function (Course Array and Student Array).

| | | PERFORMANCE LOG | | |
|---|---|---|---|---|
| Function | Token Count | Estimate | Actual Time | Rate Token/Time |
| | | | | 1.4 token/hr. |
| 3.4 | 9 | | | |
| 10.4 | 7 | | | |
| TOTAL | 16 | < 11.5 hrs. | | |

**Table 11.2. Performance log.**

Get New Student Data is not included in the estimate because that function has not changed. It continues to get the Student Record, display the Student Data, get the Update Command and New Student Data, and apply the new data to the Student Record. The only change is that Update Student Data performs additional edits when the user enters a new course code. This change has already been estimated in Check Course Update and Get New Course Data.

### Identifying the test cases

Since Check Course Update will be working with the Course Index File, tests must be built for the program to refer to the first and last entries in the index. These same tests will also cause the program to read the first and last records on the Course File.

Two other arrays need to be tested. A test case must be built that places a course code into the first and last elements of the Course Array. The first and last elements of the Student Array should also be updated by test cases.

If the user tries to enroll a student in period 2, but the Course Record shows the course is taught in period 5, an error message should appear. Also, if the user tries to add a course code to a Student Record when the course has 30 students enrolled, the program should display an error message. Both error conditions must be tested.

---

### TEST CASE LOG

| Test Case | Result |
|---|---|
| Build a course file with | ALG Period 1 on the 1st Course Record<br>SHP Period 1 on the 2nd Course Record<br>GYM Period 6 on the 99th Course Record<br>TRI Period 6 on the 100th Course Record |
| Update student with ALG period 1 | Update Student Record and Student Array in Course Record |
| Update student with TRI period 6 | Update Student Record and Student Array in Course Record |
| Update student with Course Code not on Course File | Error message - no Course Record |
| Change student's 1st period to SHP | Remove ID from ALG record<br>Add ID to SHP record |
| Change student's 6th period to GYM | Remove ID from TRI record<br>Add ID to GYM record |
| Update student ALG period 2 | Error message - wrong period |
| Enroll 29 students in ALG,<br>Update student with ALG | Updates 30th in Student Array |
| Update another student with ALG | Error message - course full |
| Delete Student Record with Course Code in Course Array | Error message - student still enrolled |

---

**Table 11.3. Test case log for Check Course Update.**

To test Check Student Update, you must be sure that student IDs are updated to the correct period on the student record and that error conditions are reported.

## TEST CASE LOG

| Test Case | Result |
|---|---|
| Build a Student File with active records in the 1st and 200th records | |
| Update 1st period course with ID number 001 | Student Array in Course Record and Student Record updated |
| Update 6th period course with ID number 200 | Student Array in Course Record and Student Record updated |
| Add student ID where student has another course that period | Error message - student enrolled in other course |
| Add student ID to course with 29 students | Updates 30th in Student Array |
| Add student ID to course with 30 students | Error message - course full |
| Delete course when Student Array contains student ID | Error message - student is still enrolled |

**Table 11.4. Test case log for Check Student Update.**

**Building the program outline**

In the program outline for Update Student Data (see Figures 9.4 and 7.4), the activity Get Grade List gets not only the grade, but also the course code and period. The data flow diagram in Figure 11.2 shows that this function has been expanded. The activity that got only the course code must now perform the work of Check Course Update, modeled in Figure 11.2. The program outline must be updated to show Check Course Update and the activities it needs to get the course code, search the Course Index File, retrieve the Course Record, add the student ID to the Student Array in the Course Record, and store the Course Record back on the Course File. These activities correspond to the data flows around Check Course Update.

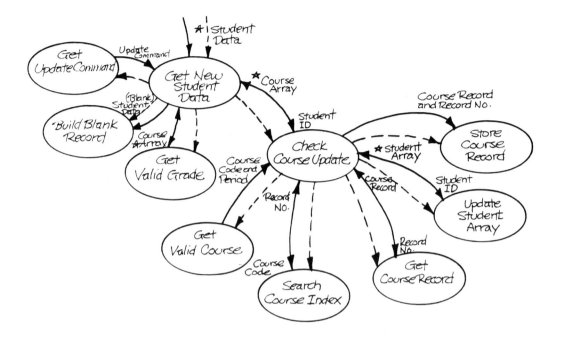

**Figure 11.4. Partial program outline for Update Student Data.**

Note that the activity to get a student's grade has been separated from the Get Course module. It is now a separate activity invoked from the Get New Student Data module.

The program outline for Update Course Data is modified by replacing Get Student Update with Check Student Update, which now gets the Student Update from the user, the Student Record from the Student File, adjusts the Course Array on the Student Record and the Student Array on the Course Record, and stores the Student Record on the Student File.

Update Course Data must also prevent the user from deleting a Course Record that contains student IDs in the Student Array. An edit can be added to Build Blank Data so that the data on the two related files remain consistent. Because the student is enrolled in a course for a particular period, the Get Period module must be changed to check the Student Array. If students are enrolled in the old period, the program should not allow the user to change the course to a different period.

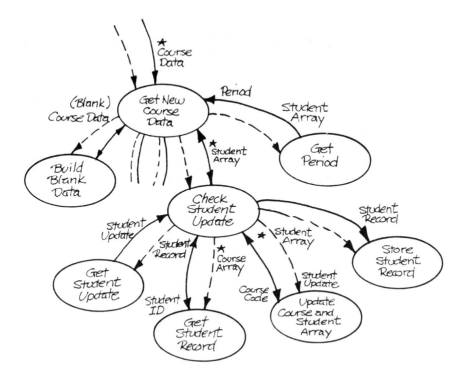

**Figure 11.5. Partial program outline for Update Course Data.**

You have completed the modeling process when the program outlines have been modified to reflect the new functions. This section demonstrates how a function that updates one file is expanded to check data on a related file and keep the data in both consistent. By updating two related files simultaneously, you reduce the number of transactions the user must enter and guarantee that data stored on one file will not contradict data stored on the other.

# 11B. Building the BASIC Program

In this section, you will learn how to write the code for a new function in a file-update program. Whenever a user updates that file, the new function will update any related files.

In the Update Student Data program, the program outline shows the activities needed to check the Course Code against the Course File and update the Course Record with the Student ID. When the counselor enters a course code, the program looks for the course on the Course Index File. If the course code is on the Course Index, the student ID is added to the Student Array on the Course Record, and the Course Record is stored on the Course File.

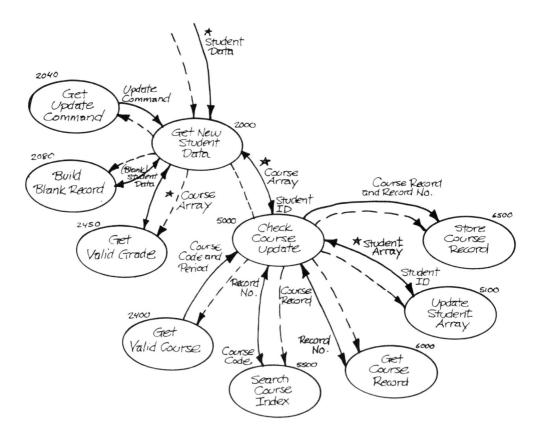

**Figure 11.6. Partial program outline for Update Student Data showing new Check Course Update activity.**

You have already assigned names to many data items in the data dictionary. However, some BASIC data names given in Chapter 10 to data items in the Course Record are the same names used in Chapter 7 for different data items in the Student Record. For example, F4$ is the Street on the Student Record, while F4$ is the Period in the Course Record. Since the Student File and Course File are referred to in the same program, you must rename the data items so that each piece of data has its own name.

---

## DATA DICTIONARY

Course Array = 6{Course + Grade}6
  CR$() GR$()

Course Data = Course Code + Teacher + Classroom + Period + Student Array
  CC$  TE$  CM$  PR%  ST%()

Course Entry = Course + Period

Course Index = 25{Course Code}25
  IC$ and CX$()

Course Record = Course Code + Teacher + Classroom + Period
  + Student Array + Status
  C1$ C2$ C3$ C4$ C5$ XC$

Course Record Number = Integer between 1 and 25
  RC%

New Course Data = [ Course Code | Teacher | Classroom | Period |
  Student Update ]

New Student Data = [ First Name | Last Name | Street | City | State |
  Zip | Class | Grade | Course Entry ]

Student Array = 30{Student ID}30
  ST%()

Student Data = First Name + Last Name + Street + City + State + Zip
  + Class + Course Array
  NF$ NL$ RD$ CI$ ST$ ZP$ CL$

Student Index = 200{Student ID}200
  IS$ and SX$()

Student Record = Student ID + Student Name + Street + City + State
  + Zip + Class + Course Array + Status
  S1$ S2$ and S3$ S4$ S5$ S6$ S7$ S8$ S9$ XS$

Student Update = [ A | D ] + Student ID
  ID%

---

**Table 11.5. Data dictionary with BASIC data names.**

The four files now used by Update Student Data are declared in the top module. Notice that the field names in Student File's FIELD statement now start with the letter S and the field names on the Course File's FIELD statement start with the letter C as defined in the data dictionary. All modules that refer to the old names (F1$, F2$, etc.) must be changed to use the new data names.

```
10 REM ----- UPDATE STUDENT DATA --------------------
11 REM
15 OPEN "R",#1,"STUDENT2"
20 FIELD #1, 2 AS S1$,20 AS S2$,10 AS S3$,20 AS S4$,15 AS S5$,
    2 AS S6$,5 AS S7$,2 AS S8$,24 AS S9$,1 AS XS$
25 OPEN "R",#2,"STINDEX"
30 FIELD #2, 120 AS IS$
35 OPEN "R",#3,"COURSES"
40 FIELD #3,3 AS C1$,20 AS C2$,3 AS C3$,2 AS C4$,60 AS C5$,1 AS XC$
50 OPEN "R",#4,"CRINDEX"
55 FIELD #4,75 AS IC$
60 DIM CX$(24),ST%(29)
65 DIM GR$(5),CR$(5),SX$(39),DL%(19)
100 E$="YES"
102 WHILE E$="YES"
103   GOSUB 300
115   GOSUB 2000
120   GOSUB 4100
121   INPUT "DO YOU WANT TO LOOK AT ANOTHER RECORD";E$
122   IF LEFT$(E$,1)="Y" THEN E$="YES" ELSE E$="NO"
123 WEND
125 CLOSE #1
126 CLOSE #2
128 CLOSE #3
129 CLOSE #4
130 CHAIN "TRANSACT"
131 REM - END UPDATE STUDENT DATA --------------------
132 REM
```

The Get Update Command activity has been expanded to include the separate Get Valid Grade function. The user enters grades and course codes separately. Build Blank Record has been changed to check for course codes in the Course Array. If the student is enrolled in a course, the record is not deleted.

```
2000 REM ----- GET NEW STUDENT DATA --------------------
2005 REM       ASSUMES VALID STUDENT DATA
2007 REM       PROMISES VALID VALUES IN STUDENT DATA
2010 REM
2011 UC$=""
2012 WHILE UC$<>"END"
2013   GOSUB 1500: GOSUB 2040
2015   IF UC$="1" THEN GOSUB 2200
2020   IF UC$="2" THEN GOSUB 2100
2021   IF UC$="3" THEN GOSUB 2600
2022   IF UC$="4" THEN GOSUB 2650
2023   IF UC$="5" THEN GOSUB 2700
2024   IF UC$="6" THEN GOSUB 2750
2025   IF UC$="7" THEN GOSUB 2300
2026   IF UC$="8" THEN GOSUB 5000
```

```
2030  IF UC$="9" THEN GOSUB 2450
2032  IF UC$="DELETE" THEN GOSUB 2080
2033 WEND
2035 RETURN
2036 REM - END GET NEW STUDENT DATA -------------------
2037 REM


2040 REM ----- GET UPDATE COMMAND(UC$) -------------------
2042 REM
2044 E%=1
2046 WHILE E%=1
2048   PRINT "ENTER UPDATE COMMAND:"
2050   PRINT "  1 - FIRST NAME"," 6 - ZIP"
2052   PRINT "  2 - LAST NAME "," 7 - CLASS"
2054   PRINT "  3 - STREET    "," 8 - COURSE"
2056   PRINT "  4 - CITY      "," 9 - GRADE"
2057   PRINT "  5 - STATE     "
2058   PRINT "  DELETE - BLANK RECORD"
2060   PRINT "  END - TO END UPDATING"
2062   INPUT UC$
2064   IF UC$="1" OR UC$="2" OR UC$="3" OR UC$="4" THEN E%=0
2065   IF UC$="5" OR UC$="6" OR UC$="7" OR UC$="8" THEN E%=0
2066   IF UC$="9" OR UC$="END" OR UC$="DELETE" THEN E%=0
2068   IF E%=1 THEN PRINT "UNRECOGNIZED COMMAND, REENTER"
2070 WEND
2072 RETURN
2073 REM - END GET UPDATE COMMAND --------------------
2074 REM


2080 REM ----- BUILD BLANK RECORD -------------------
2081 REM
2082 E%=0
2083 FOR C%=0 TO 5
2084   IF CR$(C%)<>"    " THEN E%=1
2085 NEXT C%
2086 IF E%=1 THEN PRINT "STUDENT ENROLLED IS COURSES, CANNOT DELETE"
2087 WHILE E%=0
2088   E%=1
2089   NL$=SPACE$(20) : NF$=SPACE$(10)
2090   RD$=SPACE$(20) : CI$=SPACE$(15)
2091   ST$=" " : ZP$="    " : CL$=" "
2092   FOR C%=0 TO 5
2093     CR$(C%)="   ":GR$(C%)="  "
2094   NEXT C%
2095   ZX$="X"
2096 WEND
2097 RETURN
2098 REM - END BUILD BLANK RECORD -------------------
2099 REM
```

The Check Course Update at line 5000 contains a loop that exits only when the user has entered a valid course code — one that exists on the Course File and is taught in the correct period. Get Valid Course gets a course code (C$) and period (C%) from the user. The Search Course Index module starting at line 5500 searches the Course Index File. If the record number (RC%) returned equals 0, the course code is not on the Course Index File. If the course code is found, the program retrieves the Course Record by invoking Get Course Record (GOSUB 6000). If the course is taught during the correct period, the student ID is added to the Course Record by invoking Update Student Array (GOSUB 5100).

The Update Student Array module places the student ID on the Course Record. The student may be enrolled in a different course during the same period. If so, Update Student Array must find that Course Record and remove the student ID from its Student Array. This means that Update Student Array must invoke the Search Course Index, Get Course Record, and Store Course Record modules. The code below factors the activity that puts the student ID into its own module. The program outline is also updated to reflect these changes to the program organization.

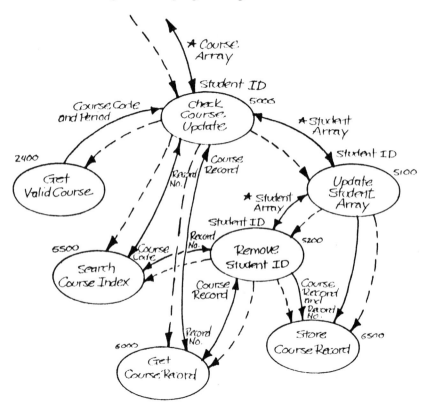

**Figure 11.7. Factored program outline for Check Course Update.**

```
5000 REM ----- CHECK COURSE UPDATE --------------------
5005 REM      ASSUMES STUDENT ID
5010 REM      PROMISES TO UPDATE COURSE ARRAY WITH VALID COURSE CODE
5015 REM
5020 GOSUB 2400
5050   IF RC%>0 THEN XR$=CR$(C%-1)
5055   IF RC%>0 THEN GOSUB 6000
5060   IF RC%>0 AND PR%=C% THEN GOSUB 5100:F1%=1
5065   IF RC%>0 AND PR%<>C% THEN PRINT CC$ " IS TAUGHT IN PERIOD " PR%:F1%=1
5070 WEND
5075 RETURN
5076 REM - END CHECK COURSE UPDATE --------------------
5077 REM
```

If the student is enrolled in a different course for the period, the student ID is taken off the old Course Record. This activity has been factored into its own module (line 5200).

```
5100 REM ----- UPDATE STUDENT ARRAY -------------------
5105 REM        ASSUMES STUDENT ARRAY AND STUDENT ID
5110 REM        PROMISES TO UPDATE STUDENT ARRAY WITH STUDENT ID
5115 REM
5120 E%=0
5125 P%=0
5130 WHILE E%=0
5135   IF ST%(P%)=0 THEN ST%(P%)=ID%:CR$(C%-1)=CC$:E%=1
5140   IF E%=0 THEN P%=P%+1
5145   IF P%>29 THEN E%=1
5150 WEND
5155 GOSUB 6500
5160 IF XR$<>"   " AND P%<30 THEN GOSUB 5200
5165 RETURN
5166 REM - END UPDATE STUDENT ARRAY -------------------
5167 REM

5200 REM ----- REMOVE STUDENT ID FROM COURSE RECORD -------------------
5201 REM
5205 CC$=XR$
5210 GOSUB 5500
5215 IF RC%>0 THEN GOSUB 5250 ELSE PRINT CC$ " NOT ON COURSE FILE"
5220 RETURN
5250 GOSUB 6000
5255 FOR P%=0 TO 29
5260   IF ST%(P%)=ID% THEN ST%(P%)=0
5265 NEXT P%
5270 GOSUB 6500
5275 RETURN
5276 REM - END REMOVE STUDENT ID FROM COURSE RECORD -------------------
5277 REM
```

The modules that search the Course Index (line 5500), get the Course Record (line 6000), and store it (line 6500) have been copied from the Update Course Data program in Chapter 10. The difference is that Search Course Index returns a record number of 0 if the course code is not found on the Course Index File. In Chapter 10, Search Course Index returned the record number of the first blank Course Record.

```
5500 REM ----- SEARCH COURSE INDEX -----------------------
5505 REM        ASSUMES VALID COURSE CODE - CC$
5510 REM        PROMISES IF CC$ ON INDEX, RC% SET TO THAT RECORD
5515 REM            IF CC$ NOT ON INDEX, RC% SET TO 0
5520 REM
5525 IR%=1
5530 RC%=0
5535 E1%=1
5540 WHILE E1%=1
5545   GOSUB 5600
5550   P%=0
5555   E2%=1
5560   WHILE E2%=1
5565     IF CC$=CX$(P%) THEN E2%=0:E1%=0:RC%=P%+(IR%*25-25)+1
```

```
5570    IF P%<24 THEN P%=P%+1 ELSE E2%=0
5575   WEND
5580   IF IR%<4 THEN IR%=IR%+1 ELSE E1%=0
5585 WEND
5590 RETURN
5591 REM - END SEARCH COURSE INDEX --------------------
5592 REM


5600 REM ----- GET COURSE INDEX RECORD --------------------
5605 REM        ASSUMES IR% BETWEEN 1 AND 4
5610 REM        PROMISES INDEX ARRAY CX$()
5615 REM
5620 GET #4,IR%
5625 FOR I%=0 TO 24
5630   CX$(I%)=MID$(IC$,I%*3+1,3)
5635 NEXT I%
5640 RETURN
5641 REM - END GET COURSE INDEX RECORD --------------------
5642 REM


6000 REM ----- GET COURSE RECORD --------------------
6005 REM        ASSUMES RECORD NUMBER - RC% BETWEEN 1 AND 100
6010 REM        PROMISES RC% COURSE DATA CC$, TE$, CM$, PR%, ST%(), AX$
6015 REM
6020 GET #3,RC%
6025 CC$=C1$
6030 TE$=C2$
6035 CM$=C3$
6040 PR%=CVI(C4$)
6045 FOR S%=0 TO 29
6050   ST%(S%)=CVI(MID$(C5$,S%*2+1,2))
6055 NEXT S%
6060 AX$=XC$
6065 RETURN
6066 REM - END GET COURSE RECORD --------------------
6067 REM


6500 REM ----- STORE COURSE RECORD --------------------
6505 REM        ASSUMES VALID COURSE DATA AND RC% BETWEEN 1 AND 100
6510 REM
6515 LSET C1$=CC$
6520 LSET C2$=TE$
6525 LSET C3$=CM$
6530 LSET C4$=MKI$(PR%)
6535 X$=""
6540 FOR S%=0 TO 29
6545   X$=X$+MKI$(ST%(S%))
6550 NEXT S%
6555 LSET C5$=X$
6560 LSET XC$=AX$
6565 PUT #3,RC%
6570 RETURN
6571 REM - END STORE COURSE RECORD --------------------
6572 REM
```

The Get Valid Course module gets the period and then the course code.  The course code is not placed in the Course Array until it has been checked against the Course Index File.

```
2400 REM ----- GET VALID COURSE --------------------
2402 REM
2404 F%=1
2406 WHILE F%=1
2408   INPUT "ENTER PERIOD 1-6: ",C%
2410   IF C%>0 AND C%<7 THEN F%=0
2412   IF F%=1 THEN PRINT "PERIOD MUST BE 1,2,3,4,5,OR 6"
2414 WEND
2416 WHILE F%=0
2418   INPUT "ENTER THREE-CHARACTER COURSE CODE: ",C$
2420   IF LEN(C$)<>3 THEN PRINT "MUST BE THREE CHARACTERS" ELSE F%=1
2422 WEND
2424 RETURN
2425 REM - END GET VALID COURSE --------------------
2426 REM


2450 REM ----- GET VALID GRADE --------------------
2451 REM
2452 F%=1
2453 WHILE F%=1
2454   INPUT "ENTER PERIOD 1-6: ",C%
2455   IF C%>0 AND C%<7 THEN F%=0
2456   IF F%=1 THEN PRINT "PERIOD MUST BE BETWEEN 1 AND 6"
2457 WEND
2458 E%=0
2459 WHILE E%=0
2460   INPUT "GRADE";G$
2461   IF G$="A" THEN E%=1
2462   IF G$="B" THEN E%=1
2463   IF G$="C" THEN E%=1
2464   IF G$="D" THEN E%=1
2465   IF G$="F" THEN E%=1
2466   IF G$="W" THEN E%=1
2467   IF G$="I" THEN E%=1
2468   IF E%=0 THEN PRINT "UNRECOGNIZED GRADE.  REENTER."
2470 WEND
2472 GR$(C%-1)=G$
2474 RETURN
2475 REM - END GET VALID GRADE --------------------
2476 REM
```

## The Update Course Data program

In order to verify that the student IDs added to the Student Array belong to active students recorded on the related file, the Update Course Data program must be changed to check the Student Update against the Student File.  Because the Student Record can be retrieved directly from the Student File by using the student ID, the program does not have to search the Student File Index.

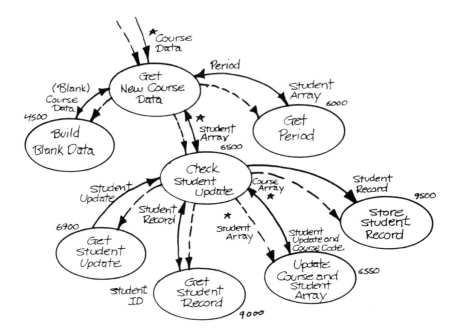

**Figure 11.8. Partial program outline for Update Course Data
showing new Check Student Update activity.**

The top module declares the files used in the program.

```
10 REM ----- UPDATE COURSE DATA --------------------
11 REM
15 OPEN "R",#1,"COURSES"
20 FIELD #1,3 AS C1$,20 AS C2$,3 AS C3$,2 AS C4$,60 AS C5$,1 AS XC$
25 OPEN "R",#2,"CRINDEX"
30 FIELD #2,75 AS IC$
35 OPEN "R",#3,"STUDENT2"
40 FIELD #3, 2 AS S1$,20 AS S2$,10 AS S3$,20 AS S4$,15 AS S5$,2 AS S6$,
     5 AS S7$,2 AS S8$,24 AS S9$,1 AS XS$
45 DIM CX$(24),ST%(29),CR$(5),GR$(5)
50 E$="YES"
55 WHILE E$="YES"
60    GOSUB 500
65    GOSUB 3000
70    GOSUB 7000
75    PRINT CHR$(26);
80    INPUT "DO YOU WANT TO LOOK AT ANOTHER COURSE";E$
85    IF LEFT$(E$,1)="Y" THEN E$="YES" ELSE E$="NO"
90 WEND
95 CLOSE #1
100 CLOSE #2
105 CLOSE #3
110 CHAIN "TRANSACT"
111 REM - END UPDATE COURSE DATA --------------------
112 REM
```

Build Blank Data now checks the Student Array for student IDs. If a student is enrolled in the course, the user is notified and the record is not deleted. Get Period is also modified to prevent changes to the period if students are enrolled.

```
4500 REM ----- BUILD BLANK DATA --------------------
4505 REM        PROMISES INITIAL VALUES IN COURSE DATA
4510 REM
4511 E%=0
4512 FOR S%=0 TO 29
4513   IF ST%(S%)<>0 THEN E%=1
4514 NEXT S%
4515 IF E%=1 THEN PRINT "STUDENTS ENROLLED IN COURSE, CANNOT DELETE"
4516 WHILE E%=0
4517   E%=1
4520   CC$="   "
4525   TE$=SPACE$(20)
4530   CM$="   "
4535   FOR S%=0 TO 29
4540     ST%(S%)=0
4545   NEXT S%
4550   PR%=0
4555   AX$="X"
4557 WEND
4560 RETURN
4561 REM - END BUILD BLANK DATA --------------------
4562 REM


6000 REM ----- GET PERIOD --------------------
6005 REM
6010 REM ** PROMISES VALID PR%
6015 E%=1
6016 FOR P%=0 TO 29
6017   IF ST%(P%)<>0 THEN E%=0
6018 NEXT P%
6019 IF E%=0 THEN PRINT "STUDENT'S ENROLLED UNDER OLD PERIOD"
6020 WHILE E%=1
6025   INPUT "ENTER PERIOD(1-6): ",PR%
6030   IF PR%<1 OR PR%>6 THEN PRINT "MUST BE 1 TO 6" ELSE E%=0
6035 WEND
6040 RETURN
6041 REM - END GET PERIOD --------------------
6042 REM
```

Check Student Update gets the Student Update, retrieves the Student Record, invokes the Update Course and Student Array module, and stores the Student Record back on the Student File.

```
6500 REM ----- CHECK STUDENT UPDATE --------------------
6505 REM        PROMISES TO UPDATE ST%() WITH STUDENT UPDATE
6510 REM
6515 GOSUB 6900
6520 GOSUB 9000
6525 GOSUB 6550
6530 GOSUB 9500
6535 RETURN
6536 REM - END CHECK STUDENT UPDATE --------------------
6537 REM
```

The Update Course and Student Array activity has been factored into two modules. One module adds a student ID and the other removes one. Both factored modules check the Student Record before changing the Student Array.

Before a student ID is added to the Student Array, the module checks whether the student is already enrolled in a course for that period (lines 6635 and 6640). If the student is not enrolled in a course, the Student Array is searched (GOSUB 6660). If the course is full, an error message is printed. If the module can add the student ID to the Student Array, the course code is placed on the Student Record (line 6645).

Before a student ID is removed from the Student Array, the course code is taken off the Student Record (line 6735) and the student ID is deleted from the Student Array (lines 6740 through 6750).

```
6550 REM ----- UPDATE COURSE AND STUDENT ARRAY -------------------
6555 REM      ASSUMES STUDENT UPDATE AND COURSE CODE
6560 REM      PROMISES TO UPDATE COURSE ARRAY AND STUDENT ARRAY
6565 REM
6570  IF U$="A" THEN GOSUB 6600
6575  IF U$="D" THEN GOSUB 6700
6580 RETURN
6581 REM - END UPDATE COURSE AND STUDENT ARRAY -------------------
6582 REM


6600 REM ----- ADD STUDENT ID TO STUDENT ARRAY -------------------
6601 REM
6635 IF CR$(PR%-1)<>"  " THEN PRINT "STUDENT HAS ANOTHER COURSE THAT PERIOD"
6640 IF CR$(PR%-1)="  " THEN GOSUB 6660
6645 IF CR$(PR%-1)="  " AND SX%<>-1 THEN CR$(PR%-1)=CC$
6650 RETURN
6651 REM - END ADD STUDENT ID TO STUDENT ARRAY -------------------
6652 REM


6660 REM ----- ADD ID% TO STUDENT ARRAY -------------------
6661 REM
6665 S%=0
6670 SX%=-1
6675 FOR S%=0 TO 29
6680   IF ST%(S%)=ID% THEN PRINT "STUDENT ALREADY ENROLLED":SX%=S%
6685   IF ST%(S%)=0 AND SX%=-1 THEN SX%=S%
6690 NEXT S%
6692 IF SX%=-1 THEN PRINT "COURSE IS FULL" ELSE ST%(SX%)=ID%
6694 RETURN
6695 REM - END ADD ID% TO STUDENT ARRAY ------------------------
6696 REM


6700 REM ----- DELETE STUDENT ID FROM STUDENT ARRAY -------------------
6701 REM
6735 IF CR$(PR%-1)=CC$ THEN CR$(PR%-1)="  ":GR$(PR%-1)="  "
6740 FOR S%=0 TO 29
6745   IF ST%(S%)=ID% THEN ST%(S%)=0
6750 NEXT S%
6755 RETURN
6756 REM - END DELETE STUDENT ID FROM STUDENT ARRAY -------------------
6757 REM
```

```
6900 REM ----- GET STUDENT UPDATE -------------------
6905 REM        PROMISES VALID STUDENT UPDATE
6910 REM
6915 E%=1
6920 WHILE E%=1
6925  INPUT "ARE YOU ADDING OR DELETING A STUDENT ID (A/D)";U$
6930  U$=LEFT$(U$,1)
6935  IF U$="A" OR U$="D" THEN E%=0 ELSE PRINT "ENTER 'A' OR 'D'"
6940 WEND
6945 E%=1
6950 WHILE E%=1
6955  INPUT "ENTER STUDENT ID";ID%
6960  IF ID%<1 OR ID%>200 THEN PRINT "MUST BE BETWEEN 1 AND 200" ELSE E%=0
6965 WEND
6970 RETURN
6971 REM - END GET STUDENT UPDATE -------------------
6972 REM
```

The Get Student Record and Store Student Record modules have been copied from the Update Student Data program.

```
9000 REM ----- GET STUDENT RECORD -------------------
9005 REM        ASSUMES ID% TO BE BETWEEN 1 AND 200
9010 REM             STUDENT FILE IS OPEN
9015 REM        PROMISES NF$, NL$, RD$, CI$, ST$, ZP$, CL$, CR$(),
9020 REM         GR$(), AND AX$ FILLED WITH DATA FROM STUDENT RECORD ID%
9025 REM
9030 GET #3,ID%
9035 NL$=S2$
9040 NF$=S3$
9041 RD$=S4$
9042 CI$=S5$
9043 ST$=S6$
9044 ZP$=S7$
9045 CL$=S8$
9050 FOR C%=0 TO 5
9051  CR$(C%)=MID$(S9$,C%*4+1,3)
9055  GR$(C%)=MID$(S9$,C%*4+4,1)
9060 NEXT C%
9065 ZX$=XS$
9070 RETURN
9071 REM - END GET STUDENT RECORD -------------------
9072 REM


9500 REM ----- STORE STUDENT RECORD -------------------
9505 REM        ASSUMES VALID STUDENT DATA, ID% BETWEEN 1 AND 200
9510 REM             STUDENT FILE OPEN
9515 REM        PROMISES TO STORE STUDENT DATA ON RECORD ID%
9520 REM
9525 LSET S1$=MKI$(ID%)
9530 LSET S2$=NL$
9535 LSET S3$=NF$
9536 LSET S4$=RD$
9537 LSET S5$=CI$
9538 LSET S6$=ST$
9539 LSET S7$=ZP$
9540 LSET S8$=CL$
```

```
9545 G$=""
9550 FOR C%=0 TO 5
9555   G$=G$+CR$(C%)+GR$(C%)
9560 NEXT C%
9565 LSET S9$=G$
9570 LSET XS$=ZX$
9575 PUT #3,ID%
9580 RETURN
9581 REM - END STORE STUDENT RECORD ------------------
9582 REM
```

After implementing these changes to the Update Student Data and Update Course Data programs, the user is able to update both related files in one transaction. When a course code is added to the Student Record, the Course Record is automatically updated with the student ID. The user does not enter the same data into the system twice, and has guaranteed consistency between the Course File and Student File.

## EXERCISE XI

The ticket seller now has two files to maintain and finds that he must enter two transactions each time a person buys tickets to a performance, one to update the Performance File and another the Patron File. He wants the program that updates the Sales File changed so that when he enters sold seats, it displays the seats available from the Performance File and updates the Performance File to mark the seats as sold.

1.  add the new function to the detailed data flow diagram of Update Sales Data; be sure to identify all data flows necessary to perform the function

2.  clarify definitions in the data dictionary when necessary

3.  estimate the job size by computing a token count; enter the token count in your performance log and estimate the time it will take to complete the task

4.  define at least four test cases that will test the resulting program

5.  identify the activities needed to perform the function and place them into a program outline

6.  modify the code in the Update Sales Data program to implement the modeled changes

# 12

# Producing a Report from Two Files

## 12A. Building the Model

Most of the work done in software development involves producing reports for the users of a system. The user wants enormous quantities of information presented in many different ways. This chapter will show how a program can access related data from two files and print the information on the same report.

### Defining the function

The counselor has asked you to produce a report that lists the courses on the Course File. Each course should be printed on a separate page. Under each course he wants a list of the students enrolled in that course and their grade. A summary must be printed for each course, showing the number of students enrolled and the grade average.

The data flow diagram shows the Course Record flowing in from the Course File, the Student Record flowing from the Student File, and the requested Course Report flowing out of the function.

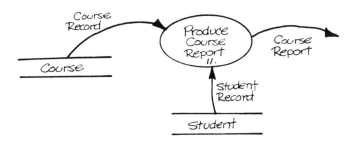

**Figure 12.1. Data flow diagram for Produce Course Report.**

## Defining the data

The data definitions for the Student Record and the Course Record are already in the data dictionary. The definition of Course Report is based on the description given by the counselor. The report consists of a series of pages. Each page contains data about a course, a list of students enrolled in the course, the number of students enrolled, and a grade average for the course.

---

### DATA DICTIONARY

Course Description = Course + Teacher + Period + Classroom

Course Report = {Page}

Course Summary = Student Count + Grade Average

Grade Average = Real number between 0.0 and 4.0

Page = Course Description + Student List + Course Summary

Student Count = Integer between 1 and 30

Student List = {Student Name + Class + Grade}30

Student Name = First Name + Last Name

---

**Table 12.1. Data dictionary for Produce Course Report.**

## Estimating the size of the program

Producing a course report requires only a small function. The initial token count is three, one for each data flow. According to the data dictionary, the course report contains two sets of braces, which means that the program requires code to keep track of the pages and the student list. To account for this code in the estimate, add two to the token count.

The Course Record contains the Student Array. Because the function uses the student IDs in the array to determine which students to list under each course, one is added to the count. Similarly, the Course Array on the Student Record is used to get the grade for the course. This set of braces adds one more to the token count.

The outgoing data flow has a new piece of data. Course Summary is updated by each incoming Student Record. The guidelines listed in your portfolio state that outgoing data not produced directly from an incoming data flow (not one-for-one) should be counted in the estimate. Therefore, one is added to the token count, making a total of eight.

### PERFORMANCE LOG

| Function | Token Count | Estimate | Actual Time | Rate Token/Time |
|----------|-------------|----------|-------------|-----------------|
| 11 | 8 | 4.5 hrs. | | 1.9 token/hr. |

**Table 12.2. Performance log for Produce Course Report.**

**Identifying the test cases**

Because the only input to the function is from the Course File and Student File, to test this function you must enter test data onto the files. If there are active records on the files, the program should produce a report with no data.

According to the data dictionary, the Student List on the Course Record holds from 0 to 30 student names. The program should be tested with one Course Record that has no students enrolled and another with 30 students.

Use a Student Record with one course code in the first period and one in the sixth to check whether the function correctly processes the Course Array of the Student Record.

### TEST CASE LOG

| Test Case | Result |
|-----------|--------|
| No records on either file | Blank report |
| Add course with no students | Course description on first page with no students listed<br>Student count = 0<br>Grade average = 0 |
| Add course with 30 students | Course description with all 30 students listed on second page<br>Student count = 30<br>Correct grade average |
| Student taking 1st- and 6th-period courses | Student listed under both courses |

**Table 12.3. Test case log for Produce Course Report.**

### Building the program outline

To build the program outline for Produce Course Report, you declare activities for each data flow. The function must get the Course Record and Student Record and then print the Course Report.

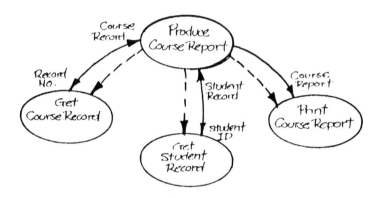

**Figure 12.2. Initial program outline for Produce Course Report.**

Review the data dictionary to identify more detailed activities that can be factored into their own modules. For example, the Course Report consists of a Course Description and Student List. You should refine the program outline to show activities that print Course Description and Student List.

In order to print the Student List, the activity must look at the Student Array and read the Student Record from the Student File. Because the Print Student list module must read the Student File, Get Student Record should be placed under Print Student List on the program outline. The top module, after reading a Course Record and printing the Course Description, invokes Print Student List to read through the Student Record and print the Student List.

As shown in Chapter 4, a report should have a heading that prints the report's name and a description of the listed data items. Page and line numbers have been added as in the Produce Grade Report program.

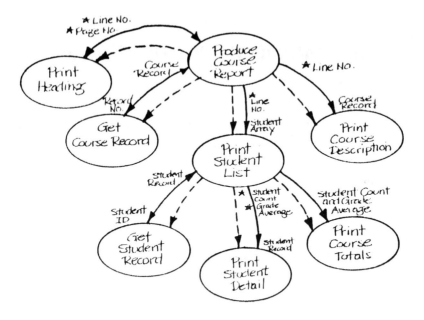

**Figure 12.3. Program outline for Produce Course Report.**

The modeling process is complete once the necessary program activities have been outlined. The function derived from this process uses the data from two related files to produce a report. The contents of the report have been defined in the data dictionary, and the program structure has been outlined. Code that implements the function must now be built.

# 12B. Building the BASIC Program

The Update Student Data and Update Course Data programs were expanded in Chapter 11 to update both files automatically when the user enters a transaction. This section will show how a BASIC program accesses two related files to include data from both files on a report.

The program outline for Produce Course Report contains two modules, Get Course Record and Get Student Record, that have already been written in the Update Student Data program. Since these modules perform the same function and produce the same data as their namesakes, you can copy them from the older program.

The starting line numbers have been assigned to each activity in the program outline shown in Figure 12.4.

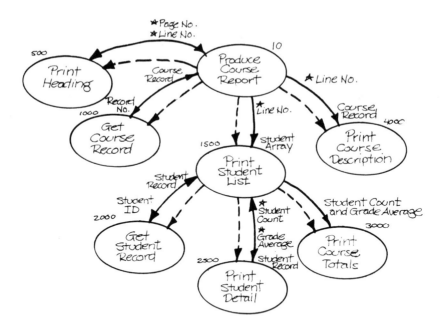

**Figure 12.4. Program outline for Produce Course Report.**

The data dictionary in Table 12.4 has been updated to include the BASIC data names used in the program.

---

## DATA DICTIONARY

Course Description = Course + Teacher + Period + Classroom
        CC$   TE$    PR%   CM$

Course Report = {Page}

Grade Average = Real number between 0.0 and 4.0
        CA!

Page = Course Description + Student List + Student Count + Grade Average

Student Count = Integer between 1 and 30
        SC%

Student List = {Student Name + Class + Grade}30
        NF$ NL$    CL$   G$

Student Name = First Name + Last Name

---

**Table 12.4. Data dictionary with BASIC data names.**

```
10 REM ----- PRODUCE COURSE REPORT --------------------
11 REM
15 OPEN "R",#1,"COURSES"
20 FIELD #1,3 AS C1$,20 AS C2$,3 AS C3$,2 AS C4$,60 AS C5$,1 AS XC$
30 OPEN "R",#2,"STUDENT2"
35 FIELD #2, 2 AS S1$,20 AS S2$,10 AS S3$,20 AS S4$,15 AS S5$,2 AS S6$,
    5 AS S7$,2 AS S8$,24 AS S9$,1 AS XS$
40 DIM ST%(29),CR$(5),GR$(5)
45 P%=1: L%=66
50 FOR RC%=1 TO 100
55   GOSUB 1000
60   IF AX$="A" THEN GOSUB 500: GOSUB 4000: GOSUB 1500
65 NEXT RC%
70 CLOSE #1
75 CLOSE #2
80 CHAIN "TRANSACT"
81 REM - END PRODUCE COURSE REPORT --------------------
82 REM


500 REM ----- PRINT HEADING --------------------
505 REM        ASSUMES L% LESS THAN OR EQUAL TO 66
510 REM           P% IS GREATER THAN 0
515 REM        PROMISES P% IS INCREMENTED BY 1 AND L% EQUALS 5
520 REM
530 FOR L%=L% TO 66
535   LPRINT
540 NEXT L%
545 LPRINT SPACES$(25); "COURSE ENROLLMENT REPORT        PAGE";P%
550 LPRINT
555 P%=P%+1
560 L%=3
565 RETURN
566 REM - END PRINT HEADING --------------------
567 REM
```

The Get Course Record and Get Student Record modules are from the Update Student Data program built in Chapter 11.

```
1000 REM ----- GET COURSE RECORD --------------------
1005 REM        ASSUMES RECORD NUMBER - RC% BETWEEN 1 AND 100
1010 REM        PROMISES RN% COURSE DATA CC$, TE$, CM$, PR%, ST%(), XC$
1015 REM
1020 GET #1,RC%
1025 CC$=C1$
1030 TE$=C2$
1035 CM$=C3$
1040 PR%=CVI(C4$)
1045 FOR S%=0 TO 29
1050   ST%(S%)=CVI(MID$(C5$,S%*2+1,2))
1055 NEXT S%
1060 AX$=XC$
1065 RETURN
1066 REM - END GET COURSE RECORD --------------------
1067 REM


1500 REM ----- PRINT STUDENT LIST --------------------
1505 REM        ASSUMES STUDENT ARRAY, ST%()
1510 REM
1515 AC%=0
1520 SC%=0
1525 CA!=0
1530 FOR I%=0 TO 29
1535   ID%=ST%(I%)
1540   IF ID%<>0 THEN GOSUB 2000: GOSUB 2500
1545 NEXT I%
1550 GOSUB 3000
1555 RETURN
1556 REM - END PRINT STUDENT LIST --------------------
1557 REM


2000 REM ----- GET STUDENT RECORD --------------------
2005 REM        ASSUMES ID% TO BE BETWEEN 1 AND 200
2010 REM            STUDENT FILE IS OPEN
2015 REM        PROMISES NF$, NL$, RD$, CI$, ST$, ZP$, CL$, CR$(),
2020 REM         GR$(), AND AX$ FILLED WITH DATA FROM STUDENT RECORD ID%
2025 REM
2030 GET #2,ID%
2035 NL$=S2$
2040 NF$=S3$
2041 RD$=S4$
2042 CI$=S5$
2043 ST$=S6$
2044 ZP$=S7$
2045 CL$=S8$
2050 FOR C%=0 TO 5
2051   CR$(C%)=MID$(S9$,C%*4+1,3)
2055   GR$(C%)=MID$(S9$,C%*4+4,1)
2060 NEXT C%
2065 ZX$=XS$
2070 RETURN
2071 REM - END GET STUDENT RECORD --------------------
2072 REM
```

As you saw in the Produce Grade Analysis program in Chapter 8, the Student File can hold grades that should not be included in the grade average. The program must ignore the grades W and I because they are incomplete and therefore have no point value.

```
2500 REM ----- PRINT STUDENT DETAIL --------------------
2505 REM        ASSUMES VALID STUDENT DATA AND SC%,CA!,AC%
2510 REM        PROMISES PRINT STUDENT DETAIL AND UPDATE SC%,CA!,AC%
2515 REM
2520 SC% = SC% + 1
2525 FOR E%=0 TO 5
2530   IF CR$(E%)=CC$ THEN G$=GR$(E%)
2535 NEXT E%
2540 LPRINT "   " NF$ " " NL$ " " CL$ " " G$
2545 L%=L%+1
2550 IF G$ = "A" THEN CA! = CA! + 4.0: AC% = AC% + 1
2555 IF G$ = "B" THEN CA! = CA! + 3.0: AC% = AC% + 1
2560 IF G$ = "C" THEN CA! = CA! + 2.0: AC% = AC% + 1
2565 IF G$ = "D" THEN CA! = CA! + 1.0: AC% = AC% + 1
2570 IF G$ = "F" THEN CA! = CA! + 0.0: AC% = AC% + 1
2575 RETURN
2576 REM - END PRINT STUDENT DETAIL --------------------
2577 REM

3000 REM ----- PRINT COURSE TOTALS --------------------
3005 REM        ASSUMES AC%,SC%,CA!
3010 REM
3015 LPRINT
3020 LPRINT "TOTAL ENROLLMENT IS: " SC%
3025 IF AC% > 0 THEN CA! = CA! / AC%
3030 LPRINT "GRADE AVERAGE IS:" CA!
3035 L%=L%+3
3040 RETURN
3041 REM - END PRINT COURSE TOTALS --------------------
3042 REM

4000 REM ----- PRINT COURSE DESCRIPTION --------------------
4005 REM        ASSUMES VALID COURSE DATA
4010 REM
4115 LPRINT CC$ " TAUGHT BY " TE$ " PERIOD " PR% " IN CLASSROOM " CM$
4120 LPRINT
4125 L%=L%+2
4130 RETURN
4031 REM - END PRINT COURSE DESCRIPTION --------------------
4132 REM
```

The program accesses two related files and combines their data in one report. This program can be run with the test data defined in section 12A; it may be turned over to the counselor when it performs as outlined.

## EXERCISE XII

The theater needs a report that lists available seats for each performance. For each row, the report should print a line with an X showing seats sold and an O marking seats available. Under this seating chart, the president wants a list of patrons who have purchased tickets for the performance and their seat assignments. The report should also list the total number of sold seats.

1.    build a data flow diagram for the report function

2.    define all new data flows in your data dictionary

3.    compute an estimate of job size

4.    build at least four test cases to verify the program

5.    build a program outline for the function

6.    write the code to implement the function

# Appendix A
# Student Portfolio

This section constitutes a suggested outline of the portfolio you should develop to record your own work. Prepare a notebook with six tabbed sections. The portfolio should contain the latest versions of data flow diagrams, data dictionary, program outlines, and code. You should also keep the test cases developed for the programs, as well as a performance log of work done. The following pages contain a brief introduction to each of the six sections; use them as the cover page to each section.

The portfolio is your complete documentation for the system. The data flow diagrams and data dictionary help you understand and define functional requirements of the system. The program outline depicts program structure, and the code defines the rules governing system functions. These four elements form a complete system model. This model, your working document, will help you understand and maintain the software. The performance log helps you evaluate future projects and your own progress. The test data are saved for retesting after system changes have been made.

# DATA FLOW DIAGRAM

The following pages contain the system's data flow diagrams. Below is a review of the data flow diagram symbols.

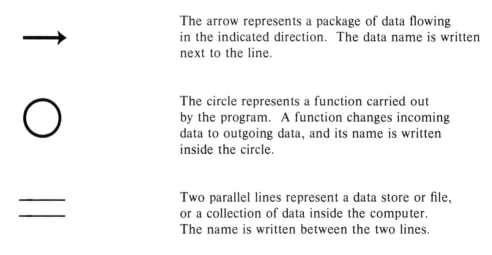

The arrow represents a package of data flowing in the indicated direction. The data name is written next to the line.

The circle represents a function carried out by the program. A function changes incoming data to outgoing data, and its name is written inside the circle.

Two parallel lines represent a data store or file, or a collection of data inside the computer. The name is written between the two lines.

# DATA DICTIONARY

The following pages contain the data dictionary, which records definitions for all data flowing through the system. Below is a summary of the data dictionary symbols.

| | |
|---|---|
| = | An equal sign means "is composed of." |
| + | A plus sign means "and." |
| [ ] | Square brackets mean "select one and only one of the enclosed items." |
| { } | Curly braces mean "iteration of." The enclosed data item is repeated a certain number of times (as in a list). If the data item must contain a minimum number of elements, you record this to the left of the braces. Maximums appear to the right of the braces. |
| ( ) | Parentheses mean "optional." The data item may or may not be present. |

# PROGRAM OUTLINE

The following pages contain the system's program outlines, whose symbols are summarized below.

A circle represents an activity to be carried out by the program.  Each activity is mapped into one or more modules of code, which performs the assigned activity.

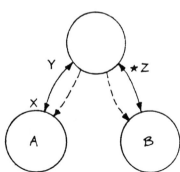

A dotted arrow between activities represents a procedure call, and identifies who initiates which activity.  Activity A coordinates activities X and Y.

The solid arrows represent data that an activity uses and produces.  Activity A assumes data X is ready for processing and promises to produce data Y.  Activity B assumes data Z is ready for processing and promises to update Z.

# PROGRAM CODE

The following pages contain the system's program code, which is based on the program outline in the previous section. The code carries out the functions defined by the data flow diagrams.

# PERFORMANCE LOG

The performance log records your progress by noting token counts — size estimates — and the time needed to build the program. With these data, you can estimate the time required to build software for new functions.

**Guidelines for computing token counts**

1.  the initial token count equals the number of data flows around the function

2.  for each data flow: if the data dictionary definition contains sets of braces, { }, and the function refers to the enclosed data, add one to the token count

3.  for each data flow: if the data dictionary definition contains sets of brackets, [ ], and the function refers to the enclosed data, add one to the token count

4.  identify any new data items on outgoing data flows:

    a.  exclude data items that are built directly (one for one) from an incoming data flow

    b.  if the new outgoing data item belongs to a set of similar data items (e.g., counts, totals) which is updated by an incoming data flow, add one to the token count for the entire set

    c.  if the new outgoing data item belongs to a set of similar data items which has only one element updated by an incoming data flow, add one to the token count for the entire set

---

## PERFORMANCE LOG

| Function | Token Count | Estimate | Actual Time | Rate Token/Time |
|---|---|---|---|---|
|  |  |  |  |  |

---

# TEST CASE LOG

The following pages contain the test cases developed during the modeling of a function. The test cases define the test data given to a program and the expected result. If the entered test case results differ, an error exists in the program.

The test case log is maintained to retest programs when changes are made.

---

### TEST CASE LOG

Test Case                          Result

---

# BASIC Language Constructs

While the BASIC language has many commands that together form millions of combinations, few of these combinations are necessary for most applications. Think of these constructs as building blocks. The following pages contain a list of constructs used in the text.

### Defining a module

Each activity on the program outline is mapped into one or more modules of code. A module is a group of statements with an identifier by which it can be invoked. In BASIC, the identifier is the line number of the module's first statement. Line numbers are assigned to each module and recorded on the program outline.

Modules are invoked by a GOSUB statement.

    GOSUB line-number

The module identified by the line number is initiated when the computer executes a GOSUB. When the computer finds a RETURN statement, the program returns to the statement following the original GOSUB.

    25 GOSUB 100
    30 PRINT X%

    100 INPUT X%
    105 X% = X% * 2
    110 RETURN

In the above example, the computer invokes the module at line number 100; that module gets an integer from the user, multiplies the number by 2, and returns to the statement following the GOSUB (30 PRINT X%).

### Two-way decision

You build an IF statement when the program must decide between two actions.

    605 IF S1$ = "YES" THEN PRINT "OK!" ELSE PRINT "SORRY"

If the condition, placed after IF, is true, the statement following THEN is executed. If the condition is false, the statement following ELSE is executed. If you want to perform more than one statement, treat the whole true or false branch as a module. Assign a starting line number and invoke the statements with a GOSUB statement.

```
605 IF S1$="YES" THEN GOSUB 690 ELSE PRINT "SORRY"

690 PRINT "OK!"
692 INPUT "ENTER NEXT ANSWER";S1$
694 RETURN
```

Your BASIC language reference manual will have more specific information about the IF statement.

**Many-way decision**

If you must choose among more than two actions, the many-way decision can be implemented using a series of IF statements.

```
100 IF UC$="THIS" THEN GOSUB 200
105 IF UC$="THAT" THEN GOSUB 250
110 IF UC$="THE" THEN GOSUB 300
115 IF UC$="OTHER" THEN GOSUB 350
```

Each IF statement tests the condition for a different value. The action to be taken is placed into its own module and invoked with a GOSUB command. Only one module is invoked, provided UC$ is not changed by modules 200, 250, 300, or 350.

**General loop construct**

Use the WHILE/WEND construct when you want the program to repeat an action.

```
115 A%=0
120 X1%=1
125 WHILE X1%=1
130 INPUT "ENTER NUMBER ";N%
135 IF N%=666 THEN X1%=0 ELSE A%=A%+N%
140 WEND
```

You first set an exit condition. In the example, the exit condition is the $X1\%=1$ following the WHILE. The condition must be true for you to go through the loop. This is done by setting X1% to 1 in line 120. The condition is checked when the WHILE statement is executed; if it is true, the body of the loop is executed. The condition is checked again after going through the loop. If it is still true, the loop is executed again.

The loop eventually must reach the objective. At this point, the exit condition is made false. In the example, when the user enters the number 666 the loop ends by setting X1% to 0. If the number is not 666, it is added to A% and the loop continues.

You should consider carefully three important steps when constructing a general loop: the beginning, bottom, and end of the loop. Make sure that you know what is happening at each point.

In the above example, A% equals 0 at the beginning of the loop and X1% equals 1 (meaning the loop is executed). At the bottom of the loop will be one of two situations. Either N% will equal 666 and X1%, 0 (meaning the loop ends), or N% will have been added to A% and X1% will still equal 1 (meaning you loop once more). After statement 140, X1% equals 0 and A% contains the sum of zero or more numbers. By checking these three points, you help ensure that the loop performs correctly.

Your language reference manual will have more information on loops under the heading WHILE.

### Alternative general loop construct

Some BASIC interpreters do not have the WHILE/WEND command. If you use such an interpreter, you must use an IF/GOTO combination to build the loop construct. The previous example appears below with an IF/GOTO construct:

```
115 A%=0
120 REM BEGINNING OF LOOP
125 INPUT "ENTER NUMBER ";N%
130 IF N%<>666 THEN A%=A%+N%
135 IF N%=666 THEN GOTO 120
140 REM END OF LOOP
```

The loop is built in the same way, checking its beginning, bottom, and end. The code will be better understood if you include remarks identifying the beginning and end of the loop.

### Counting loop construct

Establish a counting loop if the program is carrying out an action a set number of times.

```
250 FOR X1%=0 TO 5
255 PRINT AR%(X1%)
260 NEXT X1%
```

The loop sets an integer to a starting value; in the example, X1% is set to 0. If the integer is under the maximum (5 in the example), the body of the loop is executed. The statement NEXT X1% marks the end of the loop; the integer is increased by 1 and the program returns to the top of the loop. If the integer is still less than the maximum, the body of the loop is executed again. In the example, the loop is executed six times.

For more detailed information, look up the FOR statement in your BASIC language reference manual.

## Data types

There are four types of data in BASIC:

- Integer: a variable that contains any whole number between -32768 and 32767; integers are declared by placing a percent sign after the data name (e.g., N1%)

- Single Precision: a variable that contains any real number with up to 7 digits; a piece of data can be declared single precision by placing an exclamation mark after the name (e.g., N2!)

- Double Precision: a variable that contains real numbers of up to 16 digits; a double precision data item is declared by placing a number sign after the name (e.g., N3#)

- String: a variable that contains up to 255 characters; data names that contain strings are identified by a dollar sign after the name (e.g., N4$)

## Declaring arrays

You can store lists of numbers or strings in an array, a series of elements that is given one data name. Each element is referred to by the data name followed by a subscript.

Before using an array, you must tell the computer the maximum size of the list by declaring the array in a dimension statement. All arrays used in a program must be declared in a DIM statement at the beginning of the program.

For example:

```
10 DIM AR%(5), ST$(9)
```

This statement sets up an array of six integers and another of ten strings. Remember that BASIC begins with 0 when numbering arrays. The first element of the integer array can be addressed by AR%(0), the sixth element by AR%(5). If the subscript is given a name, the value of the data element can be used to address the array.

For example:

```
120 FOR C%=0 TO 9
125 PRINT ST$(C%)
130 NEXT C%
```

The above example displays all ten elements of the array ST$. C% equals 0 the first time through the counting loop and ST$(0) is displayed. The last time through, C% equals 9 and the tenth element is displayed.

Refer to the DIM statement in your language reference manual.

### Declaring random files

When a program uses a random file, it must execute an OPEN statement and FIELD statement. These commands define the file for the computer.

```
10 OPEN "R",#1,"STUDENT"
15 FIELD #1,2 AS F1$,20 AS F2$,10 AS F3$
```

The OPEN statement tells the computer that it is dealing with random file *R*. An assigned number identifies the file during the program's execution. The file is referred to as #1 in the example. The literal at the end of the OPEN statement is the file's name.

Line 15 defines a special area called a *buffer*. Each file has a buffer that acts as a staging area for data entering or leaving the file. The first two characters of the buffer are called F1$, the next twenty are called F2$, and the last ten, F3$.

The program must put data into the file's buffer before storing them on the STUDENT file. The command to move data into a file buffer is LSET.

```
500 LSET F1$=MKI$(15)
505 LSET F2$="LAST NAME"
510 LSET F3$="FIRST"
515 PUT #1,7
```

The file buffer can hold only strings. Before an integer is stored on a file, it must be converted into a string and then placed into the buffer. Line 500 converts the integer 15 to a string, which is placed in field F1$. The literal LAST NAME is placed in field F2$; the literal FIRST is placed in field F3$. After the data have been placed in the buffer, the PUT statement stores the data on the seventh record of file #1.

Before using data stored on the STUDENT file, the program must GET the record and move the data out of the buffer.

```
800 GET #1,7
805 S%=CVI(F1$)
810 L$=F2$
815 F$F3$
```

Line 800 brings the data stored on the seventh record of file #1 into the buffer. In BASIC, the data must be moved from the file buffer before any changes can be made. The command CVI(F1$) converts the string F1$ into an integer data item. The values stored in F2$ and F3$ are placed, respectively, in the data items L$ and F$.

Your language reference manual contains additional information on the LSET, CVI, and MKI commands.

# *Appendix C*
# Modeling and Coding Answers

## EXERCISE II

The data flow diagram model should show two data items, Number Of Regulars and Number of Specials, flowing into the function. The outgoing data flow, Ticket Totals, should contain the three totals.

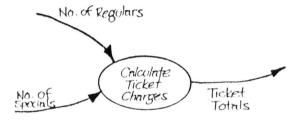

**Figure II.1. Data flow diagram for Calculate Ticket Charges.**

The data dictionary must contain definitions of data flows. The two incoming data flows are elementary items — i.e., without component parts — and need only their meaning recorded. The outgoing data flow, however, does have component parts. Ticket Totals is made up of Regular Total, Special Total, and Grand Total.

---

### DATA DICTIONARY

Number Of Regulars = an integer with a value of 0 or more

Number Of Specials = an integer with a value of 0 or more

Ticket Totals = Regular Total + Special Total + Grand Total

---

You can estimate size by counting the individual data flows around the function: two incoming and one outgoing. Since the data dictionary has no braces, the token count is three.

## PERFORMANCE LOG

| Function | Token Count | Estimate | Actual Time | Rate Token/Time |
|---|---|---|---|---|
| 1 | 3 | | | |

When building test cases, try to be as devious as possible. The data dictionary states that Number Of Regulars can equal 0. A test case with Number Of Regulars and Number Of Specials equal to 0 should produce a Grand Total of $0.

In another test case, make Number Of Regulars equal to something other than a number. An error message should result. Try a similar test on Number Of Specials.

A fourth test case can be more typical. Three regular and two special tickets should produce a grand total of $21.

## TEST CASE LOG

| Test Case | | Result | | |
|---|---|---|---|---|
| # Of Reg. | # Of Spec. | R Total | S Total | Grand |
| 0 | 0 | $0 | $0 | $0 |
| A | 2 | Error message | | |
| 1 | C | Error message | | |
| 3 | 2 | $15 | $6 | $21 |

The activities needed to perform the function are shown on the program outline. The program must get regular and special ticket quantities from the user. Once the number of tickets is known, the totals are calculated and displayed to the user.

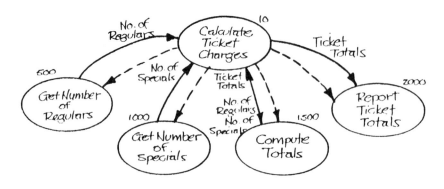

**Figure II.2. Program outline for Calculate Ticket Charges.**

Code can be written once the program outline is completed. You build one block of code for each activity declared on the program outline. Notice that starting line numbers have been added to each module.

Because BASIC allows only short, nondescriptive data names, you should record the BASIC data names in the data dictionary.

---

### DATA DICTIONARY

Number Of Regulars = an integer with a value of 0 or more
   R%

Number Of Specials = an integer with a value of 0 or more
   S%

Ticket Totals = Regular Total + Special Total + Grand Total
   RT!    ST!    GT!

---

Since the top module coordinates the lower-level activities, its code should look like this:

```
10 REM ----- CALCULATE TICKET CHARGES -------------------
11 REM
100 GOSUB 500
105 GOSUB 1000
110 GOSUB 1500
115 GOSUB 2000
120 END
121 REM - END CALCULATE TICKET CHARGES -------------------
122 REM
```

This program has no arrays, so you do not have to build a DIM statement as in the Compute GPA example in Chapter 2.

Get Number Of Regulars and Get Number Of Specials receive and check input from the user. The INPUT statement in BASIC has a built-in check; if it specifies a numeric data item and the user does not enter a number, an error message is generated.

```
500 REM ----- GET NUMBER OF REGULARS -------------------
505 REM      PROMISES R% CONTAINING THE NUMBER OF REGULAR TICKETS
510 REM
515 INPUT "HOW MANY REGULAR TICKETS";R%
520 RETURN
521 REM - END GET NUMBER OF REGULARS -------------------
522 REM

1000 REM ----- GET NUMBER OF SPECIALS -------------------
1005 REM      PROMISES S% CONTAINING THE NUMBER OF SPECIALS
1010 REM
1015 INPUT "HOW MANY SPECIAL TICKETS";S%
1020 RETURN
1021 REM - END GET NUMBER OF SPECIALS -------------------
1022 REM
```

If you check the user's input for a negative number, the modules must include a general loop construct, causing the program to loop until the user enters a positive number.

```
500 REM ----- GET NUMBER OF REGULARS --------------------
505 REM       PROMISES R% CONTAINING THE NUMBER OF REGULAR
510 REM
515 X1% = 1
520 WHILE X1% = 1
525   INPUT "HOW MANY REGULAR TICKETS";R%
530   IF R% < 0 THEN PRINT "MUST BE POSITIVE" ELSE X1% = 0
535 WEND
540 RETURN
541 REM - END GET NUMBER OF REGULARS -------------------
542 REM


1000 REM ----- GET NUMBER OF SPECIALS ------------------
1005 REM       PROMISES S% CONTAINING THE NUMBER OF SPECIALS
1010 REM
1015 X1% = 1
1020 WHILE X1% = 1
1025   INPUT "HOW MANY SPECIAL TICKETS";S%
1030   IF S% < 0 THEN PRINT "MUST BE POSITIVE" ELSE X1% = 0
1035 WEND
1040 RETURN
1041 REM - END GET NUMBER OF SPECIALS -------------------
1042 REM
```

Once the numbers have been entered, the next module — i.e., the module starting at line 1500 — can calculate totals.

```
1500 REM ----- COMPUTE TOTALS --------------------
1505 REM       ASSUMES R% IS NUMBER OF REGULARS AND S% IS NUMBER OF SPECIALS
1510 REM       PROMISES RT! CONTAINING REGULAR TOTAL
1515 REM             ST! CONTAINING SPECIAL TOTAL
1520 REM             GT! CONTAINING GRAND TOTAL
1525 REM
1530 RT! = R% * 5.00
1535 ST! = S% * 3.00
1540 GT! = RT! + ST!
1545 RETURN
1546 REM - END COMPUTE TOTALS -------------------
1547 REM
```

The last module reports the totals to the user. You use the PRINT statement at this point to display a message explaining the numbers to the user.

```
2000 REM ----- REPORT TICKET TOTALS --------------------
2005 REM       ASSUMES TICKET TOTALS (REG, SPEC, AND GRAND)
2010 REM
2015 PRINT "REGULAR TICKET TOTAL =",RT!
2020 PRINT "SPECIAL TICKET TOTAL =",ST!
2025 PRINT "THE GRAND TOTAL     =",GT!
2030 RETURN
2031 REM - END REPORT TICKET TOTALS -------------------
2032 REM
```

Run the program with the test data you prepared earlier. If the tests work as anticipated, you can be reasonably certain that the program is built correctly. You will see some differences between your solution and the answer shown above. However, as long as your code carries out the activities shown on the program outline, you have successfully completed the exercise.

Record in your performance log the time it took to complete the exercise.

# EXERCISE III

Your data flow diagram should show the Envelope Number flowing into the function. The Sales Record flows in from the file; after its data are displayed, the user enters new data and the (Updated) Sales Record is stored back on the file.

Notice a data flow in Figure III.1 labeled Total Price. The user can enter the total price along with the other data, but here, as in the Calculate Ticket Charge program, the computer calculates the total and reports it back to the user.

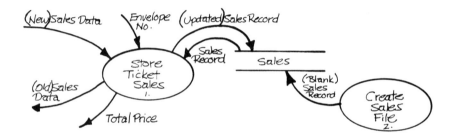

**Figure III.1. Data flow diagram for Sales File update functions.**

According to the data dictionary, a sales record contains the envelope number, the patron's name, number of regular tickets, number of special tickets, total price, and a list of one to ten seats. While the ticket seller says that seven is the largest number sold, allowing for ten seats makes the program more flexible.

Total Price is not included in the definition of Sales Data. Since the program computes this number, the user does not need to enter it.

---

## DATA DICTIONARY

Chair = Integer between 1 and 20

Envelope Number = Integer between 1 and 200

First Name = Up to 10 characters

Last Name = Up to 20 characters

Number Of Regulars = Integer

Number Of Specials = Integer

Patron Name = Last Name + First Name

Row = Letter between A and T

Sales Data = Patron Name + Number Of Regulars
  + Number Of Specials + 1 {Seat}10

Sales File = {Sale Record}200

Sales Record = Envelope Number + Patron Name + Number Of Regulars
  + Number Of Specials + Total Price + 10 {Seat}10

Seat = Row + Chair

Total Price = Dollar value

---

The initial token count for Store Ticket Sales is six tokens, one for each data flow. New Sales Data and Old Sales Data repeat data items that the function manipulates; add two to the token count for a total of eight tokens.

The program should reject as erroneous any seat in a row not between A and T, a chair of 0 or 21, and an envelope number of 0 or 201. The program should also report a last name larger than 20 characters, a first name larger than 10, and more than 10 seats. Rows equal to A and T, chairs of 1 and 20, and envelope numbers of 1 and 200 are acceptable.

You should build test cases to verify that correct data, defined in the data dictionary, are handled properly and incorrect data are reported as errors.

---

### PERFORMANCE LOG

| Function | Token Count | Estimate | Actual Time | Rate Token/Time |
|---|---|---|---|---|
| 1 | 8 | | | |
| 2 | 1 | | | |
| TOTAL | 9 | | | |

TEST CASE LOG

| Test Case | | | | | | | Result |
|---|---|---|---|---|---|---|---|
| | Characters | | | | | | |
| Envelope No. | Last | First | Reg. | Spec. | Row | Chair | |
| 0 | | | | | | | Error message |
| 201 | | | | | | | Error message |
| | 21 | | | | | | Error message |
| | | 21 | | | | | Error message |
| | | | | X | | | Error message |
| | | | | | 0 | | Error message |
| | | | | | 21 | | Error message |
| 1 | Smith | Mary | 0 | 0 | A | 1 | Update 1:   Price = $0 |
| 200 | Jones | John | 1 | 1 | T | 20 | Update 200: Price = $8 |

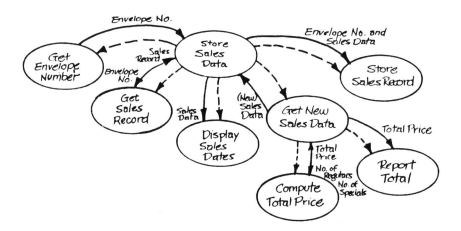

**Figure III.2. Program outline for Store Sales Data.**

The Compute Total Price and Report Total activities are placed under Get New Sales Data because they require Sales Data entered by the user.

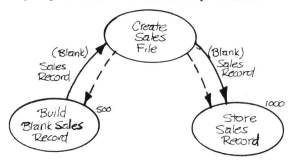

**Figure III.3. Program outline for Create Sales File.**

The data dictionary should be updated with data names used in the BASIC program.

---

## DATA DICTIONARY

Chair = Integer between 1 and 20

Envelope Number = Integer between 1 and 200
      F1$ or EV%

First Name = Up to 10 characters
      F3$ or NF$

Last Name = Up to 20 characters
      F2$ or NL$

Number Of Regulars = Integer
      F4$ or R%

Number Of Specials = Integer
      F5$ or S%

Patron Name = Last Name + First Name

Row = Letter between A and T

Sales Data = Patron Name + Number Of Regulars + Number Of Specials
      + 1 {Seat} 10

Sales File = {Sales Record} 200
      SALES

Sales Record = Envelope Number + Patron Name + Number Of Regulars
      + Number Of Specials + Total Price + 1 {Seat} 10 + Status
      F7$ or SE$()

Seat = Row + Chair
      S$

Total Price = Dollar value
      F6$ or GT!

Status = [ A | X ]
      F7$ or AX$

---

```
10 REM ----- CREATE SALES FILE -------------------
11 REM
15 OPEN "R",#1,"SALES"
20 FIELD #1,2 AS F1$,20 AS F2$,10 AS F3$,2 AS F4$,2 AS F5$,
   4 AS F6$,30 AS F7$,1 AS FX$
25 GOSUB 500
30 GOSUB 1000
35 CLOSE #1
40 END
41 REM - END CREATE SALES FILE -------------------
42 REM
```

```
500 REM ----- BUILD BLANK SALES RECORD -------------------
505 REM        PROMISES INITIALIZED RECORD
510 REM
515 LSET F1$=MKI$(0)
520 LSET F2$=STRING$(20,32)
525 LSET F3$=STRING$(10,32)
530 LSET F4$=MKI$(0)
535 LSET F5$=MKI$(0)
540 LSET F6$=MKS$(0)
545 LSET F7$=STRING$(30,32)
550 LSET FX$="X"
555 RETURN
556 REM - END BUILD BLANK SALES RECORD -------------------
557 REM

1000 REM ----- STORE SALES RECORD -------------------
1005 REM        PROMISES TO STORE 200 INITIAL RECORDS
1010 REM
1015 FOR C%=1 TO 200
1020   PUT #1,C%
1025 NEXT C%
1030 RETURN
1031 REM - END STORE SALES RECORD -------------------
1032 REM
```

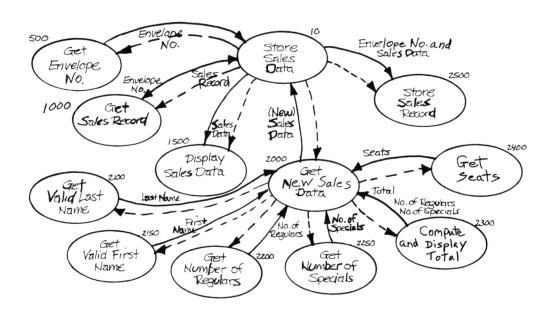

**Figure III.4. Factored program outline for Store Sales Data.**

As you start to build code, you will notice that the module performs numerous tasks. As demonstrated in Chapter 3, a more complex module requires a more detailed program outline. The module, such as Get New Sales Data, should be factored so that each piece of data is handled in its own module, making the coding easier to write and correct.

The top module declares the Sales File and steps through the activities shown on the program outline. Check that the FIELD statement in this program is identical to the FIELD in the Create Sales File program. If they differ, the program's record format will also differ from the original.

```
10 REM ----- STORE SALES DATA -------------------
11 REM
15 OPEN "R",#1,"SALES"
20 FIELD #1,2 AS F1$,20 AS F2$,10 AS F3$,2 AS F4$,2 AS F5$,4 AS F6$,30 AS F7$,1 AS FX$
25 DIM SE$(9)
30 GOSUB 500
35 GOSUB 1000
40 GOSUB 1500
45 GOSUB 2000
50 GOSUB 2500
55 CLOSE #1
60 END
61 REM - END STORE SALES DATA -------------------
62 REM


500 REM ----- GET ENVELOPE NUMBER -------------------
505 REM       PROMISES ENVELOPE NUMBER BETWEEN 1 AND 200
510 REM
515 E%=1
520 WHILE E%=1
525   INPUT "ENTER ENVELOPE NUMBER";EV%
530   IF (EV%<1) OR (EV%>200) THEN PRINT "BETWEEN 1 AND 200" ELSE E%=0
535 WEND
540 RETURN
541 REM - END GET ENVELOPE NUMBER -------------------
542 REM


1000 REM ----- GET SALES RECORD -------------------
1005 REM       ASSUMES EV% TO BE BETWEEN 1 AND 200
1010 REM             SALES FILE IS OPEN
1015 REM       PROMISES NL$,NF$,R%,S%,GT!,SE$(),AX$ FILLED WITH DATA FROM
1020 REM             SALES RECORD EV%
1025 REM
1030 GET #1, EV%
1035 NL$=F2$
1040 NF$=F3$
1045 R%=CVI(F4$)
1050 S%=CVI(F5$)
1055 GT!=CVS(F6$)
1060 FOR C%=0 TO 9
1065   SE$(C%)=MID$(F7$,C%*3+1,3)
1070 NEXT C%
1075 AX$=FX$
1080 RETURN
1081 REM - END GET SALES RECORD -------------------
1082 REM


1500 REM ----- DISPLAY SALES DATA -------------------
1505 REM       ASSUMES SALES DATA EV%,NL$,NF$,R%,S%,GT!,SE()
1510 REM
1515 PRINT "DATA FOR SALES ENVELOPE ";EV%
```

```
1520 PRINT "LAST NAME   ",NL$
1525 PRINT "FIRST NAME  ",NF$
1530 PRINT "# OF REGULAR",R%
1535 PRINT "# OF SPECIAL",S%
1540 PRINT "TOTAL PRICE ",GT!
1545 PRINT "SEATS       ",
1550 FOR C%=0 TO 9
1555   IF SE$(C%)<>"   " THEN PRINT SE$(C%);" ";
1560 NEXT C%
1565 PRINT
1570 PRINT "STATUS      ",AX$
1575 PRINT
1580 PRINT "----------------------------------"
1585 RETURN
1586 REM - END DISPLAY SALES DATA -------------------
1587 REM
```

The Get New Sales Data module must check each piece of sales data from the user. If the data are invalid, the module reports the error and repeats the process. Each piece of data should have a block of code.

```
2000 REM ----- GET NEW SALES DATA -------------------
2005 REM       PROMISES VALID VALUES IN SALES DATA
2010 REM
2015 GOSUB 2100
2020 GOSUB 2150
2025 X%=0
2030 WHILE X%=0
2035   GOSUB 2200
2040   GOSUB 2250
2045   IF R%+S%>10 THEN PRINT "NO MORE THAN 10 TICKETS" ELSE X%=1
2050 WEND
2055 GOSUB 2300
2060 GOSUB 2400
2065 RETURN
2066 REM - END GET NEW SALES DATA -------------------
2067 REM
```

Since ten is the maximum number of seats one record can hold, the program continues to loop if the total number of tickets sold — all regular and special tickets — exceeds ten.

```
2100 REM ----- GET A VALID LAST NAME(NL$) -------------------
2105 REM
2110 E%=1
2115 WHILE E%=1
2120   INPUT "ENTER LAST NAME ",NL$
2125   IF LEN(NL$)>20 THEN PRINT "ONLY 20 CHARACTERS" ELSE E%=0
2130 WEND
2135 RETURN
2136 REM - END GET A VALID LAST NAME -------------------
2137 REM

2150 REM ----- GET A VALID FIRST NAME(NF$) -------------------
2155 REM
2160 E%=1
2165 WHILE E%=1
2170   INPUT "ENTER FIRST NAME ",NF$
```

```
2175   IF LEN(NF$)>10 THEN PRINT "ONLY 10 CHARACTERS" ELSE E%=0
2180 WEND
2185 RETURN
2186 REM - END GET A VALID FIRST NAME --------------------
2187 REM

2200 REM ----- GET NUMBER OF REGULAR TICKETS --------------------
2205 REM
2210 E%=1
2215 WHILE E%=1
2220   INPUT "HOW MANY REGULAR TICKETS";R%
2225   IF R%<0 THEN PRINT "MUST BE POSITIVE" ELSE E%=0
2230 WEND
2235 RETURN
2236 REM - END GET NUMBER OF REGULAR TICKETS --------------------
2237 REM

2250 REM ----- GET NUMBER OF SPECIAL TICKETS --------------------
2255 REM
2260 E%=1
2265 WHILE E%=1
2270   INPUT "HOW MANY SPECIAL TICKETS";S%
2275   IF S%<0 THEN PRINT "MUST BE POSITIVE" ELSE E%=0
2280 WEND
2285 RETURN
2286 REM - END GET NUMBER OF SPECIAL TICKETS --------------------
2287 REM

2300 REM ----- COMPUTE GRAND TOTAL --------------------
2305 REM
2310 GT!=(R% * 5.00) + (S% * 3.00)
2315 PRINT "THE TOTAL PRICE =",GT!
2320 RETURN
2321 REM - END COMPUTE GRAND TOTAL --------------------
2322 REM
```

Get Seats edits the seat numbers as they are entered, which means checking that the first character is between A and T and the last two between 1 and 20.

A counting loop requiring the user to enter all ten seats, regardless of the number sold, would create blank seats. In the code below, the regular and special ticket quantites are used to compute the number of seats the user must enter.

```
2400 REM ----- GET SEATS --------------------
2405 REM
2410 FOR C%=0 TO 9
2415   SE$(C%)="  "
2420 NEXT C%
2425 PRINT "ENTER "; R%+S%; " SEATS.  PRESS <ENTER> AFTER EACH."
2430 FOR C%=0 TO R%+S%-1
2435   GOSUB 2450: SE$(C%)=S$
2440 NEXT C%
2445 RETURN
2447 REM
2450 E%=1
2455 WHILE E%=1
2460   INPUT "ENTER 3-CHARACTER SEAT NUMBER ";S$
```

```
2465  E%=0
2470  IF LEN(S$)<>3 THEN S$="   "
2475  IF (MID$(S$,1,1)<"A") OR (MID$(S$,1,1)>"T") THEN E%=1
2480  IF (MID$(S$,2,2)<"01") OR (MID$(S$,2,2)>"20") THEN E%=1
2485  IF E%=1 THEN PRINT "UNRECOGNIZED SEAT CODE"
2490 WEND
2495 RETURN
2496 REM - END GET SEATS ------------------
2497 REM
```

Even though the number varies among records, you know from the number of regular and special tickets how many seats the user will enter. You loop R% + S% times instead of ten.

```
2500 REM ----- STORE SALES RECORD -------------------
2505 REM       ASSUMES VALID SALES DATA, EV% BETWEEN 1 AND 200,
2510 REM               SALES FILE OPEN
2515 REM
2520 LSET F1$=MKI$(EV%)
2525 LSET F2$=NL$
2530 LSET F3$=NF$
2535 LSET F4$=MKI$(R%)
2540 LSET F5$=MKI$(S%)
2545 LSET F6$=MKS$(GT!)
2550 S$=""
2555 FOR C%=0 TO 9
2560   S$=S$+SE$(C%)
2565 NEXT C%
2570 LSET F7$=S$
2575 LSET FX$="A"
2580 PUT #1,EV%
2585 RETURN
2586 REM - END STORE SALES RECORD -------------------
2587 REM
```

Review any differences in coding answers. Your measure of success is not how closely your code matches the above, but how accurately it performs the functions declared in the data flow diagram and structured in the program outline.

Use the test cases you built to verify the code. The program should be run twice, once for a test case and again for the envelope number, to verify that the data are stored correctly. An unexpected occurrence indicates a program error. Review the program outline for the activity that should have caught the error, and correct that activity's code.

Record in the performance log the time spent on this exercise and compute a rate by dividing the token count by the time needed to complete the program. This information facilitates other job estimates.

# EXERCISE IV

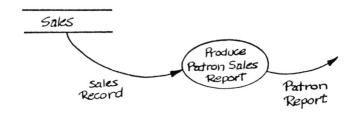

**Figure IV.1. Data flow diagram for Produce Patron Sales Report.**

The only new definition added to the data dictionary is Patron Report.

---

## DATA DICTIONARY

Chair = Integer between 1 and 20

Detail Line = Patron Name + Number Of Regulars + Number Of Specials
+ 1 {Seat} 10 + Total Price

Envelope Number = Integer between 1 and 200

First Name = Up to 10 characters

Grand Total = Dollar amount

Last Name = Up to 20 characters

Number Of Regulars = Integer

Number Of Specials = Integer

Patron Name = Last Name + First Name

Patron Report = {Detail Line} + Total Line

Regulars Sold = Integer

Row = Letter between A and T

Sales File = {Sales Record} 200

Sales Record = Envelope Number + Patron Name + Number Of Regulars
+ Number Of Specials + Total Price + 10 {Seat} 10

Seat = Row + Chair

Specials Sold = Integer

Total Line = Regulars Sold + Specials Sold + Grand Total

Total Price = Dollar amount

---

A rough estimate of the project size can be made from the information recorded in the data dictionary. The initial token count is two. The definition of Patron Report contains two braces that work with that function, and a new set of data is on the outgoing data flow (Regulars Sold, Specials Sold, and Grand Total); this gives a total token count of five.

---

### PERFORMANCE LOG

| Function | Token Count | Estimate | Actual Time | Rate Token/Time |
|---|---|---|---|---|
| 1 | 5 | | | |

---

Based on this estimate, the time required to build this program should fall between the times for the Calculate Ticket Charges and Update Sales Data programs. The token count gives you a relative measure of size.

---

### TEST CASE LOG

| Test Case | | | | Result | | |
|---|---|---|---|---|---|---|
| Record | Reg. | Spec. | Price | Reg. Sold | Spec. Sold | Grand Total |
| No records on file | | | | 0 | 0 | $0 |
| Add records 1 and 200 | | | | | | |
| 1 | 2 | 0 | $10 | | | |
| 200 | 0 | 2 | $ 6 | 2 | 2 | $16 |
| Add records 2 and 199 | | | | | | |
| 2 | 1 | 1 | $ 8 | | | |
| 199 | 1 | 1 | $ 8 | 4 | 4 | $32 |
| Add records 3 and 198 | | | | | | |
| 3 | 0 | 0 | $ 0 | | | |
| 198 | 10 | 0 | $50 | 14 | 4 | $82 |
| Add records 4 and 197 | | | | | | |
| 4 | 0 | 10 | $30 | | | |
| 197 | 5 | 5 | $40 | 19 | 19 | $152 |

You put test data on the Sales File to test the program, which should run with one file containing no active records and another with data in records 1 and 200. You also build a file with records that check the calculations for Specials Sold and Regulars Sold. You should specify the expected Grand Total in each case.

After you have written the program and run the tests, check that the patron's name is properly formated and that all seat numbers are listed.

Produce Patron Sales Report performs three basic activities: It gets the Patron Record from the Patron File, manipulates that piece of data by accumulating the total number of tickets sold and total price, and reports results by printing detail lines. You need two more activities, one to print report headings and another to print totals at the end of the report.

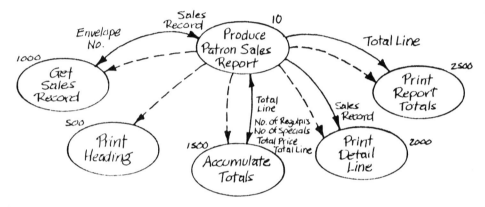

**Figure IV.2. Program outline for Produce Patron Sales Report.**

The data dictionary should be updated with the BASIC data names you have assigned.

---

## DATA DICTIONARY

Chair = Integer between 1 and 20

Detail Line = Patron Name + Number Of Regulars + Number Of Specials
        + 1 {Seat}10 + Total Price

Envelope Number = Integer between 1 and 200
        F1$ or EV%

First Name = Up to 10 characters
        F3$ or NF$

Grand Total = Dollar amount
        TS!

Last Name = Up to 20 characters
        F2$ or NL$

Number Of Regulars = Integer
      F4$ or R%

Number Of Specials = Integer
      F5$ or S%

Patron Name = Last Name + First Name

Patron Report = {Detail Line} + Total Line

Regulars Sold = Integer
      RC%

Row = Letter between A and T

Sales File = {Sales Record}200
      SALES

Sales Record = Envelope Number + Patron Name + Number Of Regulars
      + Number Of Specials + Total Price + 1{Seat}10
      F7$ or SE$()

Seat = Row + Chair

Specials Sold = Integer
      SC%

Total Line = Regulars Sold + Specials Sold + Grand Total

Total Price = Dollar amount
      F6$ or GT!

---

The top module declares the file and seat array.  After it zeros out the report totals and invokes Print Heading, the module looks at each record on the file.  If the
record is active, it invokes Accumulate Totals and Print Detail Line.  After all records
have been processed, the report totals are printed and the file closed.

```
10 REM ----- PRODUCE PATRON SALES REPORT --------------------
11 REM
15 OPEN "R",#1,"SALES"
20 FIELD #1,2 AS F1$,20 AS F2$,10 AS F3$,2 AS F4$,2 AS F5$,4 AS F6$
    ,30 AS F7$,1 AS FX$
25 DIM SE$(9)
30 RC%=0: SC%=0: TS!=0
35 GOSUB 500
40 FOR EV%=1 TO 200
45   GOSUB 1000
50   IF AX$="A" THEN GOSUB 1500: GOSUB 2000
55 NEXT EV%
60 GOSUB 2500
65 CLOSE #1
70 END
71 REM - END PRODUCE PATRON SALES REPORT --------------------
72 REM
```

```
500 REM ----- PRINT REPORT HEADING --------------------
505 REM
510 LPRINT SPACE$(25);"PATRON SALES REPORT"
515 LPRINT
520 LPRINT "  FIRST AND LAST NAME";
525 LPRINT SPACE$(13); "REG";
530 LPRINT "  SPEC";
535 LPRINT "  TOTAL"
540 LPRINT
545 RETURN
546 REM - END PRINT REPORT HEADING --------------------
547 REM
```

You copy Get Sales Record from the Store Sales Data program.

```
1000 REM ----- GET SALES RECORD --------------------
1005 REM        ASSUMES EV% TO BE BETWEEN 1 AND 200
1010 REM                 SALES FILE IS OPEN
1015 REM        PROMISES NL$,NF$,R%,S%,GT!,SE$(),AX$ FILLED WITH DATA FROM
1020 REM                 SALES RECORD EV%
1025 REM
1030 GET #1, EV%
1035 NL$=F2$
1040 NF$=F3$
1045 R%=CVI(F4$)
1050 S%=CVI(F5$)
1055 GT!=CVS(F6$)
1060 FOR C%=0 TO 9
1065   SE$(C%)=MID$(F7$,C%*3+1,3)
1070 NEXT C%
1075 AX$=FX$
1080 RETURN
1081 REM - END GET SALES RECORD --------------------
1082 REM


1500 REM ----- ACCUMULATE TOTALS --------------------
1505 REM        ASSUMES R%, S%, AND GT!
1510 REM        PROMISES TO UPDATE RC%, SC%, AND TS!
1515 REM
1520 TS!=TS!+GT!
1525 RC%=RC%+R%
1530 SC%=SC%+S%
1535 RETURN
1536 REM - END ACCUMULATE TOTALS --------------------
1537 REM

2000 REM ----- PRINT DETAIL LINE --------------------
2005 REM         ASSUMES SALES RECORD DATA
2010 REM
2015 LPRINT NF$; " "; NL$;
2020 LPRINT USING "######"; R%;
2025 LPRINT USING "#####"; S%;
2030 LPRINT USING "$$###.##"; GT!
2035 LPRINT SPACE$(13); "SEATS: ";
2040 FOR C%=0 TO 9
2045   LPRINT SE$(C%); " ";
```

```
2050 NEXT C%
2055 LPRINT
2060 RETURN
2061 REM - END PRINT DETAIL LINE -------------------
2062 REM
```

Notice that the list of assigned seats is on a separate line. Line 2030 does not end with a semicolon, so BASIC skips to the next line after printing the Grand Total. If you have room on the page for a list of ten seats (three spaces each with a space between each), you can print the data on one line. If not, you need two lines for each record.

The report totals should align with the columns of the detail line. Also, the sales total should be directly under each sales record total.

```
2500 REM ----- PRINT REPORT TOTALS -------------------
2505 REM      ASSUMES RC%, SC%, TS!
2510 REM
2515 LPRINT
2520 LPRINT SPACE$(20); "TOTAL COUNTS";
2525 LPRINT USING "#####"; RC%; SC%
2530 LPRINT
2535 LPRINT SPACE$(29); "TOTAL SALES";
2540 LPRINT USING "$$####,.##"; TS!
2545 RETURN
2546 REM - END PRINT REPORT TOTALS -------------------
2547 REM
```

This program produces a Patron Sales Report similar to the following:

---

### PATRON SALES REPORT

| First and Last Name | Reg. | Spec. | Total |
|---|---|---|---|
| TIMOTHY LENAHAN | 2 | 0 | $10 |
| Seats:  A01 A02 | | | |
| SID ALLEN | 1 | 1 | $ 8 |
| Seats:  C13 C14 | | | |
| NED ROSS | 8 | 2 | $46 |
| Seats:  F11 F12 F13 F14 F15 F16 F17 F18 F19 F20 | | | |
| Total Counts | 11 | 3 | |
| Total Sales | | | $64 |

---

# EXERCISE V

The data flow diagram for Produce Patron Sales Report does not change. The diagram for Store Sales Data, however, does change by adding a data flow carrying the user's update command to the function; its name is changed to describe its function more accurately.

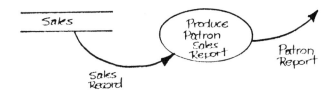

**Figure V.1. Data flow diagram for Produce Patron Sales Report.**

**Figure V.2. Data flow diagram for Update Ticket Sales.**

The data dictionary must be updated to reflect the changes in the Patron Report as well as the Update Command now going into Update Ticket Sales.

---

### DATA DICTIONARY

Patron Report = 1{Page} + Regulars Sold + Specials Sold
    + Grand Total

Page = Page Number + {Detail Line}25
        Sales Data = [ First Name | Last Name | Number Of Regulars |
        Number Of Specials | 1{Seat}10 ]

Update Command = [ 1 | 2 | 3 | 4 | 5 | END | DELETE ]

---

The number of detail lines on a page depends on the number of lines printed on that page. Line counts include the margins at the top and bottom of the page and the space needed to print the heading.

When computing an estimate, you count one token for each changed or new data flow and then add one for each changed or new set of braces or brackets. The token count for these changes is seven.

## PERFORMANCE LOG

| Function | Token Count | Estimate | Actual Time | Rate Token/Time |
|---|---|---|---|---|
| Report | 2 | | | |
| Update | 5 | | | |
| TOTAL | 7 | | | |

Tests that verify the new report structure should be built. You can use a file with 25 records followed by another with 26 to check whether a new page is started correctly.

The delete function should work for the first and last records on the file, and an error should print if the user enters an invalid update command.

## TEST CASE LOG

| Test Case | | Result |
|---|---|---|
| Delete ID Number | | |
| 1 | | Record 1 is blanked |
| 200 | | Record 200 is blanked |
| Update Command | Data | |
| 6 | | Error message |
| 0 | | Error message |
| 1 | John | Updates First Name |
| 2 | Smith | Updates Last Name |
| 3 | 2 | Updates Number Of Regulars |
| 4 | 0 | Updates Number Of Specials |
| 5 | A01 A02 | Updates Seats |
| END | | Stores data on file |

The program outline for Produce Patron Sales Report is updated to include the page number and line count. The Update Ticket Sales program outline has two new activities, one to get the update command and the other to blank the sales data.

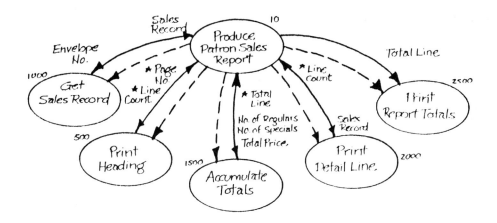

**Figure V.3. Program outline for Produce Patron Sales Report.**

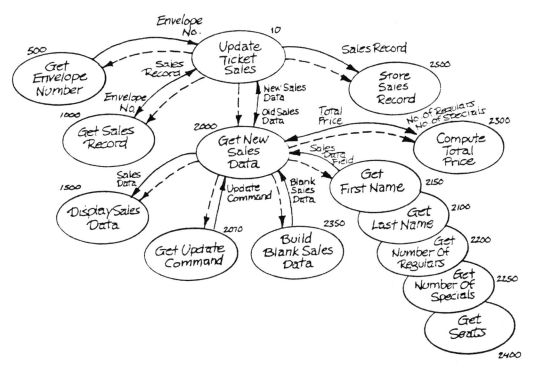

**Figure V.4. Program outline for Update Ticket Sales.**

---

## DATA DICTIONARY

Line Count  =  Integer between 1 and 66
          L%

Page Number  =  Integer greater than 0
          P%

---

```
10 REM ----- PRODUCE PATRON SALES REPORT -------------------
11 REM
15 OPEN "R",#1,"SALES"
20 FIELD #1,2 AS F1$,20 AS F2$,10 AS F3$,2 AS F4$,2 AS F5$,4 AS F6$,
    30 AS F7$,1 AS FX$
25 DIM SE$(9)
30 RC%=0: SC%=0: TS!=0
31 P%=1: L%=66
35 GOSUB 500
40 FOR EV%=1 TO 200
45   GOSUB 1000
50   IF AX$="A" THEN GOSUB 1500: GOSUB 2000
52   IF L%>54 THEN GOSUB 500
55 NEXT EV%
57 IF L%>50 THEN GOSUB 500
60 GOSUB 2500
65 CLOSE #1
70 END
71 REM - END PRODUCE PATRON SALES REPORT -------------------
72 REM


500 REM ----- PRINT REPORT HEADING -------------------
505 REM
506 FOR L%=L% TO 66
507   LPRINT
508 NEXT L%
510 LPRINT SPACE$(25);"PATRON SALES REPORT       PAGE ";P%
515 LPRINT
520 LPRINT " FIRST AND LAST NAME";
525 LPRINT SPACE$(13); "REG";
530 LPRINT " SPEC";
535 LPRINT " TOTAL"
540 LPRINT
542 P%=P%+1
544 L%=5
545 RETURN
546 REM - END PRINT REPORT HEADING -------------------
547 REM


1000 REM ----- GET SALES RECORD -------------------
1005 REM      ASSUMES EV% TO BE BETWEEN 1 AND 200
1010 REM           SALES FILE IS OPEN
1015 REM      PROMISES NL$,NF$,R%,S%,GT!,SE$(),AX$ FILLED WITH DATA FROM
1020 REM           SALES RECORD EV%
```

```
1025 REM
1030 GET #1, EV%
1035 NL$=F2$
1040 NF$=F3$
1045 R%=CVI(F4$)
1050 S%=CVI(F5$)
1055 GT!=CVS(F6$)
1060 FOR C%=0 TO 9
1065   SE$(C%)=MID$(F7$,C%*3+1,3)
1070 NEXT C%
1075 AX$=FX$
1080 RETURN
1081 REM - END GET SALES RECORD -------------------
1082 REM


1500 REM ----- ACCUMULATE TOTALS -------------------
1505 REM       ASSUMES R%, S%, AND GT!
1510 REM         PROMISES TO UPDATE RC%, SC%, AND TS!
1515 REM
1520 TS!=TS!+GT!
1525 RC%=RC%+R%
1530 SC%=SC%+S%
1535 RETURN
1536 REM - END ACCUMULATE TOTALS -------------------
1537 REM


2000 REM ----- PRINT DETAIL LINE -------------------
2005 REM         ASSUMES SALES RECORD DATA
2010 REM
2015 LPRINT NF$; " "; NL$;
2020 LPRINT USING "######"; R%;
2025 LPRINT USING "#####"; S%;
2030 LPRINT USING "$$###.##"; GT!
2035 LPRINT SPACE$(13); "SEATS: ";
2040 FOR C%=0 TO 9
2045   LPRINT SE$(C%); " ";
2050 NEXT C%
2055 LPRINT
2057 L%=L%+2
2060 RETURN
2061 REM - END PRINT DETAIL LINE -------------------
2062 REM


2500 REM ----- PRINT REPORT TOTALS -------------------
2505 REM       ASSUMES RC%, SC%, TS!
2510 REM
2515 LPRINT
2520 LPRINT SPACE$(20); "TOTAL COUNTS";
2525 LPRINT USING "#####"; RC%; SC%
2530 LPRINT
2535 LPRINT SPACE$(29); "TOTAL SALES";
2540 LPRINT USING "$$####,.##"; TS!
2545 RETURN
2546 REM - END PRINT REPORT TOTALS -------------------
2547 REM
```

---

## DATA DICTIONARY

Envelope Number = [ Integer between 1 and 200 | END ]
      EV$ / EV%

Update Command = [ 1 | 2 | 3 | 4 | 5 | END | DELETE ]
      UC$

---

```
10 REM ----- UPDATE TICKET SALES --------------------
11 REM
15 OPEN "R",#1,"SALES"
20 FIELD #1,2 AS F1$,20 AS F2$,10 AS F3$,2 AS F4$,2 AS F5$,4 AS F6$,
   30 AS F7$,1 AS FX$
25 DIM SE$(9)
30 GOSUB 500
32 WHILE EV$<>"END"
35   GOSUB 1000
40   GOSUB 2000
45   GOSUB 2500
47   GOSUB 500
48 WEND
50 CLOSE #1
55 END
56 REM - END UPDATE TICKET SALES --------------------
57 REM


500 REM ----- GET ENVELOPE NUMBER --------------------
505 REM       PROMISES ENVELOPE NUMBER BETWEEN 1 AND 200
510 REM
515 E%=1
520 WHILE E%=1
525   INPUT "ENTER ENVELOPE NUMBER OR 'END' ";EV$
527   IF EV$="END" THEN EV%=1 ELSE EV%=VAL(EV$)
530   IF (EV%<1) OR (EV%>200) THEN PRINT "BETWEEN 1 AND 200" ELSE E%=0
535 WEND
540 RETURN
541 REM - END GET ENVELOPE NUMBER --------------------
542 REM


1000 REM ----- GET SALES RECORD --------------------
1005 REM       ASSUMES EV% TO BE BETWEEN 1 AND 200
1010 REM            SALES FILE IS OPEN
1015 REM       PROMISES NL$,NF$,R%,S%,GT!,SE$(),AX$ FILLED WITH DATA FROM
1020 REM            SALES RECORD EV%
1025 REM
1030 GET #1, EV%
1035 NL$=F2$
1040 NF$=F3$
1045 R%=CVI(F4$)
1050 S%=CVI(F5$)
1055 GT!=CVS(F6$)
1060 FOR C%=0 TO 9
1065   SE$(C%)=MID$(F7$,C%*3+1,3)
1070 NEXT C%
1075 AX$=FX$
```

```
1080 RETURN
1081 REM - END GET SALES RECORD -------------------
1082 REM

1500 REM ----- DISPLAY SALES DATA -------------------
1505 REM        ASSUMES SALES DATA EV%,NL$,NF$,R%,S%,GT!,SE$(),AX$
1510 REM
1512 PRINT CHR$(26);
1515 PRINT "DATA FOR SALES ENVELOPE ";EV%
1520 PRINT "LAST NAME   ",NL$
1525 PRINT "FIRST NAME  ",NF$
1530 PRINT "# OF REGULAR",R%
1535 PRINT "# OF SPECIAL",S%
1540 PRINT "TOTAL PRICE ",GT!
1545 PRINT "SEATS      ",
1550 FOR C%=0 TO 9
1555   IF SE$(C%)<>"   " THEN PRINT SE$(C%);" ";
1560 NEXT C%
1565 PRINT
1570 PRINT "STATUS     ",AX$
1575 PRINT
1580 PRINT "----------------------------------"
1585 RETURN
1586 REM - END DISPLAY SALES DATA -------------------
1587 REM

2000 REM ----- GET NEW SALES DATA -------------------
2005 REM        ASSUMES VALID SALES DATA
2006 REM        PROMISES VALID VALUES IN SALES DATA
2007 REM
2008 UC$=""
2009 WHILE UC$<>"END"
2010   GOSUB 1500: GOSUB 2070
2015   IF UC$="1" THEN GOSUB 2150
2020   IF UC$="2" THEN GOSUB 2100
2030   IF UC$="3" THEN GOSUB 2200
2035   IF UC$="4" THEN GOSUB 2250
2040   IF UC$="5" THEN GOSUB 2400
2045   IF UC$="DELETE" THEN GOSUB 2350
2057 WEND
2058 GOSUB 2300
2060 RETURN
2061 REM - END GET NEW SALES DATA -------------------
2062 REM
```

Note that the Compute Total Price module is invoked after the user completes all updates to the record. Since the user changes the number of regulars and specials sold, the total price is computed when the user is satisfied that the data on the record are correct.

```
2070 REM ----- GET UPDATE COMMAND(UC$) -------------------
2072 REM
2073 E%=1
2074 WHILE E%=1
2076   PRINT "ENTER UPDATE COMMAND:"
2078   PRINT " 1 - FIRST NAME"
2080   PRINT " 2 - LAST NAME"
2082   PRINT " 3 - NUMBER OF REGULARS"
```

```
2084   PRINT "  4 - NUMBER OF SPECIALS"
2086   PRINT "  5 - SEATS"
2088   PRINT "  DELETE - BLANK RECORD"
2090   PRINT "  END - TO END UPDATING"
2092   INPUT UC$
2093   IF UC$="1" OR UC$="2" OR UC$="3" OR UC$="4" OR UC$="5" THEN E%=0
2094   IF UC$="END" OR UC$="DELETE" THEN E%=0
2095   IF E%=1 THEN PRINT "UNRECOGNIZED COMMAND, REENTER"
2096   WEND
2097   RETURN
2098   REM - END GET UPDATE COMMAND -------------------
2099   REM


2100   REM ----- GET A VALID LAST NAME(NL$) -------------------
2105   REM       PROMISES VALID LAST NAME AND MARKS STATUS "A"
2106   REM
2110   E%=1
2115   WHILE E%=1
2120    INPUT "ENTER LAST NAME ",NL$
2125    IF LEN(NL$)>20 THEN PRINT "ONLY 20 CHARACTERS" ELSE E%=0
2130   WEND
2132   AX$="A"
2135   RETURN
2136   REM - END GET A VALID LAST NAME -------------------
2137   REM


2150   REM ----- GET A VALID FIRST NAME(NF$) -------------------
2155   REM
2160   E%=1
2165   WHILE E%=1
2170    INPUT "ENTER FIRST NAME ",NF$
2175    IF LEN(NF$)>10 THEN PRINT "ONLY 10 CHARACTERS" ELSE E%=0
2180   WEND
2185   RETURN
2186   REM - END GET A VALID FIRST NAME -------------------
2187   REM


2200   REM ----- GET NUMBER OF REGULAR TICKETS -------------------
2205   REM       ASSUMES VALID S%
2206   REM       PROMISES VALID R%
2207   REM
2210   E%=1
2215   WHILE E%=1
2220    INPUT "HOW MANY REGULAR TICKETS";R%
2225    IF R%<0 THEN PRINT "MUST BE POSITIVE" ELSE E%=0
2227    IF R%+S%>10 THEN PRINT "NO MORE THAN 10 TICKETS":E%=1
2230   WEND
2235   RETURN
2236   REM - END GET NUMBER OF REGULAR TICKETS -------------------
2237   REM


2250   REM ----- GET NUMBER OF SPECIAL TICKETS -------------------
2255   REM       ASSUMES VALID R%
2256   REM       PROMISES VALID S%
2257   REM
2260   E%=1
2265   WHILE E%=1
2270    INPUT "HOW MANY SPECIAL TICKETS";S%
2275    IF S%<0 THEN PRINT "MUST BE POSITIVE" ELSE E%=0
2277    IF R%+S%>10 THEN PRINT "NO MORE THAN 10 TICKETS":E%=1
```

```
2280 WEND
2285 RETURN
2286 REM - END GET NUMBER OF SPECIAL TICKETS --------------------
2287 REM
```

Since the user can now update the two individually, the test for total number of tickets greater than ten has been moved into the Get Number Of Regulars and Get Number Of Specials modules.

```
2300 REM ----- COMPUTE GRAND TOTAL --------------------
2305 REM
2310 GT!=(R% * 5.00) + (S% * 3.00)
2315 PRINT "THE TOTAL PRICE =",GT!
2320 RETURN
2321 REM - END COMPUTE GRAND TOTAL --------------------
2322 REM

2350 REM ----- BLANK SALES RECORD --------------------
2352 REM
2354 NL$=SPACE$(20)
2356 NF$=SPACE$(10)
2358 R%=0
2360 S%=0
2362 FOR C%=0 TO 9
2364   SE$(C%)="  "
2366 NEXT C%
2368 GT!=0
2370 AX$="X"
2372 RETURN
2371 REM - END BLANK SALES RECORD --------------------
2374 REM

2400 REM ----- GET SEATS --------------------
2405 REM        ASSUMES VALID S% AND R%
2406 REM        PROMISES NEW SEAT ARRAY WITH S%+R% ENTRIES
2407 REM
2410 FOR C%=0 TO 9
2415   SE$(C%)="  "
2420 NEXT C%
2425 PRINT "ENTER "; R%+S%; " SEATS.  PRESS <ENTER> AFTER EACH."
2430 FOR C%=0 TO R%+S%-1
2435   GOSUB 2450: SE$(C%)=S$
2440 NEXT C%
2445 RETURN
2447 REM
2450 E%=1
2455 WHILE E%=1
2460   INPUT "ENTER 3-CHARACTER SEAT NUMBER ";S$
2465   E%=0
2470   IF LEN(S$)<>3 THEN S$="  "
2475   IF (MID$(S$,1,1)<"A") OR (MID$(S$,1,1)>"T") THEN E%=1
2480   IF (MID$(S$,2,2)<"01") OR (MID$(S$,2,2)>"20") THEN E%=1
2485   IF E%=1 THEN PRINT "UNRECOGNIZED SEAT CODE"
2490 WEND
2495 RETURN
2496 REM - END GET SEATS --------------------
2497 REM
```

```
2500 REM ----- STORE SALES RECORD --------------------
2505 REM       ASSUMES VALID SALES DATA, EV% BETWEEN 1 AND 200,
2510 REM             SALES FILE OPEN
2515 REM
2520 LSET F1$=MKI$(EV%)
2525 LSET F2$=NL$
2530 LSET F3$=NF$
2535 LSET F4$=MKI$(R%)
2540 LSET F5$=MKI$(S%)
2545 LSET F6$=MKS$(GT!)
2550 S$=''''
2555 FOR C%=0 TO 9
2560   S$=S$+SE$(C%)
2565 NEXT C%
2570 LSET F7$=S$
2575 LSET FX$=AX$
2580 PUT #1,EV%
2585 RETURN
2586 REM - END STORE SALES RECORD --------------------
2587 REM
```

# EXERCISE VI

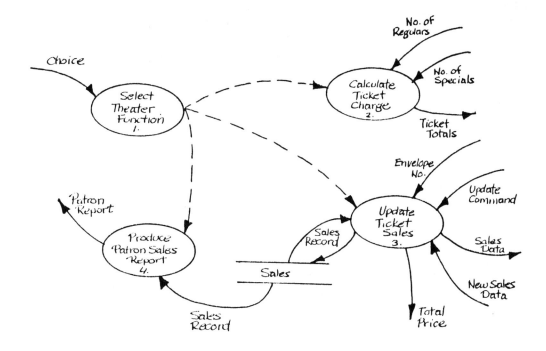

**Figure VI.1. Transaction center for theater functions.**

---

## DATA DICTIONARY

Choice = [ 1 | 2 | 3 | 0 ]
        1 - Compute Price
        2 - Update Sales Record
        3 - Produce Sales Report
        0 - End

---

## PERFORMANCE LOG

| Function | Token Count | Estimate | Actual Time | Rate Token/Time |
|----------|-------------|----------|-------------|-----------------|
| 1 | 2 | | | |

## TEST CASE LOG

| Test Case | Result |
|---|---|
| Choice | |
| 1 | Compute Price program executed |
| 2 | Update Sales program executed |
| 3 | Produce Report program executed |
| 0 | Transaction center program ends |
| 4 | Error message |

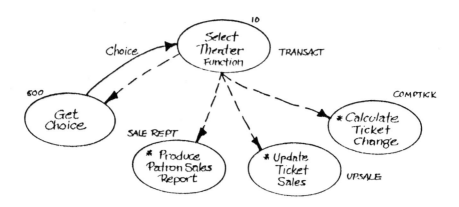

**Figure VI.2. Program outline for Select Theater Function.**

```
10 REM ----- THEATER SYSTEM TRANSACTION CENTER --------------------
11 REM
12 GOSUB 500
15 IF CH$ = "1" THEN CHAIN "COMPTICK"
20 IF CH$ = "2" THEN CHAIN "UPSALES"
25 IF CH$ = "3" THEN CHAIN "SALEREPT"
30 END
31 REM - END THEATER SYSTEM TRANSACTION CENTER --------------------
32 REM

500 REM ----- GET CHOICE --------------------
505 REM      PROMISES A CHOICE(CH$) BETWEEN 0 AND 3
510 REM
515 PRINT CHR$(26);
520 PRINT SPACE$(15);"THEATER TRANSACTION CENTER"
525 PRINT
530 PRINT SPACE$(15);"1 - COMPUTE TICKET PRICE"
535 PRINT SPACE$(15);"2 - UPDATE SALES RECORD"
540 PRINT SPACE$(15);"3 - PRODUCE SALES REPORT"
545 PRINT SPACE$(15);"0 - TO END"
550 E% = 1
```

```
555 WHILE E%=1
560   PRINT SPACE$(15);
565   INPUT CH$
570   IF CH$="1" OR CH$="2" OR CH$="3" OR CH$="0" THEN E%=0
575   IF E%=1 THEN PRINT "ENTER 1, 2, 3, OR 0"
580 WEND
585 RETURN
586 REM - END GET CHOICE -------------------
587 REM
```

The other programs should be modified to CHAIN back to the transaction center. The top module for Calculate Ticket Charges appears below.

```
10 REM ----- CALCULATE TICKET CHARGES -------------------
11 REM
15 E%=1
20 WHILE E%=1
100   GOSUB 500
105   GOSUB 1000
110   GOSUB 1500
115   GOSUB 2000
117   INPUT "DO YOU WANT TO COMPUTE ANOTHER PRICE";A$
118   IF MID$(A$,1,1)<>"Y" THEN E%=0
119 WEND
120 CHAIN "TRANSACT"
121 REM - END CALCULATE TICKET CHARGES -------------------
122 REM
```

A loop has been added that allows the user to compute a series of ticket charges without going back to the transaction center.

The top module for the sales update and sales report function appears below. The only change is the addition of the CHAIN statement.

```
10 REM ----- PRODUCE PATRON SALES REPORT -------------------
11 REM
15 OPEN "R",#1,"SALES"
20 FIELD #1,2 AS F1$,20 AS F2$,10 AS F3$,2 AS F4$,2 AS F5$,4 AS F6$,
    30 AS F7$,1 AS FX$
25 DIM SE$(9)
30 RC%=0: SC%=0: TS!=0
32 P%=1: I%=66
35 GOSUB 500
40 FOR EV%=1 TO 200
45   GOSUB 1000
50   IF AX$="A" THEN GOSUB 1500: GOSUB 2000
52   IF L%>54 THEN GOSUB 500
55 NEXT EV%
57 IF L%>50 THEN GOSUB 500
60 GOSUB 2500
65 CLOSE #1
70 CHAIN "TRANSACT"
71 REM - END PRODUCE PATRON SALES REPORT -------------------
72 REM
```

```
10 REM ----- UPDATE TICKET SALES --------------------
11 REM
15 OPEN "R",#1,"SALES"
20 FIELD #1,2 AS F1$,20 AS F2$,10 AS F3$,2 AS F4$,2 AS F5$,4 AS F6$,
    30 AS F7$,1 AS FX$
25 DIM SE$(9)
30 GOSUB 500
32 WHILE EV$ < > "END"
35   GOSUB 1000
40   GOSUB 2000
45   GOSUB 2500
47   GOSUB 500
48 WEND
50 CLOSE #1
55 CHAIN "TRANSACT"
56 REM - END UPDATE TICKET SALES --------------------
57 REM
```

# EXERCISE VII

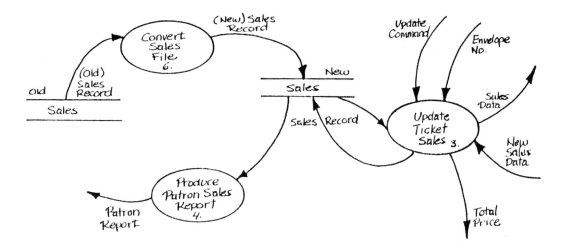

**Figure VII.1. Data flow diagram for functions affected by New Sales File.**

The brackets in the month, day, and time definitions have been included in the token count for Update Ticket Sales. The token count for the Produce Patron Sales Report is two because both data flows around the bubble have changed.

PERFORMANCE LOG

| Function | Token Count | Estimate | Actual Time | Rate Token/Time |
|---|---|---|---|---|
| 6 | 2 | | | |
| 3 | 8 | | | |
| 4 | 2 | | | |
| TOTAL | 12 | | | |

## DATA DICTIONARY

City = Update 15 characters

Day = [ 01 | 02 | ... | 31 ]

Detail Line = Patron Name + Number Of Regulars + Number Of Specials + Performance + 1{Seat}10 + Total Price

Month = [ 01 | 02 | ... | 12 ]

New Sales File = 200{Sales Record}200

New Sales Record = Envelope Number + Last Name + First Name + Number Of Regulars + Number Of Specials + Total Price + Street + City + State + Zip + Performance + 10{Seat}10

Patron Report = {Detail Line} + Total Line

Performance = Month + Day + Year + Time

Sales Data = [ Last Name | First Name | Number Of Regulars | Number Of Specials | Street | City | State | Zip | Performance | {Seat}10

State = 2 characters

Street = Up to 20 characters

Time = [ E | M ]

Total Line = Regulars Sold + Specials Sold + Grand Total

Update Command = [ 1 | 2 | 3 | ... | 10 | DELETE ]

Year = 2 digits

Zip = 5 digits

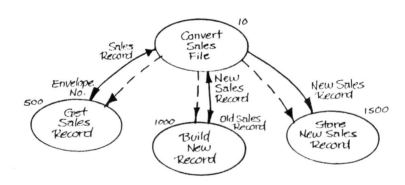

**Figure VII.2. Program outline for Convert Sales File.**

TEST CASE LOG

| Test Case | Result |
| --- | --- |
| Test the conversion by checking: | |
| Envelope #1 | Original data |
| Envelope #200 | Original data |
| Test the update function: | |

| Update code | Data | |
| --- | --- | --- |
| 5 | Street > 20 characters | Error message |
| 6 | City > 15 characters | Error message |
| 7 | State > 2 characters | Error message |
| 8 | Zip > 5 digits | Error message |
| 9 | Performance month > 12 | Error message |
| | day > 31 | Error message |
| | year > 2 digits | Error message |
| | time N | Error message |

| | |
| --- | --- |
| Update envelope #1 with valid data | Updated record |
| Delete envelope #1 | Blank record |

| | |
| --- | --- |
| Test Report Function: | |
| Run program | Same report as Produce Patron Sales Report program |

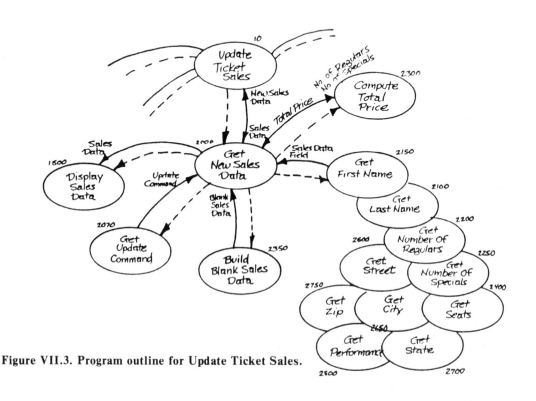

**Figure VII.3. Program outline for Update Ticket Sales.**

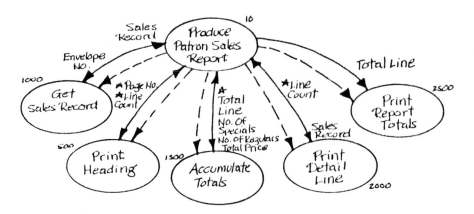

**Figure VII.4. Program outline for Produce Patron Sales Report.**

The next step is to build the code for the function outlined above. There will be one new program; two existing programs must be changed. Suggested coding answers are listed below.

The top module of the conversion program reads through the records of the Old Sales File, reformats them, and puts them on the New Sales File.

```
10 REM ----- SALES CONVERSION PROGRAM --------------------
11 REM
15 OPEN "R",#1,"SALES"
20 FIELD #1,2 AS X1$,20 AS X2$,10 AS X3$,2 AS X4$,2 AS X5$,4 AS X6$,
   30 AS X7$,1 AS XX$
25 OPEN "R",#2,"SALES2"
30 FIELD #2,2 AS F1$,20 AS F2$,10 AS F3$,2 AS F4$,2 AS F5$,4 AS F6$,20 AS F7$,
   15 AS F8$,2 AS F9$,5 AS FA$,7 AS FB$,30 AS FC$,1 AS FX$
35 PRINT "TRANSFERRING SALES RECORDS"
40 FOR EV%=1 TO 200
45   GOSUB 500
50   GOSUB 1000
55   GOSUB 1500
60 NEXT EV%
65 CLOSE #1
70 CLOSE #2
75 PRINT "CONVERSION COMPLETED"
80 END
81 REM - END SALES CONVERSION PROGRAM --------------------
82 REM

500 REM ----- GET SALES RECORD --------------------
505 REM      ASSUMES EV% BETWEEN 1 AND 200
510 REM      PROMISES SALES RECORD FOR EV% IN BUFFER
515 REM
520 GET #1,EV%
525 RETURN
526 REM - END GET SALES RECORD --------------------
527 REM
```

```
1000 REM ----- BUILD NEW SALES RECORD --------------------
1005 REM        ASSUMES VALID SALES RECORD IN BUFFER
1010 REM        PROMISES DATA TRANSFERRED TO NEW BUFFER
1015 REM
1020 LSET F1$=X1$
1025 LSET F2$=X2$
1030 LSET F3$=X3$
1035 LSET F4$=X4$
1040 LSET F5$=X5$
1045 LSET F6$=X6$
1050 LSET F7$=SPACE$(20)
1055 LSET F8$=SPACE$(15)
1060 LSET F9$=" "
1065 LSET FA$="   "
1070 LSET FB$=SPACE$(7)
1075 LSET FC$=X7$
1080 LSET FX$=XX$
1085 RETURN
1086 REM - END BUILD NEW SALES RECORD --------------------
1087 REM

1500 REM ----- STORE SALES RECORD --------------------
1505 REM        ASSUMES SALES DATA IN BUFFER
1510 PUT #2,EV%
1515 RETURN
1516 REM - END STORE SALES RECORD --------------------
1517 REM
```

You should update your data dictionary with the BASIC data names used in your programs.

---

## DATA DICTIONARY

City = Update 15 characters
        CI$ or F8$

Day = [ 01 | 02 | ... | 31 ]
        D$

Detail Line = Patron Name + Number Of Regulars + Number Of Specials +
        Performance + 1 {Seat}10 + Total Price

Month = [ 01 | 02 | ... | 12 ]
        M$

New Sales File = 200 {Sales Record}200
        SALES2

New Sales Record = Envelope Number + Last Name + First Name + Number of
        Regulars + Number Of Specials + Total Price + Street + City + State
        + Zip + Performance + 10 {Seat}10
        SE$() or FC$

Patron Report = {Detail Line} + Total Line

Performance = Month + Day + Year + Time
        PF$ or FB$

Sales Data = [ Last Name | First Name | Number Of Regulars | Number Of
        Specials | Street | City | State | Zip | Performance | {Seat}10 ]

State = 2 characters
        ST$ or F9$

Street = Up to 20 characters
        RD$ or F7$

Time = [ E | M ]
        T$

Total Line = Regulars Sold + Specials Sold + Grand Total

Update Command = [ 1 | 2 | 3 | ... | 10 | DELETE ]
        UC$

Year = 2 digits
        Y$

Zip = 5 digits
        ZP$ or FA$

---

Sample code for Update Ticket Sales is listed on the following pages.  Compare this code with your own, and look for differences between it and the previous version of this program.  The code is based on the program outline in Figure VII.2.

```
10 REM ----- UPDATE TICKET SALES --------------------
11 REM
12 OPEN "R",#1,"SALES2"
15 FIELD #1,2 AS F1$,20 AS F2$,10 AS F3$,2 AS F4$,2 AS F5$,4 AS F6$,
   20 AS F7$,15 AS F8$,2 AS F9$,5 AS FA$,7 AS FB$,30 AS FC$,1 AS FX$
20 DIM SE$(9)
25 GOSUB 500
27 WHILE EV$ < > "END"
30   GOSUB 1000
40   GOSUB 2000
45   GOSUB 2500
47   GOSUB 500
48 WEND
50 CLOSE #1
55 CHAIN "TRANSACT"
56 REM - END UPDATE TICKET SALES --------------------
57 REM

500 REM ----- GET ENVELOPE NUMBER --------------------
505 REM      PROMISES ENVELOPE NUMBER BETWEEN 1 AND 200
510 REM
515 E%=1
520 WHILE E%=1
525   INPUT "ENTER ENVELOPE NUMBER OR 'END' ";EV$
527   IF EV$="END" THEN EV%=1 ELSE EV%=VAL(EV$)
```

```
530  IF (EV%<1) OR (EV%>200) THEN PRINT "BETWEEN 1 AND 200" ELSE E%=0
535 WEND
540 RETURN
541 REM - END GET ENVELOPE NUMBER -------------------
542 REM


1000 REM ----- GET SALES RECORD -------------------
1005 REM        ASSUMES EV% TO BE BETWEEN 1 AND 200
1010 REM             SALES FILE IS OPEN
1015 REM        PROMISES NL$,NF$,R%,S%,GT!,RD$,CI$,ST$,ZP$,PF$,SE$(),AX$
1020 REM             FILLED WITH DATA FROM SALES RECORD EV%
1025 REM
1030 GET #1, EV%
1035 NL$=F2$
1040 NF$=F3$
1045 R%=CVI(F4$)
1050 S%=CVI(F5$)
1055 GT!=CVS(F6$)
1056 RD$=F7$
1057 CI$=F8$
1058 ST$=F9$
1059 ZP$=FA$
1060 FOR C%=0 TO 9
1065   SE$(C%)=MID$(FC$,C%*3+1,3)
1070 NEXT C%
1071 PF$=FB$
1075 AX$=FX$
1080 RETURN
1081 REM - END GET SALES RECORD -------------------
1082 REM


1500 REM ----- DISPLAY SALES DATA -------------------
1505 REM        ASSUMES SALES DATA
1510 REM          EV%,NL$,NF$,R%,S%,GT!,RD$,CI$,ST$,ZP$,PF$,SE$(),AX$
1511 REM
1512 PRINT CHR$(26);
1515 PRINT "DATA FOR SALES ENVELOPE ";EV%
1520 PRINT "LAST NAME   ",NL$
1525 PRINT "FIRST NAME ",NF$
1526 PRINT "STREET      ",RD$
1527 PRINT "CITY        ",CI$
1528 PRINT "STATE       ",ST$,"ZIP ",ZP$
1529 PRINT "PERFORMANCE ",
1530 PRINT LEFT$(PF$,2);"/";MID$(PF$,3,2);"/";MID$(PF$,5,2);" ";RIGHT$(PF$,1)
1531 PRINT "# OF REGULAR",R%
1535 PRINT "# OF SPECIAL",S%
1540 PRINT "TOTAL PRICE ",GT!
1545 PRINT "SEATS       ",
1550 FOR C%=0 TO 9
1555   IF SE$(C%)<>"  " THEN PRINT SE$(C%);" ";
1560 NEXT C%
1565 PRINT
1570 PRINT "STATUS    ",AX$
1575 PRINT
1580 PRINT " -----------------------------"
1585 RETURN
1586 REM - END DISPLAY SALES DATA ---------------------
1587 REM
```

```
2000 REM ----- GET NEW SALES DATA --------------------
2005 REM       ASSUMES VALID SALES DATA
2007 REM       PROMISES VALID VALUES IN SALES DATA
2010 REM
2011 UC$=""
2012 WHILE UC$<>"END"
2013   GOSUB 1500: GOSUB 2070
2015   IF UC$="1" THEN GOSUB 2150
2020   IF UC$="2" THEN GOSUB 2100
2021   IF UC$="3" THEN GOSUB 2600
2022   IF UC$="4" THEN GOSUB 2650
2023   IF UC$="5" THEN GOSUB 2700
2024   IF UC$="6" THEN GOSUB 2750
2025   IF UC$="7" THEN GOSUB 2800
2030   IF UC$="8" THEN GOSUB 2200
2035   IF UC$="9" THEN GOSUB 2250
2040   IF UC$="10" THEN GOSUB 2400
2045   IF UC$="DELETE" THEN GOSUB 2350
2057 WEND
2058 GOSUB 2300
2060 RETURN
2061 REM - END GET NEW SALES DATA --------------------
2062 REM


2070 REM ----- GET UPDATE COMMAND(UC$) --------------------
2075 REM
2076 E%=1
2077 WHILE E%=1
2078   PRINT "ENTER UPDATE COMMAND:"
2079   PRINT "  1 - FIRST NAME     6 - ZIP CODE"
2080   PRINT "  2 - LAST NAME      7 - PERFORMANCE"
2082   PRINT "  3 - STREET         8 - NUMBER OF REGULARS"
2084   PRINT "  4 - CITY           9 - NUMBER OF SPECIALS"
2086   PRINT "  5 - STATE         10 - SEATS"
2088   PRINT "  DELETE - BLANK RECORD"
2090   PRINT "  END - TO END UPDATING"
2091   INPUT UC$
2092   IF UC$="1" OR UC$="2" OR UC$="3" OR UC$="4" OR UC$="5" THEN E%=0
2093   IF UC$="6" OR UC$="7" OR UC$="8" OR UC$="9" OR UC$="10" THEN E%=0
2094   IF UC$="END" OR UC$="DELETE" THEN E%=0
2095   IF E%=1 THEN PRINT "UNRECOGNIZED COMMAND, REENTER"
2096 WEND
2097 RETURN
2098 REM - END GET UPDATE COMMAND --------------------
2099 REM

2100 REM ----- GET A VALID LAST NAME(NL$) --------------------
2105 REM
2110 E%=1
2115 WHILE E%=1
2120   INPUT "ENTER LAST NAME ",NL$
2125   IF LEN(NL$)>20 THEN PRINT "ONLY 20 CHARACTERS" ELSE E%=0
2130 WEND
2132 AX$="A"
2135 RETURN
2136 REM - END GET A VALID LAST NAME --------------------
2137 REM
```

```
2150 REM ----- GET A VALID FIRST NAME(NF$) -------------------
2155 REM
2160 E%=1
2165 WHILE E%=1
2170   INPUT "ENTER FIRST NAME ",NF$
2175   IF LEN(NF$)>10 THEN PRINT "ONLY 10 CHARACTERS" ELSE E%=0
2180 WEND
2185 RETURN
2186 REM - END GET A VALID FIRST NAME -------------------
2187 REM


2200 REM ----- GET NUMBER OF REGULAR TICKETS -------------------
2205 REM
2210 E%=1
2215 WHILE E%=1
2220   INPUT "HOW MANY REGULAR TICKETS";R%
2225   IF R%<0 THEN PRINT "MUST BE POSITIVE" ELSE E%=0
2227   IF R%+S%>10 THEN PRINT "NO MORE THAN 10 TICKETS":E%=1
2230 WEND
2235 RETURN
2236 REM - END GET NUMBER OF REGULAR TICKETS -------------------
2237 REM


2250 REM ----- GET NUMBER OF SPECIAL TICKETS -------------------
2255 REM
2260 E%=1
2265 WHILE E%=1
2270   INPUT "HOW MANY SPECIAL TICKETS";S%
2275   IF S%<0 THEN PRINT "MUST BE POSITIVE" ELSE E%=0
2277   IF R%+S%>10 THEN PRINT "NO MORE THAN 10 TICKETS":E%=1
2280 WEND
2285 RETURN
2286 REM - END GET NUMBER OF SPECIAL TICKETS -------------------
2287 REM


2300 REM ----- COMPUTE GRAND TOTAL -------------------
2305 REM
2310 GT!=(R% * 5.00) + (S% * 3.00)
2315 PRINT "THE TOTAL PRICE =",GT!
2320 RETURN
2321 REM - END COMPUTE GRAND TOTAL -------------------
2322 REM

2350 REM ----- BLANK SALES RECORD -------------------
2355 REM
2356 NL$=SPACE$(20)
2357 NF$=SPACE$(10)
2358 R%=0
2359 S%=0
2360 GT!=0
2361 RD$=SPACE$(20)
2362 CI$=SPACE$(15)
2363 ST$=" "
2364 ZP$="    "
2365 PF$=SPACE$(7)
2366 FOR C%=0 TO 9
2367   SE$(C%)="   "
2368 NEXT C%
2369 AX$="X"
2370 RETURN
2371 REM - END BLANK SALES RECORD -------------------
2372 REM
```

```
2400 REM ----- GET SEAT ARRAY --------------------
2405 REM
2410 FOR C%=0 TO 9
2415   SE$(C%)="  "
2420 NEXT C%
2425 PRINT "ENTER "; R%+S%; " SEATS.  PRESS <ENTER> AFTER EACH."
2430 FOR C%=0 TO R%+S%-1
2435   GOSUB 2450
2440   SE$(C%)=S$
2445 NEXT C%
2447 RETURN
2450 REM
2452 E%=1
2455 WHILE E%=1
2460   INPUT "ENTER 3-CHARACTER SEAT NUMBER ";S$
2465   E%=0
2470   IF LEN(S$)<>3 THEN S$="  "
2475   IF (MID$(S$,1,1)<"A") OR (MID$(S$,1,1)>"T") THEN E%=1
2480   IF (MID$(S$,2,2)<"01") OR (MID$(S$,2,2)>"20") THEN E%=1
2485   IF E%=1 THEN PRINT "UNRECOGNIZED SEAT CODE"
2490 WEND
2495 RETURN
2496 REM - END GET SEAT ARRAY --------------------
2497 REM


2500 REM ----- STORE SALES RECORD --------------------
2505 REM         ASSUMES VALID SALES DATA, EV% BETWEEN 1 AND 200,
2510 REM              SALES FILE OPEN
2515 REM
2520 LSET F1$=MKI$(EV%)
2525 LSET F2$=NL$
2530 LSET F3$=NF$
2535 LSET F4$=MKI$(R%)
2540 LSET F5$=MKI$(S%)
2545 LSET F6$=MKS$(GT!)
2546 LSET F7$=RD$
2547 LSET F8$=CI$
2548 LSET F9$=ST$
2549 LSET FA$=ZP$
2550 LSET FB$=PF$
2551 S$=""
2555 FOR C%=0 TO 9
2560   S$=S$+SE$(C%)
2565 NEXT C%
2570 LSET F7$=S$
2575 LSET FX$=AX$
2580 PUT #1,EV%
2585 RETURN
2586 REM - END STORE SALES RECORD --------------------
2587 REM


2600 REM ----- GET STREET --------------------
2605 REM
2610 E%=1
2615 WHILE E%=1
2620   INPUT "ENTER STREET ",RD$
```

```
2625  IF LEN(RD$)>20 THEN PRINT "NO MORE THAN 20 CHARACTERS" ELSE E%=0
2630 WEND
2635 RETURN
2636 REM - END GET STREET -------------------
2637 REM

2650 REM ----- GET CITY -------------------
2655 REM
2660 E%=1
2665 WHILE E%=1
2670  INPUT "ENTER CITY NAME ",CI$
2675  IF LEN(CI$)>15 THEN PRINT "NO MORE THAN 15 CHARACTERS" ELSE E%=0
2680 WEND
2685 RETURN
2686 REM - END GET CITY -------------------
2687 REM

2700 REM ----- GET STATE CODE -------------------
2705 REM
2710 E%=1
2715 WHILE E%=1
2720  INPUT "ENTER 2-CHARACTER STATE CODE ",ST$
2725  IF LEN(ST$)<>2 THEN PRINT "MUST BE 2 CHARACTERS" ELSE E%=0
2730 WEND
2735 RETURN
2736 REM - END GET STATE CODE -------------------
2737 REM

2750 REM ----- GET ZIP CODE -------------------
2755 REM
2760 E%=1
2765 WHILE E%=1
2770  INPUT "ENTER 5-DIGIT ZIP CODE ",ZP$
2775  IF LEN(ZP$)<>5 THEN PRINT "MUST BE 5 DIGITS" ELSE E%=0
2780 WEND
2785 RETURN
2786 REM - END GET ZIP CODE -------------------
2787 REM

2800 REM ----- GET PERFORMANCE CODE -------------------
2805 REM
2810 E%=1
2815 WHILE E%=1
2820  INPUT "ENTER DATE (MMDDYY) ",PF$
2825  E%=0
2830  IF LEN(PF$)<>6 THEN E%=1
2835  M$=MID$(PF$,1,2)
2840  IF M$<"01" OR M$>"12" THEN E%=1
2845  D$=MID$(PF$,3,2)
2850  IF D$<"01" OR D$>"31" THEN E%=1
2855  Y$=MID$(PF$,5,2)
2860  IF Y$<"00" OR Y$>"99" THEN E%=1
2865  T$=""
2870  IF E%=0 THEN INPUT "ENTER TIME ('E' OR 'M') ",T$
2875  IF T$<>"E" AND T$<>"M" THEN E%=1
2880  IF E%=1 THEN PRINT "UNRECOGNIZED PERFORMANCE CODE"
2885 WEND
2890 PF$=PF$+T$
```

```
2895 RETURN
2896 REM - END GET PERFORMANCE CODE -------------------
2897 REM
```

The user has asked that the Performance Code be placed on the Sales Report, which means that the Print Heading and Print Detail Line modules must be changed.

```
10 REM ----- PRODUCE PATRON SALES REPORT -------------------
11 REM
12 OPEN "R",#1,"SALES2"
15 FIELD #1,2 AS F1$,20 AS F2$,10 AS F3$,2 AS F4$,2 AS F5$,4 AS F6$,
   20 AS F7$,15 AS F8$,2 AS F9$,5 AS FA$,7 AS FB$,30 AS FC$,1 AS FX$
20 DIM SE$(9)
25 RC%=0: SC%=0: TS!=0
27 P%=1: l%=66
30 GOSUB 500
35 FOR EV%=1 TO 200
40   GOSUB 1000
45   IF AX$="A" THEN GOSUB 1500: GOSUB 2000
47   IF L%>54 THEN GOSUB 500
50 NEXT EV%
52 IF L%>50 THEN GOSUB 500
55 GOSUB 2500
60 CLOSE #1
65 CHAIN "TRANSACT"
66 REM - END PRODUCE PATRON SALES REPORT -------------------
67 REM


500 REM ----- PRINT REPORT HEADING -------------------
505 REM
506 FOR L%=L% TO 66
507   LPRINT
508 NEXT L%
510 LPRINT SPACE$(25);"PATRON SALES REPORT        PAGE ";P%
515 LPRINT
520 LPRINT " FIRST AND LAST NAME";
525 LPRINT SPACE$(13); "REG";
530 LPRINT " SPEC";
535 LPRINT " TOTAL";
536 LPRINT " PERFORMANCE"
540 LPRINT
542 P%=P%+1
544 L%=5
545 RETURN
546 REM - END PRINT REPORT HEADING -------------------
547 REM


1000 REM ----- GET SALES RECORD -------------------
1005 REM      ASSUMES EV% TO BE BETWEEN 1 AND 200
1010 REM           SALES FILE IS OPEN
1015 REM      PROMISES NL$,NF$,R%,S%,GT!,RD$,CI$,ST$,ZP$,PF$,SE$(),AX$
1020 REM           FILLED WITH DATA FROM SALES RECORD EV%
1022 REM
1025 GET #1, EV%
1030 NL$=F2$
1035 NF$=F3$
1040 R%=CVI(F4$)
1045 S%=CVI(F5$)
```

```
1050 GT!=CVS(F6$)
1051 RD$=F7$
1052 CI$=F8$
1053 ST$=F9$
1054 ZP$=FA$
1055 FOR C%=0 TO 9
1060   SE$(C%)=MID$(FC$,C%*3+1,3)
1065 NEXT C%
1066 PF$=FB$
1070 AX$=FX$
1075 RETURN
1076 REM - END GET SALES RECORD --------------------
1077 REM


1500 REM ----- ACCUMULATE TOTALS -----------------------
1505 REM        ASSUMES R%,S%,AND GT!
1510 REM        PROMISES TO UPDATE RC%,SC%,AND TS!
1515 REM
1520 TS!=TS!+GT!
1525 RC%=RC%+R%
1530 SC%=SC%+S%
1535 RETURN
1536 REM - END ACCUMULATE TOTALS --------------------
1537 REM


2000 REM ----- PRINT DETAIL LINE --------------------
2005 REM        ASSUMES SALES RECORD DATA
2010 REM
2015 LPRINT NF$; " "; NL$;
2020 LPRINT USING "######"; R%;
2025 LPRINT USING "#####"; S%;
2030 LPRINT USING "$$###.##"; GT!;
2032 LPRINT "  ";LEFT$(PF$,2);"/";MID$(PF$,3,2);"/";MID$(PF$,5,2);
2033 LPRINT " ";RIGHT$(PF$,1)
2035 LPRINT SPACE$(13); "SEATS: ";
2040 FOR C%=0 TO 9
2045   LPRINT SE$(C%); " ";
2050 NEXT C%
2055 LPRINT
2057 L%=L%+2
2060 RETURN
2061 REM - END PRINT DETAIL LINE --------------------
2062 REM


2500 REM ----- PRINT REPORT TOTALS --------------------
2505 REM        ASSUMES RC%, SC%, TS!
2510 REM
2515 LPRINT
2520 LPRINT SPACE$(20); "TOTAL COUNTS";
2525 LPRINT USING "#####"; RC%; SC%
2530 LPRINT
2535 LPRINT SPACE$(29); "TOTAL SALES";
2540 LPRINT USING "$$####,.##"; TS!
2545 RETURN
2546 REM - END PRINT REPORT TOTALS --------------------
2547 REM
```

Record in your performance log the time you took to complete the exercise.

# EXERCISE VIII

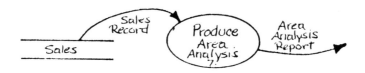

**Figure VIII.1. Data flow diagram for Produce Area Analysis.**

---

## DATA DICTIONARY

Area Analysis Report = Area Array + Total Line

Area Array = { Zip + Regulars Count + Regulars as Percentage of Area
+ Specials Count + Specials as Percentage of Area + Area Count
+ Count as Percentage of Total }

Count = Integer

Percentage = Real number between 0.0 and 100.0

Total = Integer

Total Line = Total Regulars + Regulars as Percentage of Total
+ Total Specials + Specials as Percentage of Total + Total Sold

---

The Sales Record and Area Analysis Report each count as one token; the data dictionary has one set of braces; neither the Area Array nor the Total Line is built directly from an incoming flow; the token count, therefore, is five.

---

## PERFORMANCE LOG

| Function | Token Count | Estimate | Actual Time | Rate Token/Time |
|---|---|---|---|---|
| 7 | 5 | | | |

Be sure to fill in your time estimate. When the job is complete, you should record the actual time needed to build the program. Use your test cases to verify the program.

## TEST CASE LOG

| Test Case | | | | Result | |
|---|---|---|---|---|---|
| Record | Zip | Reg. | Spec. | | |
| No records on file | | | All counts 0 | | |
| #1 | 83810 | 1 | 1 | 50% Regular | |
| | | | | 50% Special | |
| | | | | Count as % of Total | 100% |
| #200 | 83814 | 1 | 0 | 100% Regular | |
| | | | | 0% Special | |
| | | | | Count as % of Total | 33.3% |
| #2 | 83814 | 0 | 1 | 0% Regular | |
| | | | | 100% Special | |
| | | | | Count as % of Total | 50% |

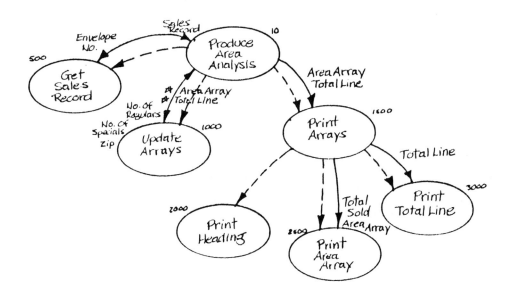

**Figure VIII.2. Program outline for Produce Area Analysis.**

---

## DATA DICTIONARY

Area Analysis Report = Area Array + Total Line

Area Array = { Zip + Regulars Count + Regulars as Percentage of Area
+ Specials Count + Specials as Percentage of Area + Area Count +
Count as Percentage of Total}
ZC$()  RC%()  SC%()

Total Line = Total Regulars + Regulars as Percentage of Total
+ Total Specials + Specials as Percentage of Total + Total Sold
TR%  TS%

Total = Integer

Count = Integer

Percentage = Real number between 0.0 and 100.0

---

The code for the top module declares the file and arrays.

```
10 REM ----- PRODUCE AREA ANALYSIS REPORT -------------------
11 REM
12 OPEN "R",#1,"SALES2"
15 FIELD #1,2 AS F1$,20 AS F2$,10 AS F3$,2 AS F4$,2 AS F5$,4 AS F6$,
   20 AS F7$,15 AS F8$,2 AS F9$,5 AS FA$,7 AS FB$,30 AS FC$,1 AS FX$
20 DIM SE$(9),ZC$(29),RC%(29),SC%(29)
25 FOR EV%=1 TO 200
30   GOSUB 500
35   IF AX$="A" THEN GOSUB 1000
40 NEXT EV%
45 CLOSE #1
50 GOSUB 1500
55 CHAIN "TRANSACT"
56 REM - END PRODUCE AREA ANALYSIS REPORT -------------------
57 REM


500 REM ----- GET SALES RECORD -------------------
505 REM       ASSUMES EV% TO BE BETWEEN 1 AND 200
510 REM              SALES FILE IS OPEN
515 REM       PROMISES NL$,NF$,R%,S%,GT!,RD$,CI$,ST$,ZP$,PF$,SE$(),AX$
520 REM           FILLED WITH DATA FROM SALES RECORD EV%
525 REM
530 GET #1, EV%
535 NL$=F2$
540 NF$=F3$
545 R%=CVI(F4$)
550 S%=CVI(F5$)
555 GT!=CVS(F6$)
560 RD$=F7$
565 CI$=F8$
570 ST$=F9$
575 ZP$=FA$
580 FOR C%=0 TO 9
```

```
585  SE$(C%)=MID$(FC$,C%*3+1,3)
590 NEXT C%
595 PF$=FB$
600 AX$=FX$
605 RETURN
606 REM - END GET SALES RECORD -------------------
607 REM
```

The block of code that adds to area arrays $RC\%()$ and $SC\%()$ has been factored into its own module. A loop set up to search the Zip Code array exits when either the zip code is found or the array is full.

```
1000 REM ----- UPDATE ARRAYS -------------------
1005 REM       ASSUMES ZP$,R%,S%
1010 REM       PROMISES TO UPDATE ZC$(),RC%(),SC%(),TR%,TS%
1015 REM
1020 N%=0
1025 E%=1
1030 WHILE E%=1
1035   IF ZC$(N%)="" THEN ZC$(N%)=ZP$
1040   IF ZP$=ZC$(N%) THEN GOSUB 1100: E%=0
1045   N%=N%+1
1050   IF N%>29 THEN PRINT "AREA ARRAY FULL - REPORT ERRONEOUS":E%=0
1055 WEND
1060 TR%=TR%+R%
1065 TS%=TS%+S%
1070 RETURN
1100 REM ** UPDATE AREA ROW
1105 RC%(N%)=RC%(N%)+R%
1110 SC%(N%)=SC%(N%)+S%
1115 RETURN
1116 REM - END UPDATE ARRAYS -------------------
1117 REM


1500 REM ----- PRINT ARRAYS -------------------
1505 REM       ASSUMES ZC$(),RC%(),SC%(),TR%,TS%
1507 REM
1510 GOSUB 2000
1515 GOSUB 2500
1520 GOSUB 3000
1525 RETURN
1526 REM - END PRINT ARRAYS -------------------
1527 REM


2000 REM ----- PRINT HEADING -------------------
2005 REM
2010 LPRINT "            AREA ANALYSIS REPORT"
2015 LPRINT
2020 LPRINT "      - - - - - - TOTALS BY AREA - - - - - - -"
2025 LPRINT " ZIP  # REG  % OF AREA   # SPEC  % OF AREA   TOTAL  % OF TOTAL"
2030 LPRINT
2035 RETURN
2036 REM - END PRINT HEADING -------------------
2037 REM
```

```
2500 REM ----- PRINT AREA ARRAY --------------------
2505 REM      ASSUMES ZC$(),RC%(),SC%(),TR%,TS%
2510 REM
2515 N%=0
2520 E%=1
2525 TT%=TR%+TS%
2530 WHILE E%=1
2535   IF ZC$(N%)<>"" THEN GOSUB 2600 ELSE E%=0
2540   N%=N%+1
2545   IF N%>29 THEN E%=0
2550 WEND
2555 LPRINT
2560 RETURN
2561 REM - END PRINT AREA ARRAY --------------------
2562 REM


2600 REM ----- PRINT AREA ROW --------------------
2602 REM
2605 LPRINT " ";ZC$(N%);" ";
2610 LPRINT USING "####";RC%(N%);
2615 LPRINT "     ";
2620 T%=RC%(N%)+SC%(N%)
2625 P!=0
2630 IF T%>0 THEN P!=RC%(N%)/T%*100
2635 LPRINT USING "###.#";P!;
2640 LPRINT "     ";
2645 LPRINT USING "####";SC%(N%);
2650 LPRINT "     ";
2655 P!=0
2660 IF T%>0 THEN P!=SC%(N%)/T%*100
2665 LPRINT USING "###.#";P!;
2670 LPRINT "     ";
2675 LPRINT USING "####";T%;
2680 P!=0
2685 IF TT%>0 THEN P!=T%/TT%*100
2690 LPRINT "     ";
2695 LPRINT USING "###.#";P!
2700 RETURN
2701 REM - END PRINT AREA ROW --------------------
2702 REM


3000 REM ----- PRINT TOTAL LINE --------------------
3005 REM      ASSUMES TT%,TR%,TS%
3010 REM
3015 LPRINT " TOTAL  ";
3020 LPRINT USING "####";TR%;
3025 LPRINT "     ";
3030 P!=0
3035 IF TT%>0 THEN P!=TR%/TT%*100
3040 LPRINT USING "###.#";P!;
3045 LPRINT "     ";
3050 LPRINT USING "####";TS%;
3055 LPRINT "     ";
3060 P!=0
3065 IF TT%>0 THEN P!=TS%/TT%*100
3070 LPRINT USING "###.#";P!;
3075 LPRINT "     ";
3080 LPRINT USING "####";TT%
3085 RETURN
3086 REM - END PRINT TOTAL LINE --------------------
3087 REM
```

The most difficult part of this program is getting the data printed in a readable format. Determining spacing and the decimal point's position are time-consuming tasks.

When the program works according to the model, record in your performance log the time you spent on this exercise.

# EXERCISE IX

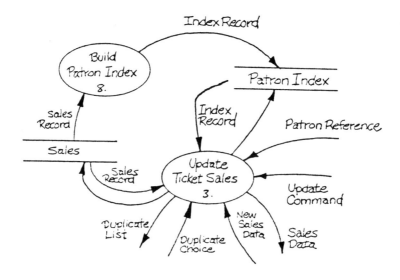

**Figure 1X.1. Data flow diagram for functions using Patron Index.**

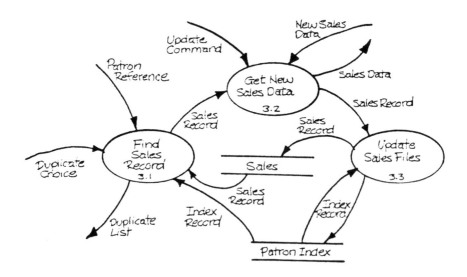

**Figure IX.2. Detailed data flow diagram for Update Ticket Sales.**

## DATA DICTIONARY

Patron Reference = [ Envelope Number | Last Name ]

Patron Index = 5 {Index Record} 5

Index Record = 40 {Abbreviated Last Name} 40

Abbreviated Last Name = 3 characters

Duplicate List = 2 {Last Name + First Name + City}

Duplicate Choice = Integer

## PERFORMANCE LOG

| Function | Token Count | Estimate | Actual Time | Rate Token/Time |
|----------|-------------|----------|-------------|-----------------|
| 8 | 2 | | | |
| 3.1 | 9 | | | |
| 3.2 | 0 | | | |
| 3.3 | 5 | | | |
| TOTAL | 16 | | | |

## TEST CASE LOG

| Test Case | Result |
|-----------|--------|
| Patron Reference: | |
| SCH when there is no SCH on the index | Error message |
| Name for record #1 | Display record #1 |
| Change name on record #1 to BAKER then enter BAK | Display the first record |
| Name for record #200 | Display record #200 |
| Change name on record #1 to FLAG then enter FLA | Display the first record |
| JON when the file contains two JONs | Display duplicate list |
| Choice 3 | Error message |
| Choice 2 | Display correct record |

You check the index by verifying that you can access the record again after a name has been added or changed.

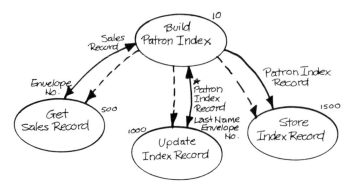

Figure IX.3. Program outline for Build Patron Index.

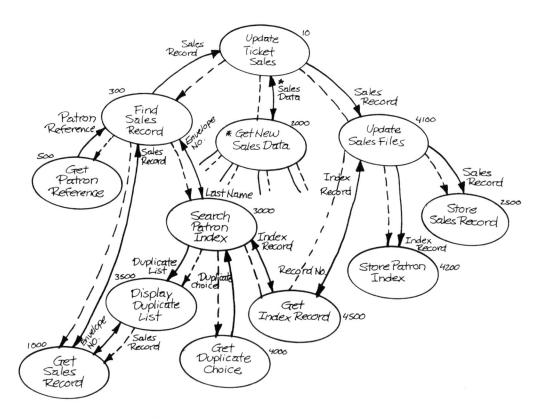

Figure IX.4. Program outline for Update Ticket Sales.

Now that you have a good model, build code for the modules on the program outlines. After you have written the code and tested the program results, compare your solution with the example below, which reads through the Sales File and creates a Patron Index File.

```
10 REM ----- BUILD PATRON INDEX --------------------
11 REM
12 OPEN "R",#1,"SALES2"
15 FIELD #1,2 AS F1$,20 AS F2$,10 AS F3$,2 AS F4$,2 AS F5$,4 AS F6$,
   20 AS F7$,15 AS F8$,2 AS F9$,5 AS FA$,7 AS FB$,30 AS FC$,1 AS FX$
20 OPEN "R",#2,"PTINDEX"
25 FIELD #2,120 AS IX$
30 DIM PX$(39)
35 PRINT "BUILDING PATRON INDEX"
40 IR%=1
45 FOR EV%=1 TO 200
50   GOSUB 500
55   GOSUB 1000
60   IF P%=39 THEN GOSUB 1500:IR%=IR+1
65 NEXT EV%
70 CLOSE #1
75 CLOSE #2
80 PRINT "PATRON INDEX CREATED"
85 END
86 REM - END BUILD PATRON INDEX --------------------
87 REM

500 REM ----- GET SALES RECORD --------------------
505 REM      ASSUMES EV% TO BE BETWEEN 1 AND 200
510 REM              SALES FILE IS OPEN
515 REM      PROMISES NL$ FROM SALES RECORD EV%
520 REM
525 GET #1, EV%
530 NL$=F2$
535 RETURN
536 REM - END GET SALES RECORD --------------------
537 REM

1000 REM ----- UPDATE INDEX RECORD --------------------
1005 REM      ASSUMES NL$,EV%
1010 REM      PROMISES TO UPDATE PX$() AND P%
1015 REM
1020 X%=INT((EV%-1)/40)
1025 P%=EV%-(X%*40)-1
1030 PX$(P%)=LEFT$(NL$,3)
1035 RETURN
1036 REM - END UPDATE INDEX RECORD --------------------
1037 REM

1500 REM ----- STORE INDEX RECORD --------------------
1505 REM      ASSUMES PX$(), IR$ BETWEEN 1 AND 5
1510 REM
1515 P$=""
1520 FOR P%=0 TO 39
1525   P$=P$+PX$(P%)
1530 NEXT P%
1535 LSET IX$=P$
1540 PUT #2,IR%
1545 RETURN
1546 REM - END STORE INDEX RECORD --------------------
1547 REM
```

Your data dictionary should be updated during the exercise. Below is a sample update.

---

### DATA DICTIONARY

Patron Reference = [ Envelope Number | Last Name ]
   EV%  EV$

Patron Index = 5{Index Record}5
   PTINDEX

Index Record = 40{Abbreviated Last Name}40
   IX$ or PX$()

Abbreviated Last Name = 3 characters

Duplicate List = 2{Last Name + First Name + City}
   DL%()

Duplicate Choice = Integer
   D%

---

The Update Ticket File program can now be changed to use the new Patron Index. In the Update Ticket Sales program, all modules under Get New Sales Data are the same. The other modules, however, must be altered to carry out the new Find Sales Record and Update Sales Files activities.

```
10 REM ----- UPDATE TICKET SALES -------------------
11 REM
12 OPEN "R",#1,"SALES2"
15 FIELD #1,2 AS F1$,20 AS F2$,10 AS F3$,2 AS F4$,2 AS F5$,4 AS F6$,
   20 AS F7$,15 AS F8$,2 AS F9$,5 AS FA$,7 AS FB$,30 AS FC$,1 AS FX$
20 OPEN "R",#2,"PTINDEX"
22 FIELD #2,120 AS IX$
24 DIM SE$(9),PX$(39),DL%(19)
25 E$="YES"
27 WHILE E$="YES"
28   GOSUB 300
30   GOSUB 1000
40   GOSUB 2000
43   GOSUB 4100
45   INPUT "DO YOU WANT TO LOOK AT ANOTHER RECORD";E$
47   IF LEFT$(E$,1)="Y" THEN E$="YES" ELSE E$="NO"
48 WEND
50 CLOSE #1
52 CLOSE #2
55 CHAIN "TRANSACT"
56 REM - END UPDATE TICKET SALES -------------------
57 REM
```

```
300 REM ----- FIND SALES RECORD --------------------
305 REM        PROMISES A VALID SALES RECORD
310 REM
315 EV%=0
320 WHILE EV%=0
325   GOSUB 500
330   IF EV$<>"  " THEN GOSUB 3000
335 WEND
340 GOSUB 1000
345 RETURN
346 REM - END FIND SALES RECORD --------------------
347 REM


500 REM ----- GET PATRON REFERENCE --------------------
505 REM        PROMISES EV% BETWEEN 1 AND 200 AND EV$="   "
510 REM           OR  EV%=0 AND EV$ CONTAINS ABBREVIATED LAST NAME
511 REM
512 PRINT CHR$(26);
515 E%=1
520 WHILE E%=1
525   INPUT "ENTER ENVELOPE NUMBER OR LAST NAME: ",EV$
526   X$=LEFT$(EV$,1)
527   IF X$>="0" AND X$<="9" THEN GOSUB 550 ELSE GOSUB 560
530 WEND
535 RETURN
536 REM - END GET PATRON REFERENCE --------------------
537 REM


550 REM ----- EDIT ENVELOPE NUMBER --------------------
551 REM
552 EV%=VAL(EV$)
554 EV$="   "
556 IF (EV%<1) OR (EV%>200) THEN PRINT "BETWEEN 1 AND 200" ELSE E%=0
557 RETURN
558 REM - END EDIT ENVELOPE NUMBER --------------------
559 REM


560 REM ----- EDIT ABBREVIATED LAST NAME --------------------
561 REM
562 EV$=EV$+"   "
564 EV$=LEFT$(EV$,3)
566 EV%=0
568 E%=0
570 RETURN
571 REM - END EDIT ABBREVIATED LAST NAME --------------------
572 REM



3000 REM ----- SEARCH PATRON INDEX --------------------------
3005 REM        ASSUMES EV$ WITH ABBREVIATED LAST NAME
3010 REM        PROMISES EV% BETWEEN 1 AND 200 IF RECORD FOUND
3015 REM           OR EV%=0 IF NO RECORD FOUND
3020 REM
3025 D%=0
3030 FOR IR%=1 TO 5
3035   GOSUB 4500
3040   FOR P%=0 TO 39
3045     IF PX$(P%)=EV$ THEN DL%(D%)=P%+(IR%*40-40)+1:D%=D%+1
3050   NEXT P%
```

```
3055 NEXT IR%
3060 IF D%=0 THEN PRINT "CANNOT FIND SALES RECORD":EV%=0
3065 IF D%=1 THEN EV%=DL%(0)
3070 IF D%>1 THEN GOSUB 3500: GOSUB 4000
3075 RETURN
3076 REM - END SEARCH PATRON INDEX -------------------
3077 REM


3500 REM ----- DISPLAY DUPLICATE LIST -------------------
3505 REM        ASSUMES DL$() WITH D% ENTRIES
3510 REM
3515 PRINT CHR$(26);
3520 PRINT "PATRONS WITH SIMILAR NAMES."
3525 PRINT
3530 FOR L%=0 TO D%-1
3535   EV%=DL%(L%)
3540   GOSUB 1000
3545   PRINT L%+1;NL$;NF$;PF$
3550 NEXT L%
3555 PRINT
3560 RETURN
3561 REM - END DISPLAY DUPLICATE LIST -------------------
3562 REM


4000 REM ----- GET DUPLICATE CHOICE -------------------
4005 REM        PROMISES USER'S CHOICE OF DL%() IN EV%
4010 REM
4015 E%=1
4020 WHILE E%=1
4025   INPUT "ENTER NUMBER OF CHOICE: ",C%
4030   IF C%<1 OR C%>D% THEN PRINT "MUST BE 1 TO ";D% ELSE E%=0
4035 WEND
4040 EV%=DL%(C%-1)
4045 RETURN
4046 REM - END GET DUPLICATE CHOICE -------------------
4047 REM


4100 REM ----- UPDATE SALES FILES -------------------
4105 REM        ASSUMES SALES DATA
4110 REM        PROMISES TO STORE SALES DATA AND UPDATE PATRON INDEX
4115 REM
4120 GOSUB 2500
4125 X%=INT((EV%-1)/40)
4130 IR%=X%+1
4135 P%=EV%-(X%*40)-1
4140 GOSUB 4500
4145 NL$=NL$+" "
4150 PX$(P%)=LEFT$(NL$,3)
4155 GOSUB 4200
4160 RETURN
4161 REM - END UPDATE SALES FILES -------------------
4162 REM
```

```
4200 REM ----- STORE PATRON INDEX -------------------
4205 REM       ASSUMES PX$(), IR%
4210 REM
4215 X$=""
4220 FOR P%=0 TO 39
4225   X$=X$+PX$(P%)
4230 NEXT P%
4235 LSET IX$=X$
4240 PUT #2,IR%
4245 RETURN
4246 REM - END STORE PATRON INDEX -------------------
4247 REM

4500 REM ----- GET PATRON INDEX -------------------
4505 REM       ASSUMES IR% BETWEEN 1 AND 5
4510 REM       PROMISES PX$() CONTAINING INDEX RECORD
4515 REM
4520 GET #2,IR%
4525 FOR I%=0 TO 39
4530   PX$(I%)=MID$(IX$,I%*3+1,3)
4535 NEXT I%
4540 RETURN
4541 REM - END GET PATRON INDEX -------------------
4542 REM
```

# EXERCISE X

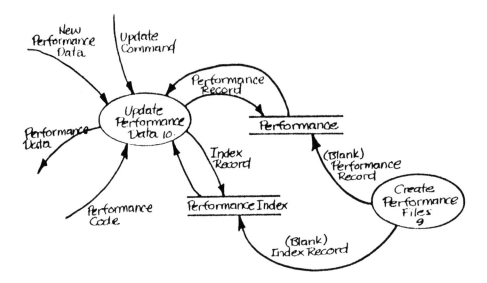

Figure X.1. Data flow diagram for functions using Performance Index.

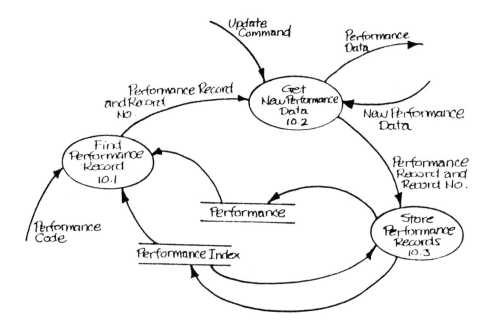

Figure X.2. Detailed data flow diagram for Update Performance Data.

---

### DATA DICTIONARY

Date = Month + Day + Year

New Performance Data = [ Date | Time | Location | 1 {Seat}400 ]

Performance Code = Date + Time

Performance Data = Date + Time + Location + 400 {Seat Sold}400

Performance File = Performance Index + 20 {Performance Record}20

Performance Index = 20 {Performance Code}20

Performance Record = Date + Time + Location + 400 {Seat Sold}400

Record Number = Integer between 2 and 21

Seat = Row + Chair

Seat Sold = [ 1 | 0 ]
        1 - Sold
        0 - Not Sold

Time = [ E | M ]

Update Command = [ 1 | 2 | 3 | 4 | END | DELETE ]
        1 - Date
        2 - Time
        3 - Location
        4 - Seat Sold

---

Performance Index is on the same file as Performance Data. The first record of the file is the index; the remaining 20 records contain performance data. The record number produced by Find Performance Record ranges from 2 through 21 because of the index record placement.

Performance Record contains the Seat Sold array. The first 20 elements of the array represent row A, the last 20 (381 - 400) represent row T. If seat A19 is sold, the number 1 is placed in the 19th position of the array. If seat T03 is sold, 1 is placed in the 183rd position of the array.

---

### PERFORMANCE LOG

| Function | Token Count | Estimate | Actual Time | Rate Token/Time |
|---|---|---|---|---|
| 9.2 | 2 | | | |
| 10.1 | 4 | | | |
| 10.2 | 11 | | | |
| 10.3 | 4 | | | |
| TOTAL | 21 | | | |

---

## TEST CASE LOG

| Test Case | Result |
|---|---|
| Enter first performance | Blank record displayed |
|     Command 1, 032485 | Updates date |
|     Command 2, E | Updates time |
|     Command 3, Kellogg High | Updates location |
|     Command 4, A01 | Updates 1st seat sold |
|     Command END | Stores data on file |
| Enter second performance | |
|     Command 5 | Error message |
|     Command 1, bad date | Error message |
|     Command 2, time N | Error message |
|     Command 3, location > 15 characters | Error message |
|     Command 4, S21 | Error message |
| Fill file with performance records | |
|     Enter 20th performance | Display blank data |
|     Enter valid data | Stores record |
| Enter 21st performance | Error message |
| Enter 1st performance | Displays data |
|     Command DELETE | Blank data |
|     Command END | Stores blank data |
| Enter 20th performance | Displays data |
|     Command DELETE | Blank data |
|     Command END | Stores blank data |

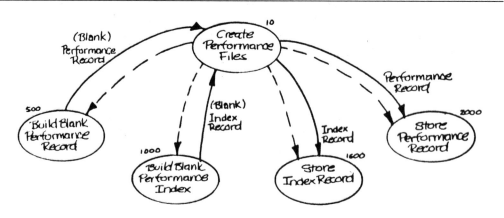

**Figure X.3. Program outline for Create Performance File.**

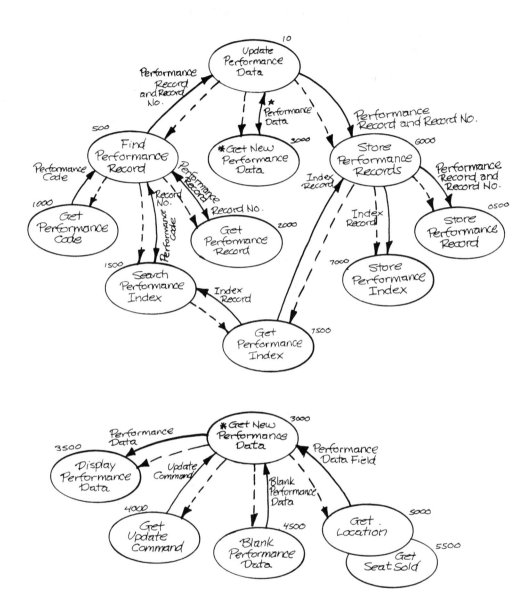

**Figure X.4. Program outline for Update Performance Data.**

You build code to fill in the program outlines and handle each module, or block of code, separately. This aids the development process by simplifying each step and reducing the number of errors in the programs.

The following data dictionary is updated with BASIC data names.

---

## DATA DICTIONARY

Date = Month + Day + Year
       F1$ or DT$

New Performance Data = [ Date | Time | Location | 1 {Seat}400 ]

Performance Code = Date + Time
       PC$

Performance Data = Date + Time + Location + 400 {Seat Sold}400

Performance File = Performance Index + 20 {Performance Record}20
       PERFORM records 2 through 21

Performance Index = 20 {Performance Code}20
       PERFORM 1st record

Performance Record = Date + Time + Location + 400 {Seat Sold}400
       LC$   F4$ thru F7$ or ST%()

Record Number = Integer between 2 and 21

Seat = Row + Chair

Seat Sold = [ 1 | 0 ]
       1 - Sold
       0 - Not Sold

Time = [ E | M ]
       F2$ or TI$

Update Command = [ 1 | 2 | 3 | 4 | END | DELETE ]
       UC$  1 - Date
             2 - Time
             3 - Location
             4 - Seat Sold

---

```
10 REM ----- CREATE PERFORMANCE FILE -------------------
11 REM
15 OPEN "R",#1,"PERFORM",428
20 FIELD #1,70 AS I1$,70 AS I2$
25 FIELD #1,6 AS F1$,1 AS F2$,20 AS F3$,100 AS F4$,100 AS F5$,
    100 AS F6$,100 AS F7$,1 AS FX$
30 DIM PI$(20),ST%(400)
35 PRINT "CREATING PERFORMANCE FILE AND INDEX"
40 GOSUB 1000
45 GOSUB 1500
50 GOSUB 500
55 GOSUB 2000
60 CLOSE #1
65 PRINT "PERFORMANCE FILE AND INDEX INITIALIZED"
70 END
71 REM - END CREATE PERFORMANCE FILE -------------------
72 REM
```

```
500 REM ----- BUILD BLANK PERFORMANCE RECORD ----------------
505 REM
510 LSET F1$=SPACE$(6)
515 LSET F2$="" "
520 LSET F3$=SPACE$(20)
525 LSET F4$=STRING$(100,48)
530 LSET F5$=STRING$(100,48)
535 LSET F6$=STRING$(100,48)
540 LSET F7$=STRING$(100,48)
545 LSET FX$="X"
550 RETURN
551 REM - END BUILD BLANK PERFORMANCE RECORD --------------------
552 REM


1000 REM ----- BUILD BLANK INDEX RECORD --------------------
1005 REM       PROMISES INITIAL VALUES IN PERFORMANCE BUFFER
1010 REM
1015 LSET I1$=SPACE$(70)
1020 LSET I2$=SPACE$(70)
1025 RETURN
1026 REM - END BUILD BLANK INDEX RECORD --------------------
1027 REM


1500 REM ----- STORE INDEX RECORD --------------------
1505 REM       ASSUMES BLANK DATA IN INDEX BUFFER
1510 REM
1520 PUT #1,1
1530 RETURN
1531 REM - END STORE INDEX RECORD --------------------
1532 REM


2000 REM ----- STORE PERFORMANCE RECORD --------------------
2005 REM       ASSUMES BLANK DATA IN THE PERFORMANCE BUFFER
2010 REM
2015 FOR PF%=2 TO 21
2020   PUT #1,PF%
2025 NEXT PF%
2030 RETURN
2031 REM - END STORE PERFORMANCE RECORD --------------------
2032 REM
```

The Performance Index requires 140 characters. Since a string in BASIC cannot exceed 128, the FIELD that holds the index on the record is halved. Similarly, the Seat Sold array, which requires 400 characters, is declared as four fields of 100 characters each.

```
10 REM ----- UPDATE PERFORMANCE DATA --------------------
11 REM
15 OPEN "R",#1,"PERFORM",428
20 FIELD #1,70 AS I1$,70 AS I2$
25 FIELD #1,6 AS F1$,1 AS F2$,20 AS F3$,100 AS F4$,100 AS F5$,
     100 AS F6$,100 AS F7$,1 AS FX$
30 DIM PI$(19),ST$(399)
35 E$="YES"
40 WHILE E$="YES"
45   GOSUB 500
50   GOSUB 3000
```

```
55   GOSUB 6000
60   PRINT CHR$(26);
65   INPUT "DO YOU WANT TO LOOK AT ANOTHER PERFORMANCE RECORD";E$
70   IF LEFT$(E$,1)="Y" THEN E$="YES" ELSE E$="NO"
75 WEND
80 CLOSE #1
85 END
86 REM - END UPDATE PERFORMANCE DATA --------------------
87 REM


500 REM ----- FIND PERFORMANCE RECORD --------------------
505 REM        PROMISES PERFORMANCE DATA AND RECORD NUMBER
510 REM
515 GOSUB 1000
520 GOSUB 1500
525 GOSUB 2000
530 IF RX$="X" THEN DT$=LEFT$(PC$,6):TI$=RIGHT$(PC$,1)
535 RETURN
536 REM - END FIND PERFORMANCE RECORD --------------------
537 REM


1000 REM ----- GET PERFORMANCE CODE --------------------
1005 REM        PROMISES PERFORMANCE CODE PC$ MADE UP OF DT$ AND TI$
1010 REM
1015 E%=1
1020 WHILE E%=1
1025   INPUT "ENTER DATE (MMDDYY) ",DT$
1030   E%=0
1035   IF LEN(DT$)< >6 THEN E%=1
1040   M$=MID$(DT$,1,2)
1045   IF M$<"01" OR M$>"12" THEN E%=1
1050   D$=MID$(DT$,3,2)
1055   IF D$<"01" OR D$>"31" THEN E%=1
1060   Y$=MID$(DT$,5,2)
1065   IF Y$<"00" OR Y$>"99" THEN E%=1
1070   TI$=""
1075   IF E%=0 THEN INPUT "ENTER TIME (E OR M) ",TI$
1080   IF TI$< >"E" AND TI$< >"M" THEN E%=1
1085   IF E%=1 THEN PRINT "UNRECOGNIZED PERFORMANCE CODE"
1090 WEND
1095 PC$=DT$+TI$
1100 RETURN
1101 REM - END GET PERFORMANCE CODE --------------------
1102 REM


1500 REM ----- SEARCH PERFORMANCE INDEX --------------------
1505 REM        ASSUMES PERFORMANCE CODE PC$
1510 REM        PROMISES IF PC$ ON INDEX RN% SET TO THAT RECORD
1515 REM               IF PC$ NOT ON INDEX RN% SET TO FIRST BLANK RECORD
1520 REM
1525 GOSUB 7500
1530 RN%=0
1535 P%=0
1540 E1%=1
1545 WHILE E1%=1
1550   IF PC$=PI$(P%) THEN E1%=0:RN%=P%+2
1555   IF PI$(P%)="     " AND RN%=0 THEN RN%=P%+2
1560   IF P%<19 THEN P%=P%+1 ELSE E1%=0
1565 WEND
```

```
1570 IF RN%=0 THEN PRINT "PERFORMANCE FILE IS FULL":RN%=2
1575 RETURN
1576 REM - END SEARCH PERFORMANCE INDEX --------------------
1577 REM

2000 REM ----- GET PERFORMANCE RECORD --------------------
2005 REM        ASSUMES RECORD NUMBER RN% BETWEEN 2 AND 21
2010 REM        PROMISES PERFORMANCE DATA DT$,TI$,LC$,ST$()
2015 REM
2020 GET #1,RN%
2025 DT$=F1$
2030 TI$=F2$
2035 LC$=F3$
2040 FOR I%=0 TO 99
2045   ST$(I%)=MID$(F4$,I%+1,1)
2050 NEXT I%
2055 FOR I%=0 TO 99
2060   ST$(I%+100)=MID$(F5$,I%+1,1)
2065 NEXT I%
2070 FOR I%=0 TO 99
2075   ST$(I%+200)=MID$(F6$,I%+1,1)
2080 NEXT I%
2085 FOR I%=0 TO 99
2090   ST$(I%+300)=MID$(F7$,I%+1,1)
2095 NEXT I%
2100 RX$=FX$
2105 RETURN
2106 REM - END GET PERFORMANCE RECORD --------------------
2107 REM

3000 REM ----- GET NEW PERFORMANCE DATA --------------------
3005 REM        ASSUMES VALID PERFORMANCE DATA
3010 REM        PROMISES VALID PERFORMANCE DATA - DT$,TI$,LC$,ST$()
3015 REM
3020 UC$=""
3025 WHILE UC$<>"END"
3030   GOSUB 3500
3035   GOSUB 4000
3040   IF UC$="DELETE" THEN GOSUB 4500
3045   IF UC$="1" THEN GOSUB 5200:RX$="A"
3050   IF UC$="2" THEN GOSUB 5300:RX$="A"
3055   IF UC$="3" THEN GOSUB 5000:RX$="A"
3060   IF UC$="4" THEN GOSUB 5100:RX$="A"
3065 WEND
3070 IF RX$="X" THEN DT$="     ":TI$="  "
3075 RETURN
3076 REM - END GET NEW PERFORMANCE DATA --------------------
3077 REM

3500 REM ----- DISPLAY PERFORMANCE DATA --------------------
3505 REM        ASSUMES PERFORMANCE DATA
3510 REM
3515 PRINT CHR$(26);
3520 PRINT "PERFORMANCE DATA        RECORD " RN%
3525 PRINT "1- DATE: ";LEFT$(DT$,2) "/" MID$(DT$,3,2) "/" RIGHT$(DT$,2) "   ";
3530 PRINT "2- TIME: ";TI$ "   ";
3535 PRINT "3- LOCATION: ";LC$ "   ";
3540 PRINT "STATUS: ";RX$
3542 X$="4- SEATING: "
3545 FOR I1%=0 TO 19
```

```
3550   PRINT X$ MID$("ABCDEFGHIJKLMNOPQRST",I1%+1,1) "  ";
3555   FOR I2%=0 TO 19
3560     P%=(I1%*20)+I2%
3565     PRINT ST$(P%);" ";
3570     IF I2%=9 THEN PRINT "    ";
3575     NEXT I2%
3580   PRINT
3585   X$="          "
3590 NEXT I1%
3595 RETURN
3596 REM - END DISPLAY PERFORMANCE DATA -------------------
3597 REM


4000 REM ----- GET UPDATE COMMAND -------------------
4005 REM        PROMISES UPDATE COMMAND, UC$ = 1,2,3,4,END
4010 REM
4015 E%=0
4020 WHILE E%=0
4025   INPUT "ENTER UPDATE COMMAND OR 'END': ";UC$
4030   IF UC$="1" OR UC$="2" OR UC$="3" OR UC$="4" OR UC$="END" THEN E%=1
4035   IF E%=0 THEN PRINT "UNRECOGNIZED UPDATE COMMAND"
4040 WEND
4045 RETURN
4046 REM - END GET UPDATE COMMAND -------------------
4047 REM


4500 REM ----- BLANK PERFORMANCE DATA -------------------
4505 REM        PROMISES BLANK VALUES IN PERFORMANCE DATA
4510 REM
4515 DT$=SPACE$(6)
4520 TI$=" "
4525 LC$=SPACE$(20)
4530 FOR I%=0 TO 399
4535   ST$(I%)="0"
4540 NEXT I%
4545 RX$="X"
4550 RETURN
4551 REM - END BLANK PERFORMANCE DATA -------------------
4552 REM


5000 REM ----- GET LOCATION -----------------------
5005 REM
5010 REM ** PROMISES VALID LOCATION, LC$
5015 E%=0
5020 WHILE E%=0
5025   INPUT "ENTER LOCATION: ",LC$
5030   IF LEN(LC$)>20 THEN PRINT "NO MORE THAN 20 CHARACTERS" ELSE E%=1
5035 WEND
5040 RETURN
5041 REM - END GET LOCATION -------------------
5042 REM


5100 REM ----- GET SEAT SOLD, ST$() -------------------
5105 REM        PROMISES TO UPDATE ST$()
5110 REM
5115 E%=0
5120 WHILE E%=0
5125   E%=1
5130   INPUT "ENTER SEAT CODE: ",SE$
5135   IF LEN(SE$)<>3 THEN PRINT "SEAT CODE MUST BE THREE CHARACTERS LONG":E%=0
```

```
5140  IF LEFT$(SE$,1)<"A" OR LEFT$(SE$,1)>"T" THEN PRINT "INVALID ROW":E%=0
5145  IF RIGHT$(SE$,2)<"01" OR RIGHT$(SE$,2)>"20" THEN
          PRINT "INVALID SEAT":E%=0
5150 WEND
5155 R$=LEFT$(SE$,1)
5160 S%=VAL(RIGHT$(SE$,2))
5165 R%=INSTR("ABCDEFGHIJKLMNOPQRST",R$)
5170 P%=(R%-1)*20
5175 P%=P%+S%-1
5180 INPUT "(S)OLD OR (N)OT SOLD";S$
5185 IF LEFT$(S$,1)="S" THEN ST$(P%)="1" ELSE ST$(P%)="0"
5190 RETURN
5191 REM - END GET SEAT SOLD -------------------
5192 REM

5200 REM ----- GET PERFORMANCE DATE -------------------
5205 REM       PROMISES VALID DATE DT$
5210 REM
5215 E%=1
5220 WHILE E%=1
5225  INPUT "ENTER DATE (MMDDYY) ",DT$
5230  E%=0
5235  IF LEN(DT$)<>6 THEN E%=1
5240  M$=MID$(DT$,1,2)
5245  IF M$<"01" OR M$>"12" THEN E%=1
5250  D$=MID$(DT$,3,2)
5255  IF D$<"01" OR D$>"31" THEN E%=1
5260  Y$=MID$(DT$,5,2)
5265  IF Y$<"00" OR Y$>"99" THEN E%=1
5270 IF E%=1 THEN PRINT "INVALID DATA - REENTER"
5275 WEND
5280 RETURN
5281 REM - END GET PERFORMANCE DATE -------------------
5282 REM

5300 REM ----- GET PERFORMANCE TIME -------------------
5305 REM       PROMISES VALID TIME TI$
5310 REM
5315 E%=1
5320 WHILE E%=1
5325  TI$=""
5330  INPUT "ENTER TIME (E OR M) ",TI$
5335  IF TI$="E" OR TI$="M" THEN E%=0
5340  IF E%=1 THEN PRINT "MUST BE E OR M"
5345 WEND
5350 RETURN
5351 REM - END GET PERFORMANCE TIME ------------------- ,
5352 REM
```

In the Seat Sold array, the first 20 elements are seats for the first row, the next 20 are for row B. The user must refer to ST$(94) when entering seat code E15. The BASIC instruction INSTR on line 5165 helps compute the index. When the program is given row E, the fifth letter in the string, line 5165 assigns the value of 5 to R%. Lines 5170 and 5175 complete the calculation.

```
6000 REM ----- STORE PERFORMANCE RECORD --------------------
6005 REM      ASSUMES RECORD NUMBER AND PERFORMANCE DATA
6010 REM      PROMISES TO STORE RECORD AND UPDATE INDEX
6015 REM
6020 GOSUB 7500
6025 PC$=DT$+TI$
6030 PI$(RN%-2)=PC$
6035 GOSUB 7000
6040 GOSUB 6500
6045 RETURN
6046 REM - END STORE PERFORMANCE RECORD --------------------
6047 REM


6500 REM ----- STORE PERFORMANCE RECORD --------------------
6505 REM      ASSUMES VALID PERFORMANCE DATA AND RECORD NUMBER
6510 REM      PROMISES TO STORE DATA ON FILE
6515 REM
6520 LSET F1$=DT$
6525 LSET F2$=TI$
6530 LSET F3$=LC$
6535 X$=""
6540 FOR I%=0 TO 99
6545   X$=X$+ST$(I%)
6550 NEXT I%
6555 LSET F4$=X$
6560 X$=""
6565 FOR I%=100 TO 199
6570   X$=X$+ST$(I%)
6575 NEXT I%
6580 LSET F5$=X$
6585 X$=""
6590 FOR I%=200 TO 299
6595   X$=X$+ST$(I%)
6600 NEXT I%
6605 LSET F6$=X$
6610 X$=""
6615 FOR I%=300 TO 399
6620   X$=X$+ST$(I%)
6625 NEXT I%
6630 LSET F7$=X$
6635 LSET FX$=RX$
6640 PUT #1,RN%
6645 RETURN
6646 REM - END STORE PERFORMANCE RECORD --------------------
6647 REM


7000 REM ----- STORE PERFORMANCE INDEX --------------------
7005 REM      ASSUMES PERFORMANCE INDEX
7010 REM
7015 X$=""
7020 FOR I%=0 TO 9
7025   X$=X$+PI$(I%)
7030 NEXT I%
7035 LSET I1$=X$
7040 X$=""
7045 FOR I%=10 TO 19
7050   X$=X$+PI$(I%)
7055 NEXT I%
7060 LSET I2$=X$
```

```
7065 PUT #1,1
7070 RETURN
7071 REM - END STORE PERFORMANCE INDEX -------------------
7072 REM


7500 REM ----- GET PERFORMANCE INDEX -------------------
7505 REM        PROMISES PI$() FILLED WITH PERFORMANCE INDEX
7510 REM
7515 GET #1,1
7520 FOR I%=0 TO 9
7525   PI$(I%)=MID$(I1$,I%*7+1,7)
7530 NEXT I%
7535 FOR I%=10 TO 19
7540   PI$(I%)=MID$(I2$,I%*7+1,7)
7545 NEXT I%
7550 RETURN
7551 REM - END GET PERFORMANCE INDEX -------------------
7552 REM
```

# EXERCISE XI

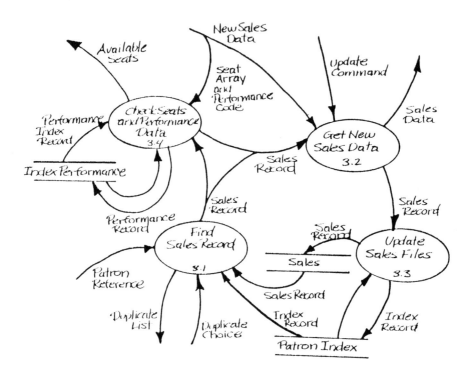

**Figure XI.1. Detailed data flow diagram for Update Ticket Sales.**

## DATA DICTIONARY

Available Seats = 20{Row}20

Row = 20{Seat Sold}20

Sales Data = [ Last Name | First Name | Number Of Regulars | Number Of
Specials | Street | City | State | Zip | Performance | Seat Array ]

Seat Array = {Seat}10

Seat Sold = [ 1 | 0 ]

Seat Array is a new data name for a series of 0 to 10 seats.

## PERFORMANCE LOG

| Function | Token Count | Estimate | Actual Time | Rate Token/Time |
|---|---|---|---|---|
| 3.4 | 12 | | | |

Check Seat and Performance Data's initial token count is seven. One token is added, however, for the set of braces in the incoming seat array. Available Seats has two sets of braces. The function refers to data within two sets of braces in the incoming Performance Index Record and the outgoing Performance Record. This gives a token count of twelve.

## TEST CASE LOG

| Test Case | Result |
|---|---|
| Performance Code that is not on the Performance Index | Error message |
| Performance Code that is first on index | Display Available Seats |
| Seat A01 where A01 is available | Updates records |
| Seat T20 where T20 is available | Updates records |
| Performance Code that is last on index | Display Available Seats |
| Seat A01 where A01 not available | Error message |
| Seat T20 where T20 not available | Error message |
| Enter more than 10 seats | Error message |
| Delete performance that has seats sold | Error message |

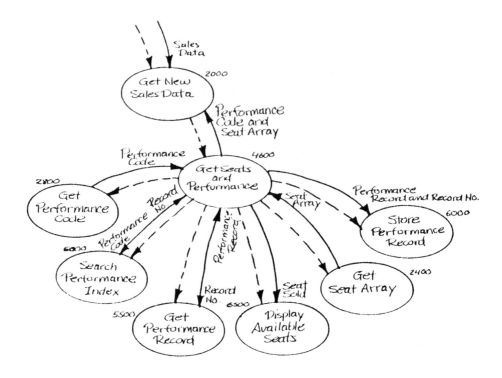

**Figure XI.2. Partial program outline for Update Ticket Sales.**

Compare your solutions with those outlined here, then build the code that performs each activity on your outline. Suggested coding answers are listed below.

```
10 REM ----- UPDATE TICKET SALES --------------------
11 REM
12 OPEN "R",#1,"SALES2"
15 FIELD #1,2 AS F1$,20 AS F2$,10 AS F3$,2 AS F4$,2 AS F5$,4 AS F6$,
   20 AS F7$,15 AS F8$,2 AS F9$,5 AS FA$,7 AS FB$,30 AS FC$,1 AS FX$
20 OPEN "R",#2,"PTINDEX"
22 FIELD #2,120 AS IX$
23 OPEN "R",#3,"PERFORM",428
24 FIELD #3,70 AS I1$,70 AS I2$
25 FIELD #3,6 AS P1$,1 AS P2$,20 AS P3$,100 AS P4$,100 AS P5$,100 AS P6$,
   100 AS P7$,1 AS XP$
26 DIM PI$(19),PT$(399)
27 DIM SE$(9),PX$(39),DL%(19)
28 E$="YES"
29 WHILE E$="YES"
30   GOSUB 300
35   GOSUB 1000
40   GOSUB 2000
43   GOSUB 4100
45   INPUT "DO YOU WANT TO LOOK AT ANOTHER RECORD";E$
```

```
47  IF LEFT$(E$,1)="Y" THEN E$="YES" ELSE E$="NO"
48 WEND
50 CLOSE #1
52 CLOSE #2
53 CLOSE #3
55 CHAIN "TRANSACT"
56 REM - END UPDATE TICKET SALES -------------------
57 REM
```

Some data names have been changed to avoid duplication.

```
300 REM ----- FIND SALES RECORD -------------------
305 REM        PROMISES A VALID SALES RECORD
310 REM
315 EV%=0
320 WHILE EV%=0
325   GOSUB 500
330   IF EV$<>"  " THEN GOSUB 3000
335 WEND
340 GOSUB 1000
345 RETURN
346 REM - END FIND SALES RECORD -------------------
347 REM


500 REM ----- GET PATRON REFERENCE -------------------
505 REM        PROMISES EV% BETWEEN 1 AND 200 AND EV$="   "
510 REM           OR  EV%=0 AND EV$ CONTAINS ABBREVIATED LAST NAME
511 REM
512 PRINT CHR$(26);
515 E%=1
520 WHILE E%=1
525   INPUT "ENTER ENVELOPE NUMBER OR LAST NAME: ",EV$
526   X$=LEFT$(EV$,1)
527   IF X$>="0" AND X$<="9" THEN GOSUB 550 ELSE GOSUB 560
530 WEND
535 RETURN
536 REM - END GET PATRON REFERENCE -------------------
537 REM


550 REM ----- EDIT ENVELOPE NUMBER -------------------
551 REM
552 EV%=VAL(EV$)
554 EV$="   "
556 IF (EV%<1) OR (EV%>200) THEN PRINT "BETWEEN 1 AND 200" ELSE E%=0
557 RETURN
558 REM - END EDIT ENVELOPE NUMBER -------------------
559 REM


560 REM ----- EDIT ABBREVIATED LAST NAME -------------------
561 REM
562 EV$=EV$+"  "
564 EV$=LEFT$(EV$,3)
566 EV%=0
568 E%=0
570 RETURN
571 REM - END EDIT ABBREVIATED LAST NAME -------------------
572 REM
```

```
1000 REM ----- GET SALES RECORD -------------------
1005 REM      ASSUMES EV% TO BE BETWEEN 1 AND 200
1010 REM           SALES FILE IS OPEN
1015 REM      PROMISES NL$,NF$,R%,S%,GT!,RD$,CI$,ST$,ZP$,PF$,SE$(),AX$
1020 REM           FILLED WITH DATA FROM SALES RECORD EV%
1025 REM
1030 GET #1, EV%
1035 NL$=F2$
1040 NF$=F3$
1045 R%=CVI(F4$)
1050 S%=CVI(F5$)
1055 GT!=CVS(F6$)
1056 RD$=F7$
1057 CI$=F8$
1058 ST$=F9$
1059 ZP$=FA$
1060 FOR C%=0 TO 9
1065   SE$(C%)=MID$(FC$,C%*3+1,3)
1070 NEXT C%
1071 PF$=FB$
1075 AX$=FX$
1080 RETURN
1081 REM - END GET SALES RECORD -------------------
1082 REM


1500 REM ----- DISPLAY SALES DATA -------------------
1505 REM      ASSUMES SALES DATA
1510 REM         EV%,NL$,NF$,R%,S%,GT!,RD$,CI$,ST$,ZP$,PF$,SE$(),AX$
1511 REM
1512 PRINT CHR$(26);
1515 PRINT "DATA FOR SALES ENVELOPE ";EV%
1520 PRINT "LAST NAME   ",NL$
1525 PRINT "FIRST NAME  ",NF$
1526 PRINT "STREET      ",RD$
1527 PRINT "CITY        ",CI$
1528 PRINT "STATE       ",ST$,"ZIP ",ZP$
1529 PRINT "PERFORMANCE ",
1530 PRINT LEFT$(PF$,2);"/";MID$(PF$,3,2);"/";MID$(PF$,5,2);" ";RIGHT$(PF$,1)
1531 PRINT "# OF REGULAR",R%
1535 PRINT "# OF SPECIAL",S%
1540 PRINT "TOTAL PRICE ",GT!
1545 PRINT "SEATS       ",
1550 FOR C%=0 TO 9
1555   IF SE$(C%)<>"   " THEN PRINT SE$(C%);" ";
1560 NEXT C%
1565 PRINT
1570 PRINT "STATUS      ",AX$
1575 PRINT
1580 PRINT "----------------------------------"
1585 RETURN
1586 REM - END DISPLAY SALES DATA -------------------
1587 REM

2000 REM ----- GET NEW SALES DATA -------------------
2005 REM      ASSUMES VALID SALES DATA
2007 REM      PROMISES VALID VALUES IN SALES DATA
2010 REM
2011 UC$=""
```

```
2012 WHILE UC$<>"END"
2013   GOSUB 1500: GOSUB 2070
2015   IF UC$="1" THEN GOSUB 2150
2020   IF UC$="2" THEN GOSUB 2100
2021   IF UC$="3" THEN GOSUB 2600
2022   IF UC$="4" THEN GOSUB 2650
2023   IF UC$="5" THEN GOSUB 2700
2024   IF UC$="6" THEN GOSUB 2750
2025   IF UC$="7" THEN GOSUB 4600
2030   IF UC$="8" THEN GOSUB 2200
2035   IF UC$="9" THEN GOSUB 2250
2045   IF UC$="DELETE" THEN GOSUB 2350
2057 WEND
2058 GOSUB 2300
2060 RETURN
2061 REM - END GET NEW SALES DATA --------------------
2062 REM
```

The Get Performance and Get Seat activities have been combined. You need the Performance Code when referring to the Performance File, which contains the information used to check seat availability.

```
2070 REM ----- GET UPDATE COMMAND(UC$) --------------------
2072 REM
2074 E%=1
2076 WHILE E%=1
2078   PRINT "ENTER UPDATE COMMAND:"
2080   PRINT "  1 - FIRST NAME      6 - ZIP CODE"
2082   PRINT "  2 - LAST NAME       7 - PERFORMANCE AND SEATS"
2084   PRINT "  3 - STREET          8 - NUMBER OF REGULARS"
2086   PRINT "  4 - CITY            9 - NUMBER OF SPECIALS"
2088   PRINT "  5 - STATE"
2089   PRINT "  DELETE - BLANK RECORD"
2090   PRINT "  END - TO END UPDATING"
2091   INPUT UC$
2092   IF UC$="1" OR UC$="2" OR UC$="3" OR UC$="4" OR UC$="5" THEN E%=0
2093   IF UC$="6" OR UC$="7" OR UC$="8" OR UC$="9" THEN E%=0
2094   IF UC$="END" OR UC$="DELETE" THEN E%=0
2095   IF E%=1 THEN PRINT "UNRECOGNIZED COMMAND, REENTER"
2096 WEND
2097 RETURN
2098 REM - END GET UPDATE COMMAND ------------
2099 REM


2100 REM ----- GET A VALID LAST NAME(NL$) --------------------
2105 REM
2110 E%=1
2115 WHILE E%=1
2120   INPUT "ENTER LAST NAME ",NL$
2125   IF LEN(NL$)>20 THEN PRINT "ONLY 20 CHARACTERS" ELSE E%=0
2130 WEND
2132 AX$="A"
2135 RETURN
2136 REM - END GET A VALID LAST NAME --------------------
2137 REM
```

```
2150 REM ----- GET A VALID FIRST NAME(NF$) --------------------
2155 REM
2160 E% = 1
2165 WHILE E% = 1
2170   INPUT "ENTER FIRST NAME ",NF$
2175   IF LEN(NF$) >10 THEN PRINT "ONLY 10 CHARACTERS" ELSE E% = 0
2180 WEND
2185 RETURN
2186 REM - END GET A VALID FIRST NAME --------------------
2187 REM

2200 REM ----- GET NUMBER OF REGULAR TICKETS --------------------
2205 REM
2210 E% = 1
2215 WHILE E% = 1
2220   INPUT "HOW MANY REGULAR TICKETS";R%
2225   IF R% <0 THEN PRINT "MUST BE POSITIVE" ELSE E% = 0
2227   IF R%+S% >10 THEN PRINT "NO MORE THAN 10 TICKETS":E% = 1
2230 WEND
2235 RETURN
2236 REM - END GET NUMBER OF REGULAR TICKETS --------------------
2237 REM

2250 REM ----- GET NUMBER OF SPECIAL TICKETS --------------------
2255 REM
2260 E% = 1
2265 WHILE E% = 1
2270   INPUT "HOW MANY SPECIAL TICKETS";S%
2275   IF S% <0 THEN PRINT "MUST BE POSITIVE" ELSE E% = 0
2277   IF R%+S% >10 THEN PRINT "NO MORE THAN 10 TICKETS":E% = 1
2280 WEND
2285 RETURN
2286 REM - END GET NUMBER OF SPECIAL TICKETS --------------------
2287 REM

2300 REM ----- COMPUTE GRAND TOTAL --------------------
2305 REM
2310 GT! = (R% * 5.00) + (S% * 3.00)
2315 PRINT "THE TOTAL PRICE =",GT!
2320 RETURN
2321 REM - END COMPUTE GRAND TOTAL --------------------
2322 REM

2350 REM ----- BLANK SALES RECORD --------------------
2351 REM
2352 NL$=SPACE$(20)
2354 NF$=SPACE$(10)
2356 R% =0
2358 S% =0
2359 GT! =0
2360 RD$=SPACE$(20)
2361 CI$=SPACE$(15)
2362 ST$="  "
2363 ZP$="     "
2364 PF$=SPACE$(7)
2365 FOR C% =0 TO 9
2366   SE$(C%) ="  "
2367 NEXT C%
```

```
2368 AX$="X"
2370 RETURN
2371 REM - END BLANK SALES RECORD --------------------
2372 REM
```

The Get Seat Array module has been changed. If the Sales Record contains seat codes in the Seat Array, the old seats are marked available on the Performance Record. Starting at line 2430, the routine computes the subscript into the Seat Array, PT$(). Get Seat Code has been expanded to check that the seat is not sold and to verify the code. The module's inner loop exits when a valid code is entered; the outer loop exits when the seat is available.

```
2400 REM ----- GET SEAT ARRAY --------------------
2402 REM
2404 FOR C%=0 TO 9
2406   IF SES(C%)<>"   " THEN S$=SES(C%):GOSUB 2430:PT$(X%)="0"
2408   SES(C%)="   "
2410 NEXT C%
2412 PRINT "ENTER "; R%+S%; " SEATS.  PRESS <ENTER> AFTER EACH."
2414 FOR C%=0 TO R%+S%-1
2416   GOSUB 2450
2418   SES(C%)=S$
2420 NEXT C%
2422 RETURN
2423 REM - END GET SEAT ARRAY --------------------
2424 REM

2430 REM ----- FIND SEAT IN PT$() --------------------
2431 REM
2432 X$=LEFT$(S$,1)
2434 X1%=VAL(RIGHT$(S$,2))
2436 X2%=INSTR("ABCDEFGHIJKLMNOPQRST",X$)
2438 X%=(X2%-1)*20+X1%-1
2440 RETURN
2441 REM - END FIND SEAT IN PT$() --------------------
2442 REM

2450 REM ----- GET SEAT CODE --------------------
2451 REM
2452 F%=1
2454 WHILE F%=1
2456   E%=1
2458   WHILE E%=1
2460     INPUT "ENTER THREE-CHARACTER SEAT NUMBER ";S$
2462     E%=0
2464     IF LEN(S$)<>3 THEN S$="   "
2466     IF (MID$(S$,1,1)<"A") OR (MID$(S$,1,1)>"T") THEN E%=1
2468     IF (MID$(S$,2,2)<"01") OR (MID$(S$,2,2)>"20") THEN E%=1
2470     IF E%=1 THEN PRINT "UNRECOGNIZED SEAT CODE"
2472   WEND
2474   GOSUB 2430
2476   IF PT$(X%)="1" THEN PRINT "SEAT ALREADY TAKEN" ELSE PT$(X%)="1":F%=0
2478 WEND
2480 RETURN
2481 REM - END GET SEAT CODE --------------------
2482 REM
```

```
2500 REM ----- STORE SALES RECORD --------------------
2505 REM        ASSUMES VALID SALES DATA, EV% BETWEEN 1 AND 200,
2510 REM             SALES FILE OPEN
2515 REM
2520 LSET F1$=MKI$(EV%)
2525 LSET F2$=NL$
2530 LSET F3$=NF$
2535 LSET F4$=MKI$(R%)
2540 LSET F5$=MKI$(S%)
2545 LSET F6$=MKS$(GT!)
2546 LSET F7$=RD$
2547 LSET F8$=CI$
2548 LSET F9$=ST$
2549 LSET FA$=ZP$
2550 LSET FB$=PF$
2551 S$=""
2555 FOR C%=0 TO 9
2560    S$=S$+SE$(C%)
2565 NEXT C%
2570 LSET FC$=S$
2575 LSET FX$=AX$
2580 PUT #1,EV%
2585 RETURN
2586 REM - END STORE SALES RECORD --------------------
2587 REM

2600 REM ----- GET STREET --------------------
2605 REM
2610 E%=1
2615 WHILE E%=1
2620   INPUT "ENTER STREET ",RD$
2625   IF LEN(RD$)>20 THEN PRINT "NO MORE THAN 20 CHARACTERS" ELSE E%=0
2630 WEND
2635 RETURN
2636 REM - END GET STREET --------------------
2637 REM

2650 REM ----- GET CITY --------------------
2655 REM
2660 E%=1
2665 WHILE E%=1
2670   INPUT "ENTER CITY NAME ",CI$
2675   IF LEN(CI$)>15 THEN PRINT "NO MORE THAN 15 CHARACTERS" ELSE E%=0
2680 WEND
2685 RETURN
2686 REM - END GET CITY --------------------
2687 REM

2700 REM ----- GET STATE CODE --------------------
2705 REM
2710 E%=1
2715 WHILE E%=1
2720   INPUT "ENTER TWO-CHARACTER STATE CODE ",ST$
2725   IF LEN(ST$)<>2 THEN PRINT "MUST BE TWO CHARACTERS" ELSE E%=0
2730 WEND
2735 RETURN
2736 REM - END GET STATE CODE --------------------
2737 REM
```

```
2750 REM ----- GET ZIP CODE -------------------
2755 REM
2760 E%=1
2765 WHILE E%=1
2770  INPUT "ENTER FIVE-DIGIT ZIP CODE ",ZP$
2775  IF LEN(ZP$)<>5 THEN PRINT "MUST BE FIVE DIGITS" ELSE E%=0
2780 WEND
2785 RETURN
2786 REM - END GET ZIP CODE -------------------
2787 REM

2800 REM ----- GET PERFORMANCE CODE -------------------
2805 REM
2810 E%=1
2815 WHILE E%=1
2820  INPUT "ENTER DATE (MMDDYY) ",XF$
2825  E%=0
2830  IF LEN(XF$)<>6 THEN E%=1
2835  M$=MID$(XF$,1,2)
2840  IF M$<"01" OR M$>"12" THEN E%=1
2845  D$=MID$(XF$,3,2)
2850  IF D$<"01" OR D$>"31" THEN E%=1
2855  Y$=MID$(XF$,5,2)
2860  IF Y$<"00" OR Y$>"99" THEN E%=1
2865  T$=""
2870  IF E%=0 THEN INPUT "ENTER TIME (E OR M) ",T$
2875  IF T$<>"E" AND T$<>"M" THEN E%=1
2880  IF E%=1 THEN PRINT "UNRECOGNIZED PERFORMANCE CODE"
2885 WEND
2890 XF$=XF$+T$
2895 RETURN
2896 REM - END GET PERFORMANCE CODE -------------------
2897 REM

3000 REM ----- SEARCH PATRON INDEX -------------------
3005 REM      ASSUMES EV$ WITH ABBREVIATED LAST NAME
3010 REM      PROMISES EV% BETWEEN 1 AND 200 IF RECORD FOUND
3015 REM          OR EV%=0 IF NO RECORD FOUND
3020 REM
3025 D%=0
3030 FOR IR%=1 TO 5
3035  GOSUB 4500
3040  FOR P%=0 TO 39
3045   IF PX$(P%)=EV$ THEN DL%(D%)=P%+(IR%*40-40)+1:D%=D%+1
3050  NEXT P%
3055 NEXT IR%
3060 IF D%=0 THEN PRINT "CANNOT FIND SALES RECORD":EV%=0
3065 IF D%=1 THEN EV%=DL%(0)
3070 IF D%>1 THEN GOSUB 3500: GOSUB 4000
3075 RETURN
3076 REM - END SEARCH PATRON INDEX -------------------
3077 REM

3500 REM ----- DISPLAY DUPLICATE LIST -------------------
3505 REM      ASSUMES DL$() WITH D% ENTRIES
3510 REM
3515 PRINT CHR$(26);
3520 PRINT "PATRONS WITH SIMILAR NAMES."
3525 PRINT
3530 FOR L%=0 TO D%-1
```

```
3535  EV%=DL%(L%)
3540  GOSUB 1000
3545  PRINT L%+1;NL$;NF$;PF$
3550 NEXT L%
3555 PRINT
3560 RETURN
3561 REM - END DISPLAY DUPLICATE LIST -------------------
3562 REM


4000 REM ----- GET DUPLICATE CHOICE -------------------
4005 REM        PROMISES USERS CHOICE OF DL%() IN EV%
4010 REM
4015 E%=1
4020 WHILE E%=1
4025   INPUT "ENTER NUMBER OF CHOICE: ",C%
4030   IF C%<1 OR C%>D% THEN PRINT "MUST BE 1 TO ";D% ELSE E%=0
4035 WEND
4040 EV%=DL%(C%-1)
4045 RETURN
4046 REM - END GET DUPLICATE CHOICE -------------------
4047 REM


4100 REM ----- UPDATE SALES FILES -------------------
4105 REM        ASSUMES SALES DATA
4110 REM        PROMISES TO STORE SALES DATA AND UPDATE PATRON INDEX
4115 REM
4120 GOSUB 2500
4125 X%=INT((EV%-1)/40)
4130 IR%=X%+1
4135 P%=EV%-(X%*40)-1
4140 GOSUB 4500
4145 NL$=NL$+" "
4150 PX$(P%)=LEFT$(NL$,3)
4155 GOSUB 4200
4160 RETURN
4161 REM - END UPDATE SALES FILES -------------------
4162 REM


4200 REM ----- STORE PATRON INDEX -------------------
4205 REM        ASSUMES PX$(), IR%
4210 REM
4215 X$=""
4220 FOR P%=0 TO 39
4225   X$=X$+PX$(P%)
4230 NEXT P%
4235 LSET IX$=X$
4240 PUT #2,IR%
4245 RETURN
4246 REM - END STORE PATRON INDEX -------------------
4247 REM


4500 REM ----- GET PATRON INDEX -------------------
4505 REM        ASSUMES IR% BETWEEN 1 AND 5
4510 REM        PROMISES PX$() CONTAINING INDEX RECORD
4515 REM
4520 GET #2,IR%
4525 FOR I%=0 TO 39
4530   PX$(I%)=MID$(IX$,I%*3+1,3)
4535 NEXT I%
```

```
4540 RETURN
4541 REM - END GET PATRON INDEX --------------------
4542 REM
```

If the user enters a performance code that differs from the code on the sales record, the seats reserved on the old performance record must be released.

```
4600 REM ----- GET SEATS AND PERFORMANCE --------------------
4605 REM        PROMISES PERFORMANCE CODE PF$, SEAT ARRAY,SE$() AND
4610 REM               UPDATE TO PERFORMANCE RECORD
4615 REM
4620 IF R%+S%=0 THEN PRINT "PLEASE ENTER NUMBER OF TICKETS":Z1%=1 ELSE Z1%=0
4625 WHILE Z1%=0
4630   GOSUB 2800
4635   IF PF$="     " THEN PF$=XF$
4640   IF XF$<>PF$ THEN GOSUB 5000:GOSUB 5500:GOSUB 4800:GOSUB 6000
4645   PF$=XF$
4650   GOSUB 5000
4655   IF RN%=0 THEN PRINT "NO PERFORMANCE " PF$ " ON FILE":PF$="     "
4660   IF RN%>0 THEN GOSUB 5500:GOSUB 6500:GOSUB 2400:GOSUB 6000:Z1%=1
4665 WEND
4670 RETURN
4671 REM - END GET SEATS AND PERFORMANCE ------------------------
4672 REM

4800 REM ----- MARK OLD SEATS AVAILABLE --------------------
4801 REM
4802 FOR C%=0 TO 9
4804   IF SE$(C%)<>"     " THEN S$=SE$(C%):GOSUB 2430:PT$(X%)="0"
4806   SE$(C%)="     "
4808 NEXT C%
4810 RETURN
4811 REM - END MARK OLD SEATS AVAILABLE --------------------
4812 REM
```

The modules Search Performance Index, Get Performance Record, and Store Performance Record have been copied from the Update Performance Data program.

```
5000 REM ----- SEARCH PERFORMANCE INDEX --------------------
5005 REM        ASSUMES PERFORMANCE CODE PF$
5010 REM        PROMISES IF PF$ ON INDEX RN% SET TO THAT RECORD
5015 REM               IF PF$ NOT ON INDEX RN% SET TO 0
5020 REM
5025 GOSUB 5100
5030 RN%=0
5035 P%=0
5040 E1%=1
5045 WHILE E1%=1
5050   IF PF$=PI$(P%) THEN E1%=0:RN%=P%+2
5060   IF P%<19 THEN P%=P%+1 ELSE E1%=0
5065 WEND
5075 RETURN
5076 REM - END SEARCH PERFORMANCE INDEX --------------------
5077 REM
```

```
5100 REM ----- GET PERFORMANCE INDEX -------------------
5105 REM      PROMISES PI$() FILLED WITH PERFORMANCE INDEX
5110 REM
5115 GET #3,1
5120 FOR I%=0 TO 9
5125   PI$(I%)=MID$(I1$,I%*7+1,7)
5130 NEXT I%
5135 FOR I%=10 TO 19
5140   PI$(I%)=MID$(I2$,I%*7+1,7)
5145 NEXT I%
5150 RETURN
5151 REM - END GET PERFORMANCE INDEX -------------------
5152 REM


5500 REM ----- GET PERFORMANCE RECORD -------------------
5505 REM      ASSUMES RECORD NUMBER RN% BETWEEN 2 AND 21
5510 REM      PROMISES PERFORMANCE DATA DT$,TI$,LC$,PT$()
5515 REM
5520 GET #3,RN%
5525 DT$=P1$
5530 TI$=P2$
5535 LC$=P3$
5540 FOR I%=0 TO 99
5545   PT$(I%)=MID$(P4$,I%+1,1)
5550 NEXT I%
5555 FOR I%=0 TO 99
5560   PT$(I%+100)=MID$(P5$,I%+1,1)
5565 NEXT I%
5570 FOR I%=0 TO 99
5575   PT$(I%+200)=MID$(P6$,I%+1,1)
5580 NEXT I%
5585 FOR I%=0 TO 99
5590   PT$(I%+300)=MID$(P7$,I%+1,1)
5595 NEXT I%
5600 RX$=XP$
5605 RETURN
5606 REM - END GET PERFORMANCE RECORD -------------------
5607 REM


6000 REM ----- STORE PERFORMANCE RECORD -------------------
6005 REM      ASSUMES VALID PERFORMANCE DATA AND RECORD NUMBER
6010 REM      PROMISES TO STORE DATA ON FILE
6015 REM
6020 LSET P1$=DT$
6025 LSET P2$=TI$
6030 LSET P3$=LC$
6035 X$="""
6040 FOR I%=0 TO 99
6045   X$=X$+PT$(I%)
6050 NEXT I%
6055 LSET P4$=X$
6060 X$="""
6065 FOR I%=100 TO 199
6070   X$=X$+PT$(I%)
6075 NEXT I%
6080 LSET P5$=X$
6085 X$="""
6090 FOR I%=200 TO 299
6095   X$=X$+PT$(I%)
6100 NEXT I%
```

```
6105 LSET P6$=X$
6110 X$=""
6115 FOR I%=300 TO 399
6120   X$=X$+PT$(I%)
6125 NEXT I%
6130 LSET P7$=X$
6135 LSET XP$=RX$
6140 PUT #3,RN%
6145 RETURN
6146 REM - END STORE PERFORMANCE RECORD -------------------
6147 REM


6500 REM ----- DISPLAY AVAILABLE SEATS -------------------
6505 REM       ASSUMES SEAT SOLD, PT$()
6510 REM
6515 PRINT CHR$(26);
6520 PRINT "AVAILABLE SEATING(0-AVAILABLE, 1-SOLD): "
6525 PRINT "  1            10  11            20"
6530 FOR I1%=0 TO 19
6535   PRINT MID$("ABCDEFGHIJKLMNOPQRST",I1%+1,1) " ";
6540   FOR I2%=0 TO 19
6545     P%=(I1%*20)+I2%
6550     PRINT PT$(P%);" ";
6555     IF I2%=9 THEN PRINT "   ";
6560   NEXT I2%
6565   PRINT
6570 NEXT I1%
6580 RETURN
6581 REM - END DISPLAY AVAILABLE SEATS -------------------
6582 REM
```

# EXERCISE XII

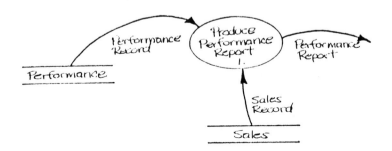

**Figure XII.1. Data flow diagram for Produce Performance Report.**

---

## DATA DICTIONARY

Page = Seating Chart + Patron List + Total Count

Patron List = {Patron Name + Seat List}

Performance Report = {Page}

Row = 20 {Seat Sold} 20

Seating Chart = 20 {Row} 20

Seat List = {Seat} 10

Total Count = Integer between 0 and 200

---

## PERFORMANCE LOG

| Function | Token Count | Estimate | Actual Time | Rate Token/Time |
|----------|-------------|----------|-------------|-----------------|
| 11 | 8 | | | |

Three data flows around Produce Performance Report and five sets of braces in the Performance Report definition give a total token count of eight.

## TEST CASE LOG

| Test Case | Result |
| --- | --- |
| No records on either file | Blank report |
| Performance on first record: No sales | Performance description with no sales |
| Performance on last record: Full house | Performance description with all seats marked sold |
| Sales file with sales on first and last records | Patron list contains correct names |

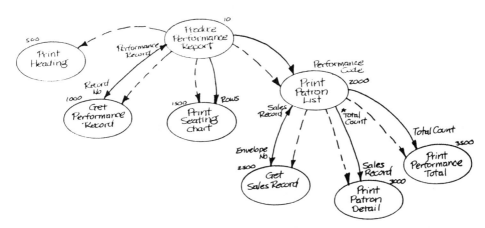

**Figure XII.2. Program outline for Produce Performance Report.**

## DATA DICTIONARY

Page = Seating Chart + Patron List + Total Count

Patron List = {Patron Name + Seat List}
     NF$ NL$

Performance Report = {Page}

Row = 20 {Seat Sold} 20

Seating Chart = 20 {Row} 20
     PT$()

Seat List = {Seat} 10
     SE$()

Total Count = Integer between 0 and 200
     TC%

```
10 REM ----- PRODUCE PERFORMANCE REPORT -------------------
11 REM
15 OPEN "R",#1,"SALES2"
20 FIELD #1,2 AS F1$,20 AS F2$,10 AS F3$,2 AS F4$,2 AS F5$,4 AS F6$,
     20 AS F7$,15 AS F8$,2 AS F9$,5 AS FA$,7 AS FB$,30 AS FC$,1 AS FX$
25 OPEN "R",#2,"PERFORM",428
30 FIELD #2,6 AS P1$,1 AS P2$,20 AS P3$,100 AS P4$,100 AS P5$,
     100 AS P6$,100 AS P7$,1 AS XP$
35 DIM PT$(399),SE$(9)
40 P%=1: L%=66
45 FOR RN%=2 TO 20
50   GOSUB 1000
55   IF RX$="A" THEN GOSUB 500: GOSUB 1500: GOSUB 2000
60 NEXT RN%
65 CLOSE #1
70 CLOSE #2
75 CHAIN "TRANSACT"
76 REM - END PRODUCE PERFORMANCE REPORT -------------------
77 REM


500 REM ----- PRINT HEADING -------------------
505 REM
510 IF L%>66 THEN L%=L%-66
515 FOR L%=L% TO 66
520   LPRINT
525 NEXT L%
530 LPRINT SPACE$(20);"PERFORMANCE STATUS REPORT        PAGE ";P%
535 LPRINT
540 P%=P%+1
545 L%=3
550 RETURN
551 REM - END PRINT HEADING -------------------
552 REM


1000 REM ----- GET PERFORMANCE RECORD -------------------
1005 REM        ASSUMES RECORD NUMBER RN% BETWEEN 2 AND 21
1010 REM        PROMISES PERFORMANCE DATA DT$,TI$,LC$,PT$()
1015 REM
1020 GET #2,RN%
1025 DT$=P1$
1030 TI$=P2$
1035 LC$=P3$
1040 FOR I%=0 TO 99
1045   PT$(I%)=MID$(P4$,I%+1,1)
1050 NEXT I%
1055 FOR I%=0 TO 99
1060   PT$(I%+100)=MID$(P5$,I%+1,1)
1065 NEXT I%
1070 FOR I%=0 TO 99
1075   PT$(I%+200)=MID$(P6$,I%+1,1)
1080 NEXT I%
1085 FOR I%=0 TO 99
1090   PT$(I%+300)=MID$(P7$,I%+1,1)
1095 NEXT I%
1100 RX$=XP$
1105 RETURN
1106 REM - END GET PERFORMANCE RECORD -------------------
1107 REM
```

```
1500 REM ----- PRINT SEATING CHART --------------------
1505 REM      ASSUMES SEAT SOLD, PT$() AND PERFORMANCE DATA
1510 REM
1515 LPRINT "SEATING FOR THE ";
1520 LPRINT LEFT$(DT$,2) "/" MID$(DT$,3,2) "/" RIGHT$(DT$,2) " ";
1525 LPRINT TI$ "   PERFORMANCE";
1530 LPRINT " AT " LC$
1535 LPRINT "AVAILABLE SEATING (0-AVAILABLE, 1-SOLD): "
1540 LPRINT "      1              10  11              20"
1545 L% = L% + 3
1550 FOR I1% = 0 TO 19
1555   LPRINT "     " MID$("ABCDEFGHIJKLMNOPQRST",I1% + 1,1) " ";
1560   FOR I2% = 0 TO 19
1565     I% = (I1%*20) + I2%
1570     LPRINT PT$(I%);" ";
1575     IF I2% = 9 THEN LPRINT "    ";
1580   NEXT I2%
1585   LPRINT
1590 NEXT I1%
1595 LPRINT
1600 L% = L% + 22
1605 RETURN
1606 REM - END PRINT SEATING CHART --------------------
1607 REM


2000 REM ----- PRINT PATRON LIST --------------------
2005 REM      ASSUMES PERFORMANCE DATE AND TIME, DT$,TI$
2010 REM
2015 PC$ = DT$ + TI$
2020 TS! = 0
2025 RC% = 0
2030 SC% = 0
2035 FOR EV% = 1 TO 200
2040   GOSUB 2500
2045   IF AX$ = "A" AND PC$ = PF$ THEN GOSUB 3000
2050 NEXT EV%
2055 GOSUB 3500
2060 RETURN
2061 REM - END PRINT PATRON LIST --------------------
2062 REM
```

For each performance record, you read through the entire sales file. If the performance code on the sales record matches the performance code on the performance record, the patron has tickets for the current performance.

```
2500 REM ----- GET SALES RECORD --------------------
2505 REM      ASSUMES EV% TO BE BETWEEN 1 AND 200
2510 REM            SALES FILE IS OPEN
2515 REM      PROMISES NL$,NF$,R%,S%,GT!,RD$,CI$,ST$,ZP$,PF$,SE$(),AX$
2520 REM            FILLED WITH DATA FROM SALES RECORD EV%
2525 REM
2530 GET #1, EV%
2535 NL$ = F2$
2540 NF$ = F3$
2545 R% = CVI(F4$)
2550 S% = CVI(F5$)
2555 GT! = CVS(F6$)
```

```
2556 RD$=F7$
2557 CI$=F8$
2558 ST$=F9$
2559 ZP$=FA$
2560 FOR C%=0 TO 9
2565   SE$(C%)=MID$(FC$,C%*3+1,3)
2570 NEXT C%
2572 PF$=FB$
2575 AX$=FX$
2580 RETURN
2581 REM - END GET SALES RECORD -------------------
2582 REM


3000 REM ----- PRINT PATRON DETAIL -------------------
3005 REM       ASSUMES SALES RECORD DATA AND TS!,RC%,SC%
3010 REM       PROMISES TO UPDATE TS!,RC%,SC%
3015 REM
3020 TS!=TS!+GT!
3025 RC%=RC%+R%
3030 SC%=SC%+S%
3035 LPRINT NF$; " "; NL$;
3040 LPRINT USING "######"; R%;
3045 LPRINT USING "#####"; S%;
3050 LPRINT USING "$$###.##"; GT!
3055 LPRINT SPACE$(13); "SEATS:  ";
3060 FOR C%=0 TO 9
3065   LPRINT SE$(C%); " ";
3070 NEXT C%
3075 LPRINT
3080 L%=L%+2
3085 RETURN
3086 REM - END PRINT PATRON DETAIL -------------------
3087 REM


3500 REM ----- PRINT REPORT TOTALS -------------------
3505 REM       ASSUMES RC%, SC%, TS!
3510 REM
3515 LPRINT
3520 LPRINT SPACE$(20); "TOTAL COUNTS";
3525 LPRINT USING "#####"; RC%; SC%
3530 LPRINT
3535 LPRINT SPACE$(29); "TOTAL SALES";
3540 LPRINT USING "$$####,.##"; TS!
3545 RETURN
3546 REM - END PRINT REPORT TOTALS -------------------
3547 REM
```

After the program has been tested, you should complete your entry in the performance log: Enter the time you took to complete the exercise and compute a work rate. Remember that these numbers will help with future projects.

# Afterword

My objective in writing this book is to present a simplified, yet reasonably complete view of the software development process. To many people in the field, the book may seem a simplistic treatment of a complex activity. This may be true.

I have presented the basics of at least ten disciplines, each with only a cursory summary: systems analysis; software design; software testing, estimating, and measurement; file definition and organization; program maintenance, coding, and coding style. Often, these activities have been presented without being identified as separate skills.

Although it is impossible to master fully all skills that make up application software development, the new professional must be at least familiar with them. He or she must have a preliminary sense of how these skills fit together, for this understanding forms a context on which specific study can be based.

To the student: This book is only an introduction to building quality application software. Each aspect of the discipline should now be thoroughly investigated. From the beginning, however, you must concentrate on building reliable, understandable systems.

# Index